Six Religions in the Twentieth Century

W. Owen Cole, B.A., B.D., M. Phil., Ph.D., Dip.Ed

Principal Lecturer and Head of Religious Studies, West Sussex Institute of Higher Education, Bishop Otter College, Chichester

with additional material by

Peggy Morgan, B.A., M.A., Cert. Ed.

Lecturer, Westminster College, Oxford

Hulton Educational

This revised and expanded edition first published
in Great Britain as
Six Religions in the Twentieth Century, 1984
by Hulton Educational Publications Ltd
Ellenborough House
Wellington Street
Cheltenham GL50 1YD

Reprinted 1986 (twice) 1987, 1993, 1994

Originally published in Great Britain as
Five Religions in the Twentieth Century, 1981
by Hulton Educational Publications Ltd

ISBN 0 7175 1290 8

Printed and bound in Great Britain at
The Bath Press, Avon.

The cover photograph shows a group of
Hindus taking part in an act of worship called havan
described on page 126.

Contents

continued

DEDICATION AND ACKNOWLEDGEMENTS

This book is offered with warm affection to the friends of many faiths from whom I have acquired the knowledge and insights contained in it and especially to members of Leeds Council of Christians and Jews, Concord, and the Yorkshire Committee for Community Relations. I dedicate it too to those students of James Graham College, whom I had the joy of teaching, who are now helping to build a multifaith Britain.

While it is impossible to acknowledge by name everyone who has helped me to write this book, a special word of gratitude must be expressed to Douglas Charing, Ahmed Shuttari, Jean O'Gorman, Bill Snelson, Vimal Khadke, Len Abramson and Piara Singh Sambhi, my guides over the years, and Peter Woodward, as well as Mr. Marsh and his staff. Anything that is good in this book owes much to their wisdom. Its errors and faults are the sole responsibility of the author.

Scriptural texts quoted in this book are taken from the following sources: The New English Bible; The Jerusalem Mass Sheet, the National Liturgical Commission of England and Wales; The Qur'an Basic Teachings, Islamic Foundation, Leicester; Islamic Correspondence Course, Riadh El-Droubie, Minaret House, Croydon; Authorised Jewish Prayer Book. Selected Buddhists texts have been reproduced from the following translations: T. Ling, *The Buddha's Philosophy of Man*, Dent; W. Rahula, *What the Buddha Taught*, Gordon Fraser; *Sacred Texts of the World*, ed. N. Smart and R. Hecht, Macmillan; *Abhidharma*, vol. 39, Pali Text Society; E. Conze, *Buddhist Scriptures*, Penguin Books Ltd.; C. Luk, *Vimalikirti Nirdesa Sutra*, Shambala Publications; L. Hurvitz, *Scripture of the Lotus Blossom of the Fine Dharma*, Columbia University Press; *World of the Buddha*, ed. L. Stryk, Anchor Press. The quotation which appears on the back cover is taken from 'Many Tributaries' by the Right Reverend George Appleton, published in *The Daily Telegraph*, 10th September, 1983.

PREFACE TO SIX RELIGIONS IN THE TWENTIETH CENTURY

Almost as soon as *Five Religions in the Twentieth Century* had been published it became apparent that the book would benefit from the addition of Buddhism. The present expanded volume, which now covers six religions, has been made possible with the great help of my friend Peggy Morgan to whom I owe a considerable debt. It is not easy to fit into the existing mould of a book, but Peggy has undertaken the task with her usual care, patience and enthusiasm. Elizabeth Smith of Hulton has borne the burden of transforming the old book into the present one. Peggy and I are grateful to her for the sensitive way that she has carried out this difficult task. Any improvements that this book has when compared with its parent must be accredited to Peggy, Elizabeth and a number of teachers who drew my attention to factual errors. These, I hope, will now be fewer. Should any remain they are my sole responsibility.

Finally, when this book was being revised my colleague John Rankin announced his retirement from the staff of West Sussex Institute of Higher Education, but not, I am sure from his many educational interests. Religious Studies owes much to him for the way it has developed recently and I am particularly indebted for the opportunities and encouragement he has given me here in West Sussex. Perhaps in this book, which owes much to his influence, my debt can gratefully be acknowledged and my gratitude expressed.

W.O.C.

Thanks are due to Barney Aldridge, who drew the plans, maps and diagrams, and to the following for kind permission to reproduce copyright photographs: The Rev. J. C. Allen, 44, 104, 219; The British Museum (by courtesy of the Trustees), 28, 227; Camera Press (Text and Illustrations) Ltd., 221, photo by William MacQuitty; The Council of Christians and Jews, 65, 135, 251, 256; The Daily Telegraph, 62; The Jewish Education Bureau, 8 Westcombe Avenue, Leeds LS8 2BS, 15; Keystone Press Ltd., 18, 127, 129, 170, 187, 230, 232, 236; The Mansell Collection, 22, 37, 95; Minaret House, 197; The National Children's Home, 271; Bury Peerless, 47, 166, 245; The Pitt Rivers Museum, University of Oxford, 156; Michael Pye, 263; Ronald Sheridan Photo-Library, 225, photo by Allan Eaton; Topham Picture Library, 88, 146.

SYMBOLS

HINDUISM OM or AUM. It symbolises what we cannot speak of, ultimate reality, Brahman, all that is.

JUDAISM The Star of David (Magen David). A famous Jew, Franz Rosenschweig, 1886–1929, said the six points stood for God, the world and man, and God's three great acts of Creation, Revelation and Redemption. Found on the flag of Israel.

BUDDHISM The wheel is the symbol of Buddhist teaching or Dharma. The Buddha's first sermon is called 'Turning the Wheel of the Dharma'. The wheel often has eight spokes, which stand for the Eightfold Path.

CHRISTIANITY The cross, signifying the death of Jesus on behalf of mankind, came to be used by Christians as a symbol of the meeting place between man and God.

ISLAM The Stars and the Moon are essential aids to people of hot desert countries who often travel by night. The stars guide, the moon lights the way. Islam guides and illumines man on the journey of life. Seen on the flags and stamps of many Muslim countries.

SIKHISM The Khanda is the name of the two-edged sword, symbolising God's concern for truth and justice. It is also the name of the complete symbol of two-edged sword, circle (representing the unity of God, the one reality) and two swords showing God's concern for temporal and spiritual power.

The letters CE and BCE which appear after dates in this book stand for Common Era and Before the Common Era. They refer to the period starting in AD1, as the Christian Era. A note on calculating the corresponding Christian and Muslim years will be found on page 275.

INTRODUCTION

This book is concerned with the main beliefs and practices of the six religions which are most strongly represented in the late twentieth century. In order of age these are Hinduism, Judaism, Buddhism, Christianity, Islam and Sikhism. They all began in Asia, though we are used to thinking of Judaism and Christianity as western and the others as eastern. In this introductory section we shall try to relate the religions to one another, bearing in mind their respective histories and time-scales. We shall also consider how best to study someone else's religion. In the rest of the book we shall examine such things as the scriptures, worship and festivals found in the six different faiths.

The beginnings of religion

Religion may be as old as man himself. Wherever archaeologists have been able to discover not merely the bones of our ancestors, but also something of the way in which they lived, evidence has been found which points to some kind of religious belief. For example, they buried their dead, which suggests that they believed in some type of continued existence beyond the grave. However, it was not until man began to write that it was possible to learn anything certain about his beliefs. Two of the religions in this book —those which became Hinduism and Judaism—started before man could write.

Hinduism is linked with some cities in the plain of the river Indus, in what is now Pakistan, and with a large group of tribes or a race of people called the Aryans, who captured the Indus valley towns nearly four thousand years ago. Judaism's story begins with a man called Abraham who left his kinsfolk in the Tigris-Euphrates plain to go to the land of Canaan, later known as Palestine and now called Israel. Abraham may have lived at the time when the Aryans were settling in north India. About eleven hundred years after Abraham, a man named Siddhartha Gautama taught in north-east

India. He was given the title Buddha, Enlightened One. His followers became a religious group separate from the faith—later called Hinduism—which was the predominant religion of India at that time.

Some seventeen hundred years after the time of Abraham a Jew named Jesus was born. Those who came to believe in him as the promised deliverer of the Jewish people and saviour of the world eventually broke away from Judaism and became Christians.

Five hundred years later, in Arabia, a man named Muhammad became aware that he was called to be God's messenger. Those who accepted the message which he preached, and that included some Jews and Christians, became known as Muslims. Finally, just over five hundred years ago, in North India, not far from the ancient cities of the Indus valley — though they had by then disappeared and no one knew of their existence until the twentieth century—a man named Nanak was born who became the religious teacher or Guru of the Sikhs.

The map below shows the area of Asia where all these religions began. You might compare it with the map on page 9, which shows where the religions are to be found today, and also study the time-line on page 11 showing the relative age of each of the six religions.

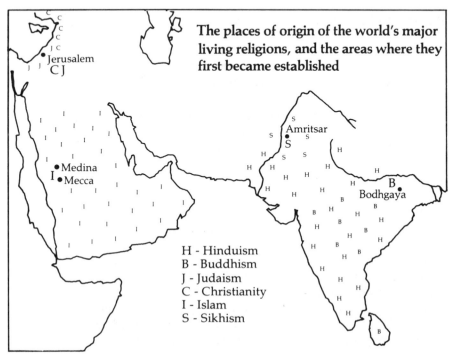

The places of origin of the world's major living religions, and the areas where they first became established

H - Hinduism
B - Buddhism
J - Judaism
C - Christianity
I - Islam
S - Sikhism

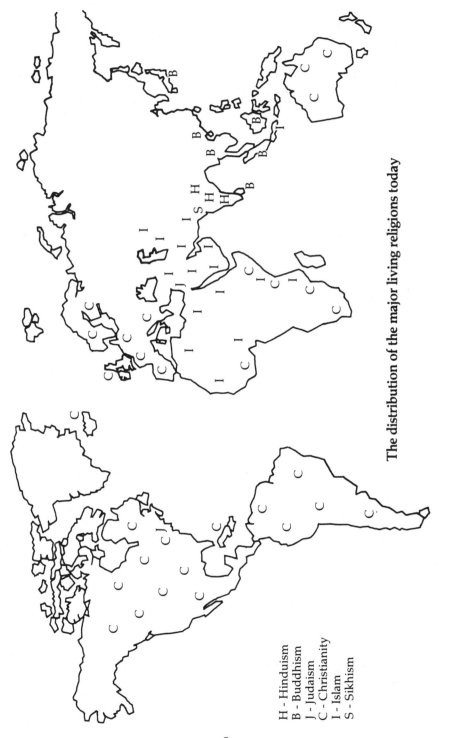

The distribution of the major living religions today

H - Hinduism
B - Buddhism
J - Judaism
C - Christianity
I - Islam
S - Sikhism

The six religions: how they arrived in the Western World

None of these six religions is native to Britain. This apparently obvious statement needs to be made because it is possible to hear people speak of Judaism, Hinduism, Buddhism, Islam and Sikhism as 'foreign' religions! Presumably what they mean is that Christianity has been in Europe, America, but not Africa, for a much longer time than the rest.

During the two hundred years after the ministry of Jesus, Christianity spread to India, Africa and Europe. Some of its early expansion through the Roman Empire is described in the Acts of the Apostles, one of the books of the Christian New Testament. However, that story ends with the great missionary, St. Paul, in Rome. It is only possible to guess at the way Christianity reached Spain, Gaul (modern France) or Britain. Probably it was brought by traders and merchants. The first named Christians linked with the British Isles are Julian, Aaron and Alban, three men who died there for their faith. The date might have been about 305, but if Alban was really sentenced to death by an Emperor, as accounts of his trial claim, the date could have been between 208 and 212 when Septimus Severus and his sons were campaigning in the island.

Judaism seems to have come to Britain in the wake of the Norman conquerors, some time after 1066. Soon Jews were to be found in such large cities as York, London and Lincoln, where the oldest surviving house in Britain is called the Jew's House. However, medieval England was not a happy place for Jews. They were persecuted in Lincoln and in 1190 the entire Jewish population of York, which had sought refuge in Clifford's Tower, was massacred when it emerged under the promise of safe conduct. One hundred years later Edward I expelled those Jews who remained.

The present Jewish population of the British Isles began to settle in 1655 when Oliver Cromwell readmitted them. However, they were few in number and it was only at the end of the nineteenth century that the ancestors of most Jews now living in Britain came. Persecutions in Russia and other parts of Europe forced the communities of those regions to move westwards. Many Jews found refuge in Britain; others went to America.

In the nineteen-thirties persecution broke out in Germany and the lands which the Germans occupied, Austria and Czechoslovakia. Again refugees came to Britain. Now there are about 400 000 British Jews, living mainly in such large cities as London, Manchester and Leeds.

Buddhism first arrived in Britain through the work of scholars

TIME LINE OF MAJOR RELIGIOUS EVENTS

Note: Most BCE dates can only be regarded as approximate

2000 INDUS VALLEY (date of beginning uncertain)
CIVILISATION

c 1750 ARYANS ENTER INDIA   c 1800 THE HEBREW PATRIARCHS

1720 HYKSOS RULE IN EGYPT BEGINS

c 1650 HEBREWS SETTLE IN EGYPT

1280 EXODUS

1000   1000 DAVID BECOMES KING (captures Jerusalem)

961–922 SOLOMON (builds Temple in Jerusalem)

597 and 587 CHALDEAN (Babylonian) CAPTURE OF JERUSALEM. EXILE IN BABYLON.

563 BIRTH OF SIDDHARTHA (later known as BUDDHA)

538 CYRUS ALLOWS EXILES TO RETURN TO PALESTINE

483 DEATH OF BUDDHA

165 JERUSALEM TEMPLE REDEDICATED AFTER GREEK OCCUPATION

BCE/CE   7 BCE-5CE BIRTH of JESUS of NAZARETH

29–33 CRUCIFIXION of JESUS

66–73 JEWISH RISING AGAINST ROME

70 FALL OF JERUSALEM TEMPLE

313 EMPEROR CONSTANTINE's EDICT OF TOLERATION (Christianity recognised as a legal religion in the Roman Empire)

570 BIRTH of MUHAMMAD (d. 632)

610 CALL of MUHAMMAD

622 HIJRA (Year One of MUSLIM CALENDAR)

710 MUSLIMS FIRST ENTER INDIA   632–661 PERIOD of the FOUR RIGHTLY-GUIDED CALIPHS

1000   1469 BIRTH of GURU NANAK (d. 1539)
1521 MUGHALS BEGIN TO CONQUER INDIA   1468–1708 PERIOD of the TEN GURUS of the SIKHS

11

and translators. British people like Christmas Humphreys became Buddhists in the early years of this century, and the present Buddhist Society was founded in 1923. Monks from Burma, Thailand, Sri Lanka and Japan, including Westerners trained in these countries, now live in England, teaching Dharma to a rapidly increasing British Buddhist community. A further impetus to Buddhism in Britain had come at the end of the Second World War, with the return of soldiers who had served in south-east Asia and become interested in Buddhist ideas. Tibetan lamas who left Tibet after the Chinese invasion in the 1950s are an important focus of teaching, and more recently Vietnamese refugees have also settled in Britain.

Muslims came to Britain in the late nineteenth century. The first settlers were seamen who were paid off, jumped ship or, quite simply, were dismissed without pay by the captains or owners. Their descendants are found in Cardiff, Liverpool and other ports. Other Asians, Sikhs and Hindus, as well as Muslims, came as traders after the First World War.

The nineteen-fifties saw a boom in British industry, and with it the need for workers in textiles, clothing and various types of engineering. The more poorly paid jobs in hospitals and public transport also could not attract enough workers, even though some traditional industries like mining or shipbuilding were declining, and many men were unemployed. London Transport and other employers recruited in India, Pakistan and the Caribbean when they could not attract native Britons. By 1960 Hindus, Muslims, Sikhs and West Indians were to be found in most of the larger cities of West Yorkshire, the Midlands and Lancashire, as well as London, where labour shortages had existed. To these were added Asians from East Africa when, after independence, Kenya, Uganda and the other new nations adopted Africanisation policies.

It is not easy to say how many Hindus, Buddhists, Muslims and Sikhs are now living in Britain, any more than it is possible to count the number of practising Christians. Censuses record where people were born; they do not ask questions about which religion they belong to. Perhaps they should. A very rough estimate would suggest that the number of Muslims in Britain approaches the million mark, while there are about 300 000 Hindus and the same number of Sikhs. The Muslims come from African countries like Egypt and Nigeria and from East Africa also. Others come from Iraq, Persia and Cyprus though the majority have come from Pakistan and Bangla Desh. The Hindus and Sikhs are of Indian origin, coming either from that country directly or indirectly via East Africa. Small numbers of Buddhists come from China, Tibet,

Vietnam or India. There are many more British Buddhists who are very well established. Their number is approximately 100 000.

In the drama of human migration — which is at least as old as man's recorded history — they represent the latest act. From lands formerly colonised by European powers they have moved to the countries that ruled over them before 1945 and made new homes there. As Indians and West Indians have come to Britain, so Indonesians and Algerians have migrated to the Netherlands and France.

How to study religion

The reader of this book is likely to come to the religions mentioned in it with knowledge of one of them and possessing a 'folklore' understanding of others. Long ago, when Christianity was in its infancy, rumours persisted that Christians ate human flesh in their secret gatherings. In later times Christians have sometimes been the sources of misunderstandings, about Judaism and Islam especially, the faiths with which they have had most contact. For example, some people are still inclined to say that Christianity is a religion revealed by God, while all the others are human searches for God. It is a matter of fact that all the faiths examined in this book claim to be rooted in ultimate reality, to have as their source a truth which is transcendent and which some call God, but to which others give a non-personal title.

The reader may also be attached to one of these faiths, perhaps as a worshipping believer. Yet the attachment may sometimes contain an element that the reader does not suspect—one of suspicion, dislike, or even rejection. Christianity or Judaism, Islam, Sikhism, Buddhism or Hinduism may be the faith of the reader's family but a faith which he or she personally has turned against. Affection or disenchantment pose particular problems for the student of religion. We find it difficult to be objective about our likes and dislikes, our hatreds or prejudices and our friends, the things we believe in or those we have come to regard as no longer meaningful or helpful.

People hold strong views about religion. Christian Catholics have burned Christian Protestants and Protestants have hanged, drawn and quartered Catholics. Christian has fought Muslim in the Crusades and Jews were massacred by the Christian population of York in the Middle Ages.

13

Attitudes and understanding

Almost everyone has some attitude to religion. The atheist may not be content to say that he does not believe in the existence of God. He may well want to condemn religion as superstitious nonsense, fit only for those who enjoy fairy tales or who are afraid of the dark. The person who doesn't know whether he believes in a God or not, the agnostic, is likely sometimes to ask whether a religious view of life can be helpful to him in solving his problems.

In this book we are not concerned with whether one religion is true and another false — for two reasons. First, there seems to be no method of answering religious claims about truth. We may believe something, but we cannot prove it in the way that we can prove that London is two hundred miles (320 km) from Leeds or that the sun is still shining on a dull day when it is hidden by the clouds. Most religions would say that people live by trust or faith, that they have the freedom to accept or reject the transcendent dimension in their lives.

There is another reason why we are not concerned with answering the question. The first task of the student is to understand a religion — not to form attitudes to it. Therefore, in this book we shall be finding out what people do and believe and the reason for their beliefs and actions. *How? when? where? what?* will be questions that are asked many times, but we shall also ask *why?* Some questions lie beyond the scope of this book — why are some people religious and others are not? Why do some need to believe in God when others don't? How does prayer work? These are matters which men and women have discussed and argued about since writing was invented and probably long before. They are the issues to consider once this study has been completed.

In this book we shall try to get as close as possible to the ideas and actions we are examining, to the kind of thought that passes through a Muslim's mind as he prepares to say his prayers, or the feelings that a Christian may have on receiving the bread and wine at a Communion service. Some of the things we come across may seem strange to us, and we may be inclined to say 'how odd'; but we must remind ourselves that our task is not to comment and approve or disapprove, but to understand. Everything seems queer to someone. Fancy kicking a blown-up leather bag around a field for ninety minutes or trying to hit a little white ball into a small hole. . . But footballers and golfers would not like us to dismiss what they enjoy doing as odd or silly.

So we come to the religions of the world to find out what they teach. We do not come to give the stamp of our approval or to thrust our own opinions upon those who practise them.

Visits and visitors

You may be able to gain a better understanding of a religion by visiting one of its places of worship or inviting a member of the faith to speak to you. If you do either of these, however, it is as well to bear a few points in mind.

When you are writing to invite a speaker to address you, mention why you are studying the particular religion and list the special aspects that you would like him to describe. Such information helps your guest to prepare his talk in a way that will be profitable and interesting for you. Similarly, if you are arranging a visit you should explain beforehand exactly what you are hoping to see and hear about

Remember, too, that most of the people you will approach are busy, and it may be necessary to plan weeks or months ahead. However, they are always pleased when an interest is shown in their religion. If you show consideration—and also appreciation—they will always respond generously.

A visit to a succah in a synagogue. The rabbi is holding the four species used during the Succoth festival and carried to the Temple in ancient times by pilgrims. They are palm branches, myrtle and willow leaves and a citron. (*Jewish Education Bureau*)

The plan and purpose of this study

The rest of this book will examine certain aspects of the six religions covered; sacred writings, worship, festivals and pilgrimages, and significant personalities such as Jesus, Buddha and Muhammad. The topic index at the end of the book should make it possible for those who wish to find out what a number of religions teach about 'prayer' or 'worship' to discover the relevant material easily.

Three final points remain to be made:

1. Beware of falling into the trap of thinking that, for example, all Christians or all Jews are alike. Not every Englishman likes cricket; many Welshmen don't play rugby. In the same way, some Sikhs cut their hair, some Christians don't go to church, some Hindus are not vegetarians, some Christians are.

2. In this book we shall describe the religion of the Sikh who keeps his hair uncut and the Christian who is a churchgoer; otherwise the book would be full of 'ifs' and 'buts'. However, we shall try to penetrate the deep concerns which all Christians, Hindus, Buddhists, Muslims, Sikhs and Jews share.

3. Our purpose is to learn, analyse and understand, not to criticise or judge. We hope, therefore, that whatever faith the readers of this book may belong to, they will have found the approach sympathetic and will feel that we have stood respectfully on their particular holy ground and helped them also to stand on the holy ground of others.

CHAPTER ONE
MESSENGERS

To find an appropriate name to describe such men as Moses, Siddhartha, Jesus, Muhammad or Guru Nanak is not easy. Sometimes books call them the founders of Judaism, Buddhism, Christianity, Islam and Sikhism, but that is not a very satisfactory title. Each of these faiths, in common with many which are not mentioned in this book, claims that the authority and power for what it teaches lie in some way beyond the limitations of human existence.

The transcendent reality, which is beyond the world of human history, as well as active within it, is what is called 'God' in Judaism, Christianity, Islam and Sikhism. For each of these God is their founder, and consequently Judaism, Islam and Sikhism regard Moses, Muhammad and Guru Nanak as messengers and nothing more. Christians, however, although they believe that Jesus was divine and that in some special way he was God, see differences between Christianity as it now exists anywhere in the world and the community of Jesus and his first disciples. Some Christians find it hard, therefore, to say that Jesus founded the church, for the church is an institution which grew up after his ministry.

Sometimes what is beyond the world and gives meaning to the world is not a personal God but a reality beyond even personhood. Hindus talk about the non-personal Brahman as well as using personal names. Buddhists talk about a final state called Nirvana. Siddhartha was an ordinary human being who realised this state and taught others how to realise it too. Something of its beauty and power are present in his life after his enlightenment, but he is not 'sent'. The title 'messenger' is appropriate, because he had a message to teach.

In this section we are not going to examine the life-stories of the messengers in detail. Instead we are going to consider how they are regarded by those who have accepted the message which they gave to the world.

17

ॐ Hinduism

There is no messenger, or even a group of men, to whom Hinduism can look with any certainty and identify as the people through whom God revealed himself. Seven rishis or wise men are mentioned in the ancient myths of Hinduism, but no details of their lives are known and they are probably to be regarded as representatives of the human race, rather than historical figures. These rishis became the constellation Ursa Major, the Great Bear, when their earthly task of guidance had come to an end. There they still help the traveller to find his way. It is said that these men overheard the wisdom being spoken by the gods and passed it on to mankind. This wisdom is the content of the first of the Hindu scriptures, the Vedas, the books of knowledge.

Brahmins. One group of men has become important in Hinduism, on account of this idea of divine wisdom heard by men. These are the Brahmins, the successors of the rishis. The word Brahmin refers

A Hindu priest teaches a group of devotees in India.

to the group of men from whom the Hindu priesthood is drawn and to the priests themselves. Only Brahmins may become priests, though not all do. It is correct to say, then, that every priest is a Brahmin but not all Brahmins are priests. 'Brahmin' comes from a word in the ancient religious language of Sanskrit related to a term meaning 'breath'. The idea is that God—Brahman is the name used for God in Hinduism — is the being who gives the breath of life which creates and sustains the universe. The Brahmin is the one through whom this breath, in the form of divine wisdom, reaches men. It is the duty of the Brahmin to offer worship to God and to teach men the sacred wisdom of the Vedas.

Gurus. The Brahmins taught, and still teach, the Vedas, but another group of teachers has appeared over the centuries. These are called Gurus. Some of them are Brahmins, but many are not. Some of them have based their teaching on the Vedas, but many have not. Hindus believe that within all living things—animals and plants as well as humans—there exists an indestructible eternal atman, a soul, for want of a better word. Some Hindus consider this atman to be part of Brahman, that is God, in the same way that a drop of water is part of the sea. Some Hindus think that the atman has some kind of separate existence, like the planets going around the sun. All tend to agree that man's problem is that he is not aware of this true nature as a spiritual being and instead thinks that it is the body that is eternal. Consequently he spends his time feeding it, dressing it, and trying to amass wealth to make it comfortable. He seems to fail to realise that one day the body will perish. The function of the spiritual guide, whether he be a Brahmin priest or a Guru, is to persuade men to recognise their true nature so that the soul may be freed from its body-prison. If the truth is not realised, the soul must return again into another body and keep on doing so until finally it gains its freedom.

The Brahmin or the Guru helps the soul to know its true identity and to waken it from its sleep, so that freedom may be gained. Perhaps because these guides can be so important in the everyday life of a Hindu, historical figures of the past have never acquired the significance of men like Moses, Siddhartha, or Jesus. The Vedas may be the world's oldest scripture, Hindu rituals may go back to people who lived in India four thousand years ago, but Hinduism seems to emphasise experience more than history, and the man who matters is the one who can provide you with enlightenment and liberation now.

✡ Judaism

A number of men and women have played their part in the development of the religion of Judaism. The most famous fall into two groups, the patriarchs and the prophets. Abraham and his descendants Isaac and Jacob are the patriarchs. Of these the first is the most important.

Abraham. Abraham came from an area which has been called the cradle of civilisation, the land at the mouth of the rivers Tigris and Euphrates in present-day Iraq. At some point in his life Abraham left Ur for a city about eight hundred miles (1300 km) to the north-west, called Haran. He didn't settle there, but became aware that God was directing him to a land some six hundred miles (920 km) to the south-west, a country on the Mediterranean coast, Canaan. Abraham is portrayed in the Bible as a man who trusted the promises of God contained in these words:

> 'Go from your country and your kindred and your father's house to the land which I will show you. And I will make of you a great nation, and I will bless you, and make your name great, so that you will be a blessing. I will bless those who bless you, and him who curses you I will curse; and in you all the families of the earth will be blessed.'
>
> (Genesis 12:1–3)

Abraham's travels did not end when he reached Canaan. It is clear from the Bible that he was a nomad, but Canaan seems to have been his base.

The Covenant. In Chapter 17 of Genesis the story is told of an agreement, or covenant, which the God who had led Abraham from Ur and Haran to Canaan made with him. Abraham was to walk before God and be blameless, that is, he was to worship this God who had revealed himself to him and to serve him only. God, in turn, promised that he would make Abraham the father of many people and give him and his descendants the land of Canaan 'for an everlasting possession'.

The account of Abraham's relationship with God is to be found in the Bible in Chapters 12–25 of the book of Genesis. Many of the episodes are strange to our experience and difficult to understand, but they hinge on this idea of a covenant relationship between God and a man who has been described elsewhere in the Bible as 'God's friend' (James 2:23).

The covenant with Abraham was renewed with Isaac, his son, and with Jacob, his grandson (see Genesis 26:23–25, 28:10–17).

However, these were covenants made with individuals. The next important stage in the religious development of the Hebrew people came some hundreds of years later.

The Hebrews in Egypt. About 1720 BCE some invaders from the east conquered Egypt. These people, known as the Hyksos, were inclined to be sympathetic to other foreigners who came to settle in the land. Perhaps this was why a group of Hebrews who found their way to Egypt, the family of Jacob, was received favourably and given land where they could live and keep their flocks. Somewhere near 1550 BCE the Hyksos rulers were overthrown, and it is likely that those they had favoured were regarded with suspicion by the new Pharaohs. It is not surprising to find the Bible describing the changed fortunes of the Hebrews who now became slaves (Exodus 1:8–14).

From among the slaves came a man called Moses. His story is a fascinating one, and even his name has something unusual about it. It is apparently incomplete. In its present form it seems to mean nothing and all names originally had a meaning. It may be a short-ened form of Ramses or Tothmoses, son of Ra, or son of Toth, two of the Egyptian gods. Later Biblical writers, refusing to accept the idea that a Hebrew prophet could be called after an Egyptian god, may have removed the first part of his name. That he did have such a name is not improbable, for the Bible itself states that he was brought up in the Egyptian court as the son of Pharaoh's daughter. (Exodus 2:10, where a more contrived explanation of his name is given.) This period at court was to stand Moses in good stead later in his life when he found himself leader of the Hebrew slaves, trying to persuade the Pharaoh to let them leave Egypt for the land of the ancestors, Canaan.

However, before that happened Moses' fortunes took an unex-pected turn. Though he lived like a prince he had never forgotten his own people. One day when he saw a slave being whipped by the taskmaster he killed the Egyptian, and immediately became an outlaw wanted by the very people who had brought him up. He fled from Egypt into the Sinai desert where he fell in with a nomadic family of herdsmen. There he married and learned the lore of the desert, especially how to survive in a region of little water and vegetation. This period of his life was also brought to a dramatic end, this time by an experience of the presence of God. It is known as the story of the burning bush. (Exodus 3:1–6).

The Bible suggests that this was the significance of the incident. The God of Abraham, Isaac, Jacob, and Moses' own father, revealed himself to Moses and commanded him to return to Egypt to deliver

21

Moses and the Burning Bush by D. Deti. An artist's attempt to portray Moses' experience of being confronted by God. The account is found in the Bible, Exodus 3.

the Hebrew people. It is tempting to spend time trying to explain the mystery of God manifesting himself through a bush which burned but was not consumed. However, the Bible says that Moses, once his doubts about his ability to accomplish the mission had been dispelled, set off immediately for Pharaoh's court, stopping only to take his leave of his father-in-law.

The deliverance.   Back in Egypt Moses was no longer a wanted man. There was a new ruler who was not concerned about events before his reign, though he shared a fear of the Hebrews and was making their slavery harsher than ever. Moses gained an audience with this Pharaoh and tried to persuade him to let the slaves go. Though Moses pointed to the finger of God being active in a series of calamities befalling the Egyptians, the Pharaoh would not free the slaves. Only the death of the Pharaoh's own son convinced him, and within a few days of giving his permission he had changed his mind again. Though the army which Pharaoh sent after the Hebrews perished, the problems of Moses and his people had only just begun. In their long wanderings through the desert the Hebrews would often have returned to slavery and would have starved had not Moses found food, using skills acquired during his own exile, and helped them to build up faith in the power of God to deliver them. This, according to the Bible, was the time when the faith and religion of the Jewish people were formed. They entered the desert a rabble and emerged a nation.

The people of the Covenant.   At Mount Sinai the Hebrews were made the people of the Covenant, and a priesthood was established to maintain it through worship. The great festivals of Passover, Pentecost, Tabernacles (or Booths), and the Day of Atonement are all associated with the Exodus in the Hebrew Bible. So is the giving of the Torah. This is the name by which the first five books of the Bible are known, but far more important, it refers to the teaching contained in them. Torah means 'teaching', and the tradition of Judaism is that Moses received not only the Ten Commandments at Sinai (Exodus 20:1–17), but the whole of the Torah which he later wrote down.

Moses was allowed to see the Promised Land, but not to enter it (Deuteronomy 32:48–52 and 34:1–12). This final pronouncement on his life puts him in his place in the Hebrew tradition. He was but a man, no more, though a great servant of God. The Hebrew nation, which at Sinai had become the people of the Covenant, was greater than Moses or any other man or woman. So was the Torah, the books in which details of the Covenant were recorded, the teachings by which the covenanted people were to live. After Moses came many other spokesmen, the prophets who were charged with the task of keeping Israel faithful to the Covenant, but of Moses the Bible says:

> 'And there has not risen a prophet since in Israel like Moses, whom the Lord knew face to face, none like him for all the signs and wonders which the Lord sent him to do in the land of Egypt, to Pharaoh and to all his servants and to all his land, and for all the great and terrible deeds which Moses wrought in the sight of all Israel.'
>
> (Deuteronomy 34:10–12)

Buddhism

The central story in the Buddhist tradition is about a prince who became a pauper in order to discover the meaning of life. The example of his search is important for Buddhists, who believe that what he discovered and taught is the truth about the way things are.

Siddhartha the Prince. Siddhartha was born about 563 BCE in north-east India. Siddhartha was his personal name. His clan name was Gautama and the title 'Buddha' was given to him after he became 'Awakened' or 'Enlightened'. He can also be called Shakyamuni, the sage of the Shakya tribe; Bodhisattva, a being capable of enlightenment; Bhagavan, Lord; and Tathagata. This last title is a synonym for Buddha, and its exact meaning is debated. His father, Suddhodana, and his mother, Mahamaya, ruled an area which was called Magadha. He was born at Lumbini, near Kapilavatthu, their capital. The site is in present-day Nepal.

At the time of Siddhartha's conception his mother dreamed that a white elephant (a rarity, so a symbol of greatness) entered her side; and it was recorded that right from the beginning the boy was extraordinary. After his birth the wise teachers at his father's court said that he would be either an emperor or a great religious teacher. There were many holy men in India at this time, like the Hindu gurus already mentioned. They chose lives of hardship, often alone in the forests, or as wanderers. They sought answers to the deepest problems of life, and felt that this quest demanded leaving ordinary family commitments. Suddhodana did not want his son to choose such a life, so he made sure that Siddhartha saw nothing which might disturb his happiness with the world.

The boy's youth within the palace gardens was one of comfort and enjoyment. All knowledge of suffering and death was kept

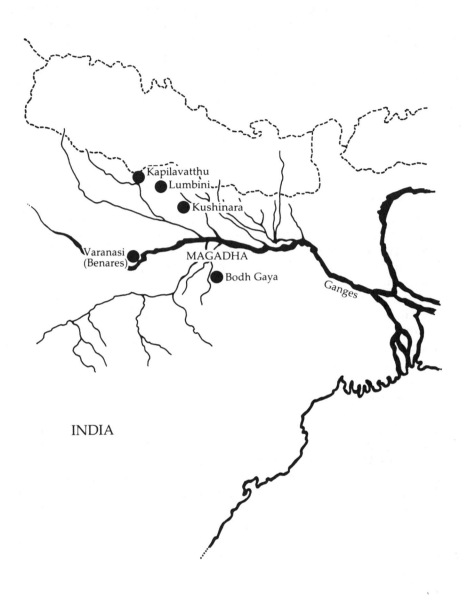

**Map of north-east India at the time of the
Buddha's birth**

from him and he was surrounded by pleasure and riches. He was married to a beautiful wife, who had a son called Rahula. Despite all this, Siddhartha became restless and eventually persuaded his charioteer to take him outside the palace gates and into the villages. There he had four experiences which are called the 'Four Signs'. These changed his whole life. The first three were the sight of an old man, a sick man and a corpse. The prince asked his charioteer whether he, Siddhartha, could ever be like this, and was amazed to be told that these states were a part of life. The fourth sign was a wandering ascetic. The charioteer explained that the man was trying to understand the impermanence and suffering of life. Siddhartha decided he wanted a happiness and peace that were not dependent on youth and wealth. One night he made 'The Great Renunciation'. Leaving his sleeping wife and son in the care of his family, he said goodbye to his charioteer, cut off his own beautiful black hair with his sword and wandered away on his search.

A life story is a good way of teaching a religion. Siddhartha's renunciation is acted out by many boys and girls in Buddhist countries at initiation ceremonies which are described in Chapter Five. They dress up in royal clothes and ritually abandon them for two simple pieces of cloth, to show that they want to follow in his footsteps. This is their religious ideal, even if they go on to live ordinary lives afterwards.

Gautama the ascetic. After he left home Gautama, as he is frequently called, was helped by two meditation teachers. Both taught him all they could, but he did not feel that he had found his goal. He continued to wander, at one stage with five other ascetics. They fasted so strictly that Gautama's stomach touched his backbone. By now he had experienced the extremes of luxury and deprivation, but was still not at peace. Much to the disgust of his five friends, he began to eat and drink a little food regularly. He continued to travel alone until he found a pleasant spot under a fig tree, regarded as a sacred species in India. This was at Bodh Gaya. The tree was later called the 'Bodhi' or 'Enlightenment' Tree. He decided to stay at Bodh Gaya and meditate until he reached enlightenment.

During his trance he struggled with Mara, The Evil One, who sent his beautiful daughters to distract Gautama. They did not succeed, and Gautama is often portrayed with his hand touching the earth, asking it to bear witness to the fact that, through many previous births and his attainments in this last life, he is now worthy to attain enlightenment. When he at last realised the wisdom he had been looking for it was obviously not easy to put

26

into words. It is rather like trying to describe happiness, or being in love. Gautama had felt bound or trapped in a world that was stained by insecurity and self-centredness, where people grew old and died in bewilderment. He now found himself in a state of great clarity in which he felt no sense of self and others as separate entities, a sense of freedom from that insecurity that arises from self-centredness. Since there was no longer a sense of self, there was also no fear for the self and no fear of dying. His mind rested at peace, in complete freedom and fearlessness. This peace, which comes when people are no longer obsessed with any kind of self-centredness, is the enlightenment which Buddhists call anatman (not-self) and is Nirvana.

The Buddha teaches. It is now appropriate to call Gautama 'Buddha', the title for an enlightened being. He knew how difficult it would be to teach about enlightenment and how unwilling people might be to make the effort to follow his path. The stories say that one of the great Indian gods, Brahma, asked the Buddha to help the world by teaching the Dharma (Truth) he had found. For Buddhists, gods are high beings who live longer than men, but they are not creators or immortal; only enlightenment and the state of Nirvana last forever.

The Buddha felt compassion for all beings and decided to teach, beginning with the five ascetics he already knew. They had thought he had taken a 'soft option' and were now surprised at his new radiance and sense of authority. His first sermon was in a deer park at Benares. He was thirty-five years old, and until he died about 483 BCE, at the age of eighty, he travelled about north-east India and was willing to help everybody, whatever their class or stage of spiritual development. The only thing he refused to do was enter into theoretical speculations, which he considered not helpful for attaining Nirvana. These included questions about the origins of the universe and where a buddha goes at death. The Buddha said that debating such questions was like being a man shot by a poisoned arrow. The man would not have the arrow removed until he knew everything about the person who had shot him; his caste, and whether he was tall or short, whether his complexion was black or brown, where he came from and what kind of bow and arrow he had used. The Buddha said the man would die and should be asking about a cure.

The Buddha emphasised practice rather than theory in various ways. He said that people can only help others out of the muddy rut in which they are stuck if they are on firm ground themselves. He knew that sermons were not necessarily the best way of helping

Buddha in full lotus posture of meditation. This shows the enlightenment.
(*Reproduced by courtesy of the Trustees of the British Museum*)

people. When Kisogotami came to him with her dead child in her arms, completely absorbed in her grief and asking him to help her, he sent her to collect a grain of mustard seed from any house in the town where no one had died. Her visits to the houses showed her that her suffering was not unique. She cremated her son and returned to the Buddha, realising the impermanence of life, and acknowledged him as her teacher. His own path to the 'Deathless', or Nirvana, had been through experience. He asked others to test what he said in their lives and not to follow him blindly.

The Buddha's first teaching in the deer park at Benares describes a middle way between the extremes of self-indulgence and self-denial. It is important for all Buddhists, and is presented as a doctor's diagnosis of the impermanent and unsatisfactory condition of people. It also showed the cure that lay in a life of morality, meditation and wisdom. Much of the Buddha's teaching is preserved in numerical lists which are easy to remember. The first sermon includes the Four Noble Truths and the Noble Eightfold Path.

The Four Noble Truths

1. *Life is unsatisfactory.*   Instead of running smoothly, life is full of ups and downs. Its unsatisfactoriness is called dukkha, a word which suggests restlessness and suffering.

2. *Dukkha arises.*   This takes the form of a kind of thirst (tanha) of selfish desire which is linked with ignorance, greed and hatred.

3. *Dukkha can cease.*   To achieve this state (nirodha) one must follow certain moral and spiritual disciplines.

4. *The way is laid down in the Noble Eightfold Path.*   This is described below. Each of the eight stages must be 'right', which means appropriate or effective.

The Noble Eightfold Path

1. *Right understanding (wisdom).*   This involves seeing life as it is, in all its impermanence and unsatisfactoriness.

2. *Right thought (wisdom).*   Here one acknowledges the power of one's mind, which should be filled with thoughts of loving-kindness and compassion.

29

3. Right speech (morality).   Such speech ranges from not telling lies to not gossiping.

4. Right action (morality).   Such action is not taking life, stealing or indulging in sexual misconduct.

5. Right livelihood (morality).   One must be careful to have a job which does not involve one in destroying life or hurting people.

6. Right effort (meditation).   This is needed to think about what one says and does.

7. Right awareness (meditation).   One must be wholly alert or awake in life.

8. Right concentration (meditation).   With this one achieves a deeper level of attentiveness, characterised by peace and calm.

After a long life of teaching the Buddha died at the age of eighty. He realised he had a stomach upset, and died while calmly reclining on his right side between two trees. He reminded his followers that he had been no more than their teacher and that they must now be self-reliant and pass on the Dharma which he had given them. After his death he was cremated and his remains divided and buried in mounds which became the pilgrimage centres, described in Chapter Four.

The Sangha, the community of world-renouncers and house-holders.   After his death, the message of any great religious leader is passed on by the community he leaves behind. The Buddhist community consists of two groups: those who continued to lead ordinary lives with jobs and families—householders or upasikas, laymen and laywomen—and those who gave up a settled life to meditate and teach Dharma—world-renouncers or bhikkhus, monks and nuns. The word Sangha is commonly used just for the monks and nuns.

The relationship between the two groups was established during the Buddha's lifetime. Householders offer monks food, clothes and somewhere to live. They thank the monks for this opportunity. Monks are highly respected by householders, who see them as experts in meditation and the scriptures and close to Nirvana. Householders hope that in a future birth they may be world-renouncers. It is possible, in theory, for a householder to attain Nirvana (see Vimalikirti in Chapter Two). It is, however, more difficult to attain enlightenment as a lay-person. Jobs and families bring too many distractions. In return for the laity's material support, monks and nuns teach, help with pastoral problems and offer the inspiration of a life lived close to the example of the Buddha. The moral life of the householder is based on generosity and loving-kindness for all living things. The ascetic life of the monks shows that the roots of happiness lie in a calm and peace that comes from within.

The Three Refuges.   Monks and householders declare themselves to be followers of the Buddha by 'taking refuge', by repeating three times:

> 'I take my refuge in the Buddha.'
> 'I take my refuge in the Dharma.'
> 'I take my refuge in the Sangha.'

Because the Buddha, Dharma and Sangha are treasured above everything else these declarations are also called the Three Jewels.

The Ten Precepts.   Householders and monks promise the first five of these:

1. To refrain from killing or harming living things.
2. To refrain from taking what is not given.
3. To refrain from indulging in sensual pleasures.
4. To refrain from false and wrong speech.
5. To refrain from drink or drugs which cloud the mind.

If householders stay with monks for a retreat (described in Chapter Five) they take three, or sometimes five more precepts, making eight or ten in all. Boys training to be monks observe all ten. Fully-ordained monks, who have to be over twenty, add to these precepts many more monastic rules. These include owning only necessities like their bowl for food, a razor for shaving the head and beard, and their robes. The rest of the Ten Precepts are:

6. To refrain from eating after midday.
7. To refrain from involvement in dancing, acting or music.
8. To refrain from using ornaments or perfumes.
9. To refrain from using a high or big bed.
10. To refrain from handling gold or silver.

THE INFLUENCE OF THE BUDDHA

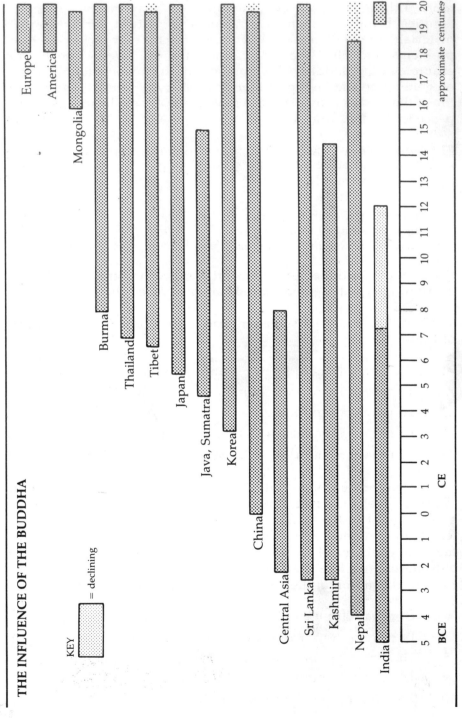

KEY

☐ = declining

| Europe | America | Mongolia | Burma | Thailand | Tibet | Japan | Java, Sumatra | Korea | China | Central Asia | Sri Lanka | Kashmir | Nepal | India |

BCE 5 4 3 2 1 0 1 2 3 4 5 6 7 8 9 10 11 12 13 14 15 16 17 18 19 20

CE

approximate centuries

The message in the practice. Buddhists have developed many different ways of talking about the Buddha's message and following his path. The southern Buddhism of Sri Lanka, Burma and Thailand tries to stay close to the original teaching of the Buddha and his first followers. This path is called Theravada, or the way of the Elders. The northern areas of India, with China and Japan, follow the Mahayana. Mahayana means great or superior vehicle or way. A great vehicle can take more people to enlightenment. The Mahayana claims that its greater variety of paths and practices grows naturally from the seeds of the Buddha's teaching. Within the Mahayana there are schools like Zen and Pure Land Buddhism. Mahayana Buddhists call Theravadins the Hinayana, the little or inferior vehicle. Hinayana is a term that Theravadins dislike, as it seems to them to be an unkind insult. Tibetan Buddhists belong to a third way, the Vajrayana. They say it is a fast vehicle, named after the thunderbolt which takes a direct and powerful route to its goal and must be treated with care. Buddhists have always travelled widely and taught the Dharma in the language and customs of the people. In the twentieth century all the main schools have come to the west.

The place of the Buddha in Buddhism

To a historian, Siddhartha Gautama Buddha is the man who stands at the beginning of the religion which we call Buddhism. Buddhists talk about him in another way. He discovered Dharma, the truth about the way things are. This truth involves seeing how unsatisfactory life is as long as we cling to our obsession with ourselves. When we lose ourselves in love, compassion and sympathetic joy we find a peace which passes all understanding and lasts forever. That truth, or Dharma, not the person of the Buddha, is the foundation of Buddhism. Theravada Buddhists emphasise that he was just a man who became enlightened, taught others the truth he had found and then died. He has passed beyond this world to Nirvana and is no longer accessible to us. He helps us through the teaching he left behind, and through the example of his life. He is not unique. There were other buddhas before him in the cycles of world history and there is at least one more to come. Each buddha goes through many lives of preparation in animal and human births. The accounts of these births are called Jataka Tales, and are some of the most popular stories in the Buddhist world. They illustrate generosity, patience, truthfulness and love. One example is of a monkey king who let his tribe escape over his back—which acted as a bridge over a chasm—until he fell

33

exhausted to the ground. Another is of a prince who gave his life to a tigress who had cubs to feed, but was too weak to hunt for food.

People are helped and Buddhism thrives when a buddha is alive and when the Dharma is taught after his death; but there are times in the cycles of history when the Dharma is neglected, when truth is lost and people have to wait for it to be discovered by another buddha.

Although for Theravada Buddhists the Buddha is no more than a man, they have such confidence in him, such love and gratitude for his memory, that the word 'faith' is appropriate. Images of him are honoured with the kind of words and actions that the east traditionally used in the presence of a king. These words and actions will be described in Chapter Three.

Mahayana Buddhists believe that, as well as buddhas in world history, there are celestial or cosmic buddhas, who have their own realms or Pure Lands. These are paradise worlds in which it is possible to be reborn. Both there and on earth they, like the bodhisattvas, can use skilful means to help beings to enlightenment. The most famous of these is Amitabha (Chinese) or Amida (Japanese). People who call on his name in faith will be reborn in his Happy or Pure Land, and there his skill helps them to Nirvana.

Buddhists also honour bodhisattvas. Because a bodhisattva is a being on his way to full Buddhahood it is a possible title for Gautama before his enlightenment. Beings who have taken a vow to become fully enlightened buddhas are called bodhisattvas. This vow must be taken in the spirit of complete selflessness. It is sometimes expressed as, 'may I not enter Nirvana until I have brought all beings to supreme enlightenment.' This bodhisattva vow is undertaken, like the refuges and precepts, by many Mahayana Buddhists. One of the most famous bodhisattvas is Avalokitesvara, the Bodhisattva of Infinite Compassion. Bodhisattvas are not limited to the world, but can dwell on celestial plains, where they are active in the world, rather like gods. In China and Japan, Avalokitesvara has a female form and name, Kuan-yin or Kwannon. In Tibet his name is Chenresig. Another famous bodhisattva is Manjusri, whose characteristic is Infinite Wisdom.

In the Mahayana and Vajrayana traditions, what is most central is not the emphasis on an individual buddha as teacher, but the ever-present spiritual force which shines out in all buddhas and bodhisattvas. These beings are representations, or emanations, of the ultimate, which can be called enlightenment, Nirvana, Dharma or Tathata (suchness). One way of talking about the unity which they all represent is to call it the Dharma-Kaya or Truth-Body. This lies behind them all and is beyond conception. Another way is to talk about the Buddha-Nature or Tathagatha-Garbha. The last term means the seed or heart of enlightenment, which is present in all beings, waiting to be realised, like the moon behind a cloud or the oak tree dormant in the acorn. In buddhas and bodhisattvas the bright moon of enlightenment shines forth for all to see. In other beings it is covered by the clouds of ignorance and delusion.

✠ Christianity

The prophetic voice had been silent in Judaism for many centuries until it spoke again through John the Baptist and Jesus of Nazareth. Christians believe that John the Baptist was the Elijah figure spoken of by Malachi:

> 'Behold I will send you Elijah the prophet before the great and terrible day of the Lord comes. And he will turn the hearts of fathers to their children and the hearts of children to their fathers, unless I come and smite the land with a curse.' (Malachi 4:5–6)

God's Messiah. There were Jewish traditions that said that God would send his Messiah one day. He would be a man of King David's family, an anointed deliverer (Messiah simply meant 'anointed' originally) who would restore the fortunes of Israel. Many people are called 'anointed' in the Jewish Bible, among them Aaron, the brother of Moses whom he anointed priest, King David, and a non-Jew, Cyrus, the Persian king who is called 'the Lord's anointed' (Isaiah 45:1). However, by the time of Jesus Messiah had come to have a more precise meaning. It was used to refer to a man that God would send to drive out the Roman occupying power, and restore Israel to the greatness it had enjoyed in the time of King David. Before Jesus, and in the fifty years after his ministry, there were a number of 'Messiahs', each of whom came to a painful end. Jesus differs from the other claimants because he believed that he was a spiritual Messiah called to restore the faith of Israel and lead it in its task of carrying God's covenant to the world. Some Jews may have hoped for a Messiah of this kind. A group whose writings were discovered only in the nineteen-fifties, the community of the Dead Sea Scrolls, who lived at Qumran, may have hoped for a spiritual leader. Yet most Jews rejected Jesus' Messiahship and could not agree that the Biblical passages on which Christians based his claims were Messianic. At best, Judaism regards Jesus as a rabbi, a religious teacher, at worst one of many mistaken Messiahs.

The Christian gospels say that Jesus was born in Bethlehem in southern Palestine, the city of King David, during the reign of Herod the Great. The land of Jesus' birth, Palestine, was a puppet state of the Roman Empire and passed under direct Roman rule on Herod's death in 4 BCE. (Owing to miscalculations it seems that the Christian Era now commonly used in calendars throughout the world is four years out of 'true'.) The town in which Jesus grew up was Nazareth, in Galilee, the northern region of Palestine and he was first known in history as Jesus of Nazareth. When he was about thirty years old a preacher named John the Baptist, one of Jesus' kinsmen, began calling his fellow Jews to repent and prepare for the coming of the Messiah and the kingdom of God.

The work and teaching of Jesus. This seems to have been the signal for Jesus to start his work. He went about Galilee healing the sick and teaching, and gathering around him a group of disciples, mostly Galilean Jews like himself. His mission seems to have been summed up in some words of the prophet Isaiah which he read during a synagogue service in Nazareth and used as the text of his sermon:

> 'The spirit of the Lord is upon me. He has anointed me to preach the goods news to the poor, he has sent me to proclaim liberty to the captives; and recovery of sight to the blind, to set free the oppressed, to announce the year when the Lord will deliver his people.'
>
> (Isaiah 61:1–2, quoted Luke 4:18–19)

In the book of Isaiah these words are a great message of hope, but no more. Yet when they came from Jesus' lips they seemed to amount to a claim that he was God's special messenger, the anointed one. This was too much for many of his fellow-citizens, who could not believe that such a messenger could come from the household of the village carpenter.

The view of religion presented by Jesus did not go explicitly against the Judaism of his day. He went to the Temple and worshipped in the synagogue, he kept the festivals, and was a good Jew. He emphasised the free response of each individual to God in such a way that he put God higher than the Torah, or worship in the Temple. Nevertheless, there was nothing particularly new in this. Many of the Hebrew prophets to whom he often referred had preached similar ideas. When he summed up the Torah in two commandments, 'Love the Lord your God with all your heart and with all your mind and with all your strength, and love your neighbour as yourself,' (Matthew 22:37) Jesus was quoting from the Torah —perhaps the best-known words of the Bible among Jews (Deuter-

A Russian icon. Icons are believed to be one of the channels through which God's blessings are communicated to Christians.

onomy 6:4, 5 and Leviticus 19:18). Even when he addressed God as 'my father', and used a word which means the equivalent of 'daddy', 'Abba', this familiarity would not have been thought offensive. Jesus' blasphemy lay in claiming to be divine.

It was another teaching of Jesus which provoked hostility and his execution. This was that he was the Messiah who would establish the kingdom of God. The claim was contained in his Nazareth sermon and explains why his words were received with such anger. Such a teacher could not be tolerated when he spoke similar words in Jerusalem. Therefore Jesus was arrested, tried and crucified, either as a rebel (John 19:12) or as a religious teacher whose doctrine threatened the safety of Judaism (John 11:47–51). However, according to the gospel accounts, within three days of his death, Jesus' disciples came to believe that he had risen from the dead, and testified that they had not only seen him, they had even shared a meal with him. They also claimed that they had witnessed his bodily ascension into heaven from the Mount of Olives, the place where some Jews believed that the Messiah would make his appearance.

The message of the apostles. After these events, the twelve disciples went out proclaiming the good news of the coming of God's kingdom in the person of Jesus, the Messiah of the Jews and the saviour of all mankind. From this time the twelve disciples became known as apostles, which means appointed messengers. The same word is also applied later to Paul, even though he was not a disciple during Jesus' ministry. These words of the apostle Peter give some idea of the message:

'Men of Israel, listen to me: I speak of Jesus of Nazareth, a man singled out by God and made known to you through miracles, portents, and signs, which God worked among you through him, as you well know. When he had been given up to you, by the deliberate will and plan of God, you used heathen men to crucify and kill him. But God raised him to life again, setting him free from the pangs of death because it could not be that death should keep him in its grip.

For David says of him:

'I foresaw that the presence of the Lord would be with me always,
For he is at my right hand so that I may not be shaken;
Therefore my heart was glad and my tongue spoke my joy;
Moreover, my flesh shall dwell in hope,
For thou wilt not abandon my soul to Hades,
Nor let thy loyal servant suffer corruption,

Thou hast shown me the ways of life,
Thou wilt fill me with gladness of thy presence.'

'Let me tell you plainly, my friends, that the patriarch David died and was buried, and his tomb is here to this very day. It is clear therefore that he spoke of a prophet who knew that God had sworn to him that one of his own direct descendants should sit on his throne; and he said he was not abandoned to Hades, and his flesh never suffered corruption, he spoke with foreknowledge of the resurrection of the Messiah. The Jesus we speak of has been raised by God, as we can all bear witness. Exalted thus with God's right hand, he received the Holy Spirit from the Father, as was promised, and all that you now see and hear flows from him. For it was not David who went up to heaven; his own words are: "The Lord said to my Lord, 'Sit at my right hand until I make your enemies your footstool.' " Let all Israel then accept as certain that God has made this Jesus, whom you crucified, both Lord and Messiah.'

(Acts 2:22–36)

This sermon contains most of the claims of Christianity. Jesus was sent by God. Even his death was part of God's plan, and the fact that God raised him from the dead is proof of this. The Hebrew scriptures foretold this event. (Here Peter refers to verses in Psalms 132:16, and 110, which tradition says were written by King David.) Jesus is clearly God's Messiah and the Lord. By 'Lord', Peter presumably meant he was the person to whom men should give their allegiance, the ruled appointed by God. As Messiah Jesus was not only to be a deliverer, he was also to be the lord. However, Peter had not a military ruler in mind. He mentions another passage from the Scripture, 'I shall pour out my spirit on all flesh' (Joel 2:28–32), and says that this promise had been fulfilled in him and the other followers of Jesus and that whoever believed in Jesus would enjoy the same assuring and vitalising experience. (Acts 2:14–36).

Peter's first sermon did not include the claim that Jesus was God's son. This was not a part of his argument in preaching to the citizens of Jerusalem. However, when Christians began to tell the Gentile world about Jesus they made full use of it, for the idea of a Messiah meant nothing to people who were not Jews.

The Christian view of Jesus. Christians believe that Jesus was more than a prophet, that he stood in a special relationship to God, that of a son to his father. They also believe that his death was no terrible tragedy but the supreme way chosen by God to show his love for mankind and to re-establish his covenant, not with an individual like Abraham, or a nation like Israel, but with all humanity. By faith in this view of Jesus, anyone may enter into this new covenant. This was the message preached by the followers of Jesus. This message of God's covenant with all mankind came to be known in English as the Gospel, from an old English word godspel meaning 'good news.'

✳ Islam

Muhammad's early years. In the year 570 of the Christian Era a child was born in the Arabian city of Mecca. His name was Muhammad. His father had died a few months before his birth and his mother died when he was about the age of six. The boy grew up in the care of an uncle and eventually became the agent of a business woman named Khadija, who traded with such distant cities as Gaza and Damascus. Recognising Muhammad to be a trustworthy man, Khadija married him. He was twenty-five years old at the time and she was some years older, though perhaps not aged forty, as a tradition states, for she and Muhammad had six children, four daughters and two sons, the latter dying in infancy.

Muhammad became increasingly dissatisfied with the way of life which he saw around him in Mecca. In the nomadic camps which he had visited on his journeys he had found generosity and brotherliness. In Mecca the wealthy cared only about themselves and business success. The poor and orphans, those among whom Muhammad had grown up, were neglected. The religious life of Mecca was equally unsatisfactory. The moon and many gods made of stone or wood were worshipped by the population. These, Muhammad felt, had no power because they had no reality. Through meeting Christians and Arabs who believed that there was only one God, Muhammad had been brought to the position of rejecting the expression of religion which he found in Mecca. How long this crisis lasted and how he dealt with it is not known. As with Moses, Jesus, Guru Nanak and many other messengers of God these are 'hidden years' a period of frustrating silence.

The vision in the cave. At the end of this time Muhammad at every opportunity would seek solitude in a cave on one of the hills outside Mecca. Here, on a night which has come to be called the night of power, Muhammad had a vision of a glorious being who appeared high up in the sky near the horizon but then approached him until he was only two bow-shot lengths away. This being, whom Muhammad later realised was the angel Gabriel, commanded Muhammad, 'Iqra', which means 'Recite', or 'Read'. When Muhammad, who had been overcome by awe and astonishment, said that he could not read, Gabriel assured him that his task was not to read books written by men, but to preach the message of a book God would reveal to him through the angel.

Naturally this experience perplexed and disturbed Muhammad, but his wife and his cousin, a Christian named Waraqah, encouraged him to believe that he had been called to be a prophet. The revelations continued, though only once more did he actually receive a vision of Gabriel, and Muhammad began preaching to the people of Mecca. The year was probably 610, dated by the Christian calendar.

The message of Muhammad. The message that Muhammad preached was not well received by most of the population of Mecca. He insisted that they should worship the one God; in Arabic those words are translated by 'Allah'. He said that this God required them to be compassionate, to live as brothers rather than for themselves. The messenger found himself opposed by many of the citizens of Mecca, deserted by his own clan, and a widower, for his wife died in 619. Each year the Arabs made a pilgrimage to the Ka'ba, a cube-shaped building in Mecca. During the pilgrimage of 620 a group of men from Medina, a town about two hundred miles (320 km) to the north of Mecca, met Muhammad and were impressed by the message they heard him preach. The following year five of these six men returned, bringing seven others, influential members of Medinan society. They, too were impressed and made a promise to accept Muhammad as a prophet and to obey him. A trusty Muslim, who could remember accurately the teachings revealed by Gabriel to Muhammad, was sent with these twelve men to Medina. By 622 the number of Muslim pilgrims from Medina was seventy-five, representing all the clans of the city.

The Hijra. Medina was a town torn by civil unrest. Different factions took to the streets, roaming the countryside around and fighting. It was impossible to find a leader who could unite the community. Muhammad seemed to provide the answer to strife. Already members of every clan accepted him as a prophet; if all would pledge loyalty to him there might be peace. So, in September 622, Muhammad, already known as Al-Amin, the Trustworthy, slipped away from Mecca where a plot had been made to kill him, and became the leading citizen of Medina. Although many of the

Jews and Christians of Medina refused to recognise Muhammad as a messenger of God, the city became a Muslim community ruled by the revelations given to the Prophet. The significance of Muhammad's migration to Medina proved to be so great that eventually it was made the first year of the Muslim calendar. Dates in Muslim books are often given as AH or BH, that is after the Hijra, or before the Hijra, the Hijra being the Arabic word meaning 'emigration'. During the next eight years many tribes accepted Muhammad's leadership. Finally in 630 the people of Mecca received the citizen they had once despised as the Prophet he claimed to be. His enemies were reconciled, the idols of the Ka'ba that he had preached against were destroyed. The peace of Islam had been established in Arabia. Muhammad died in 632 CE, the leader of a successful movement. Mecca had become the focal point of Islam, though the Prophet died and was buried in the city that had first recognised him, Medina.

The Muslim view of Muhammad. When Muhammad died, his faithful companion Abu Bakr, whom the Prophet chose to lead the Muslims in prayer after his death, announced to the crowd, 'O ye people, if anyone worships Muhammad, Muhammad is dead, but if anyone worships God, he is alive and dies not.' These words contain an important teaching about the Prophet of Islam. He was a man, and nothing more. The Qur'an describes him as the Seal of the Prophets, that is the last and the greatest, but it always insists that God has no son, and that only God is worthy of worship. No Muslim worships the Prophet and Muslims are indignant if they are called Muhammadans, or if Muhammad is called the founder of Islam. There is no one the Muslims respect more than the Prophet, but admiration stops far short of worship.

Muhammad is honoured in a number of ways. When a Muslim speaks his name it is followed by 'peace be upon him', and this invocation of blessing is also frequently found written in books after the Prophet's name. However, it must be noted that similar respect is frequently paid to Jesus, Abraham, Noah, and the rest of the prophets who were sent by God in the centuries before Muhammad.

Muslims believe that Adam, Noah, Abraham, Jacob, Moses, Jesus and many other men whose names are to be found in the Jewish and Christian scriptures were also prophets. God gave them the same message as he entrusted to Muhammad. Though the prophets were faithful, their hearers were not. The Jews ignored the warnings of the prophets time and again. The Christians accepted the prophet Jesus but committed the blasphemy of raising

42

him to the status of God. Therefore, it was necessary for the compassionate and merciful God to give mankind a last chance. This time he chose to send his prophet to the Arabs, not the Jews. According to the teachings of Islam, Muhammad was only the last prophet of many, but the Muslim community is the only one which has recorded God's message without corrupting it (in the Qur'an), and has obeyed it faithfully.

Of all Muslims Muhammad is regarded as the perfect example. His conduct and even his dress are worthy of being copied. He expressed a preference for simple cotton garments, rather than silks, and said, 'Wear white garments for they are the best.' Fashion among Muslims has taken these considerations into account. More important were the Prophet's examples of generosity, kindness and respect for the elderly, which Muslims follow with great sincerity.

Imitating the Prophet's example does not, however, permit the drawing of portraits of him, or the carving of statues. These can easily become objects of worship. During the Middle Ages, some artists in Persia and other parts of the Muslim world did produce pictures of the Prophet, but the community as a whole deeply disapproves of such portraits.

Respect for the Prophet Muhammad is kept within strict limits within Islam. There has been a natural tendency for legends to grow up around him and tales of the miracles he performed to be told. However, the pious Muslim, much as he may reverence the Prophet, is fully aware of his words:

'I have no power to benefit, nor power to hurt, but as God wills.
Had I knowledge of the unseen I would have acquired much good,
and evil would not have touched me. I am only a warner, and a
bearer of good tidings to a people believing.'

(Sura 7:188)

These words are probably the best summary that can be given of the task which God entrusted to Muhammad and his place in Islam.

The rightly guided Caliphs. After the Prophet Muhammad's death, leadership of the Muslim community passed in turn to four of his companions; these are known as the four rightly guided Caliphs. The word 'caliph' is a shortened form of the Arabic phrase, Khalifat-ur-basul-Allah, 'successor to the messenger of God'.

Abu Bakr. The first Caliph was Muhammad's closest companion, Abu Bakr. The Prophet once said of him, 'If I were to take a friend other than my Lord, I would take Abu Bakr as a friend.' During his brief leadership (632–634) he consolidated the community, warded

43

off attacks on Mecca, and collected together the verses of the Qur'an. Abu Bakr is also remembered for his piety, his kindness, and the use of what little wealth he possessed to care for orphans and free slaves.

This beautiful mosque, known as the Dome of the Rock, stands on the site of Herod's Temple. The Dome was begun in 687 and took about four years to build

Umar. Umar was Caliph for ten years (634–644). During this period the Arab empire spread into Syria, Iraq and Egypt and the great cities of Damascus, Jerusalem and Alexandria were occupied. He provided a system of wages for his soldiers so that they should not have to loot the towns they captured to obtain a reward for fighting. He introduced a tax system and cared for the poor and elderly out of public funds. Perhaps most important was his treatment of Jewish and Christian subjects. Their rights and privileges are summed up in the contract he made with the Christians of Jerusalem:

> 'This is the protection which the servant of God, Umar, the Ruler of the Believers, has granted to the people of Eiliya (Jerusalem). The protection is for their lives and properties, their churches and crosses, their sick and healthy and for all their co-religionists. Their churches shall not be used for habitation, nor shall they be demolished, nor shall any injury be done to them or to their compounds, or to their crosses, nor shall their properties be injured in any way. There shall be no compulsion for these people

44

in the matter of religion, nor shall any of them suffer any injury on account of religion. . . . Whatever is written herein is under the covenant of God and the responsibility of His Messenger, of the Caliphs and of the believers and shall hold good as long as they pay *Jizya* (the tax for their defence) imposed on them.'

Uthman. Uthman (644–656) was married to two of Muhammad's daughters, to Ruqayya, and after her death to Kultum. Under Uthman's guidance an authoritative version of the Qur'an was published and copies were sent to the principal cities of the Muslim world. Towards the end of his reign civil unrest broke out and the Caliph met his end at the hands of an assassin.

Ali. Ali (656–661) was the Prophet's cousin and married Muhammad's youngest daughter Fatima. Of him Muhammad said, 'You are my brother in this world and the next.' He had been a close adviser to the three earlier Caliphs and only assumed the leadership of Islam with the utmost reluctance. He attempted to restore order by dismissing the provincial governors whose injustices had apparently forced their subjects to rebel. However, the rulers of Syria and Egypt stood out successfully against him and when Ali was killed by an assassin during the holy month of Ramadan, the unity of Islam under one undisputed leader finally came to an end. Though the ruler of Syria took the title of Caliph, and it became hereditary, it never held the same significance for Islam as it had in the days of the rightly guided Caliphs who had been companions of the Prophet.

Sikhism

The Sikh faith was revealed through the messengers who lived in north India between 1469 and 1708 CE. These men were called the Sikh Gurus. In an earlier section the role of the Hindu guru has been described. It is to enlighten the disciple so that he may become like his teacher, a person free from the threat of rebirth; one who will live eternally with Brahman when the spirit is released from the body at death. The particular emphasis of the Sikh Gurus, and the political circumstances of sixteenth-century and seventeenth-century India, resulted in a movement within Hinduism emerging as an independent religion.

The Sikh Gurus all came from the protector or warrior class of Hindu society. They were Kshatriyas. Therefore they had a right to study the Vedas, but not to teach them. However, they insisted that their revelation came to them direct from God, not from the Vedas, and that it was he who gave them a message to preach, and authority to proclaim it. The essence of their preaching was that there is only one God, who is the creator and sustainer of all life. People of all classes, Brahmins and Shudras, men and women, rich and poor, are equally in his care and may receive enlightenment and spiritual liberation in this present life. God takes the initiative in bringing man spiritual freedom. All man has to do is respond to his grace with faithful obedience. Such a person should live a useful existence as a householder, serving God through worship, honest hard work, and being generous to the poor and needy.

Guru Nanak (1469–1539). The first of the Gurus was called Nanak. He was born in a village called Talwandi, some miles from Lahore, the largest city in the Punjab region of north India. Talwandi is now in the country of Pakistan. Nanak grew up as a Hindu, and according to the stories of his childhood quickly mastered the sacred language of Sanskrit. That part of India was already under Muslim rule and when Nanak was a young man he entered the employment of the local government official. In his service he learned about the religion of Islam. Although Nanak grew up familiar with two great religious traditions, he does not seem to have been able to solve his own spiritual quest. A crisis occurred in his life when he was about thirty years of age and it was as a consequence of this that he became a spiritual guide to others, a Guru.

God calls him. Like most Hindus, Nanak bathed in the local river each morning. One day he failed to reappear. The river was dragged but no sign of Nanak could be found. Three days later, when all hopes of discovering him alive had gone, he reappeared. He told his friends that he had been taken to God's court and there given a cup of nectar to drink, with the instructions that he should rejoice in God's name and teach others to do so. Nanak, henceforth known as Guru Nanak, described this experience in one of his hymns:

> 'I was a minstrel out of work,
> The Lord gave me employment.
> The mighty One instructed me,
> 'Night and day, sing my praise.'
> The Lord summoned the minstrel
> To his High Court.
> On me he bestowed the robe of honouring
> him and singing his praise.
>
> On me he bestowed the Nectar in a cup,
> The nectar of his true and holy name.

Guru Nanak. A traditional portrait of the kind found in most Sikh homes.

Those who at the bidding of the Guru
Feast and take their fill of the Lord's holiness
Attain peace and joy.
Your minstrel spreads your glory
By singing your word.
Nanak, through adoring the truth
We attain to the all-highest.'

(AG 150)

The Guru left his work as an accountant to become a full-time preacher, helping men and women to know the God who was quietly present in their hearts.

The journeys. Guru Nanak's missionary journeys occupied the next twenty years of his life, until about 1521. He then settled down in a village called Kartarpur, and there he established the first Sikh community. The word 'Sikh' comes from a Punjabi verb, sikhna meaning 'to learn', and was the name that came to be applied to the disciples of Guru Nanak who gathered around him to receive his teachings. Besides the message which the Sikhs found in the Guru's many hymns the community needed someone to care for them and lead them when Guru Nanak died. Therefore, at some stage in his ministry at Kartarpur, Guru Nanak chose a man called Lehna to be his successor, and trained him to assume leadership of the Sikhs. This man's name he changed to Angad, which means 'my limb', suggesting that the new Guru was an extension of himself. The Sikhs are extremely insistent on the belief that each Guru was faithful to the same message that Guru Nanak first preached. As one Sikh put it:

'The divine light is the same, the life form is the same, the king has merely changed the body.'

(AG 966)

The ten Gurus. Although each of the Gurus is regarded as equally important by the Sikhs, each being a messenger of God, some achieved more in developing the Sikh community and religion than others. The full list of Gurus reads:

1. Guru Nanak (1469–1539)
2. Guru Angad (1539–1552)
3. Guru Amar Das (1552–1574)
4. Guru Ram Das (1574–1581)
5. Guru Arjan (1581–1606)

 6. Guru Hargobind (1606–1644)
 7. Guru Har Rai (1644–1661)
 8. Guru Har Krishan (1661–1664)
 9. Guru Tegh Bahadur (1664–1675)
10. Guru Gobind Singh (1675–1708)

Briefly, the other Gurus are remembered for the following deeds.

Guru Angad consolidated the community and gathered together the hymns of Guru Nanak, a task which the first Guru may have begun before his death.

Guru Amar Das assembled the Sikhs at his headquarters, a village called Goindwal, three times a year, at the time of Hindu festivals. This had the effect of making Sikhs decide between serving their Guru or observing Hindu rituals; they could not be both Sikh and Hindu.

Guru Ram Das began the building of Amritsar, the place which was to become the centre of Sikhism.

Guru Arjan completed Amritsar and built other towns. He collected the hymns of his four predecessors, himself, and some Hindu and Muslim holy men, and produced the first version of the Sikh scriptures. It was given the title Adi Granth. He was arrested by the Mughal rulers of north India, died in captivity and is therefore revered as the first martyr-Guru of the Sikhs.

Guru Hargobind was a hunter and warrior rather than a composer of hymns and a man renowned for his piety. Under his leadership the Sikhs began to arm themselves to join in uprisings against the Mughal rule.

Guru Har Rai was leader for seventeen uneventful years and was succeeded by a child of five, *Guru Har Krishan*. Most of his short reign of three years was spent under house-arrest, where he died of smallpox.

Guru Tegh Bahadur, the ninth guru was the youngest son of Guru Hargobind. Twice he had been passed over when the Sikh leader was being selected. He combined the qualities of a number of his predecessors, being a pious man who composed hymns, and a soldier who joined in the fight of Indian nationalists against Mughal rule. After a period of imprisonment he died a martyr's death in Delhi.

Guru Gobind Singh was responsible for bringing the line of human Gurus to an end. Before he died of wounds received at the hands of an assassin, he installed the scripture which Guru Arjan had compiled and he had revised, as Guru. Some years earlier, in

49

1699, he introduced a new rite of initiation into the Sikh faith, and gave the men and women who joined this community, the Khalsa or 'pure ones', the common surname Kaur or Singh, which means princess or lion respectively. They also adopted a uniform, part of which, in the case of men, is the turban.

The place of the Gurus in Sikhism.   The ten Gurus are highly respected by the Sikh community as messengers through whom God has spoken and revealed himself. However, reverence must not be confused with worship. Only God is worshipped by Sikhs. Although pictures of the Gurus may be found in Sikh homes and places of worship (these are called gurdwaras), Sikhs should not bow to them or garland them, as is the Hindu practice in their homes and temples. In fact the tenth Guru said, 'The Khalsa is my other self, in it I live and move and have my being.' Consequently on one occasion when his hard-pressed soldiers told him to leave them and raise another army he acknowledged their equality and reluctantly obeyed their command. However, the ten Gurus do belong to a special class of men and women, a few people whose birth is regarded as non-karmic.

According to Hindu teaching anyone who does not attain spiritual liberation (moksha) during his or her present life, must be born into this world again as a consequence of conduct while on earth. Such rebirth must continue until the effect of bad works is exhausted and liberation is achieved. Sikhs believe that the Gurus were perfect men who had no need to be reborn because of past deeds; the reason why they came back to earth was that God wanted them to be his messengers. The consequence of this belief can be found in many of the traditions associated with Guru Nanak and his successors. For example, the Guru is described as being able to talk at birth, and is said to have been much cleverer than the Hindu priest who was given the task of educating him. The explanation of this precociousness lies in the fact that the Guru was already perfect; he had nothing to learn. According to this view, Guru Nanak's experience of being taken to God's court was not one of enlightenment, for he was already enlightened. It was the signal for him to begin the task God had predestined him to do.

Although the Sikhs naturally give pride of place to their own Gurus, they are also ready to recognise such men as the Buddha, Moses, Jesus, Muhammad, or a famous Hindu of the twentieth century, Gandhi, as similar beings who were sent into this world to reveal God's message. They could not, however, accept the belief of either Hindus or Christians that God is ever born himself. The way in which God reveals himself, according to the Sikh, is that he speaks to mankind. God is man's teacher, the unique Guru from whom his messengers learn their wisdom.

Questions

1. *Explain the importance of* **two** *messengers of God within their own traditions.*

2. *How does the Christian view of Jesus differ from Jewish or Muslim views?*

3. *Brahmins, Bodhisattvas or Bhikkus, Gurus, Prophets, Rabbis, Apostles and Caliphs feature in the religions you have studied. Explain what part each of these adherents or followers plays in his particular religion. How do they differ?*

4. *The following important words occur in this chapter: revelation; God; soul; liberation; covenant; prophesy; gospel; worship; resurrection, Allah; Enlightenment, Dharma and Nirvana. What particular significance has each of these abstract words in relation to one or other of the religions? Briefly describe what is meant by each word.*

5. *Describe the experience that caused* **two** *messengers, from different faiths, to begin their work.*

6. *Outline the lives of* **two** *messengers before they began their work.*

7. *How did the early career of Moses or Muhammad prepare him for his later task as God's servant and messenger?*

8. *What specific task did* **two** *of the messengers seek to accomplish? Tell the story of their achievement.*

9. *Outline briefly the careers of* **two** *of the religious messengers you have studied (not from the same faith). Explain how members of their faiths regard them.*

CHAPTER TWO
SCRIPTURES

The truth in books or sacred teachings

Each of the six religions being studied in this book has its sacred scriptures. The full meaning of this phrase will only become clear as each scripture is studied in detail and the information is put together in our minds. For the moment, a scripture may be regarded as a book or set of books teaching about the truth, the reality which is beyond our world. They present in written form the divinely revealed or specially discovered teaching associated with the messengers.

Sometimes the period of revelation or discovery is very long—perhaps the best part of a thousand years in the cases of Hinduism, Judaism and Buddhism, if one takes account of all the schools. Sometimes it is much shorter. In nearly two hundred years the Sikh teachings were revealed and assembled and the standard text of the Qur'an was finalised in the Caliphate of Uthman, perhaps by 651 CE, only forty years after Muhammad had received his first revelation. The position of the Christian Bible is very unusual when compared with the others, for it includes the scriptures of another faith, the Hebrew or Jewish Bible. It might, therefore, be argued that it took nearly fifteen hundred years to produce, even though the New Testament books were written in the space of between forty and a hundred years. However, the length of the process has no significance; it is the source of the teachings that matters in the mind of believers.

In every one of these religions there is an eagerness to say that the word contained in the scriptures is not man's wisest thoughts but God's revelation; in one sense it is the 'Word of God', or, to put it in language more appropriate to Buddhism, it is Dharma, truth and teaching which is beyond conventional truth and purely human wisdom, and links us to what is changeless and eternal. This belief in the divine origin of the teaching contained in the scriptures is a feature of the six faiths. Whatever view each religion may have of the scriptures of the other faiths, it agrees that these (and the scriptures of other religions) form a unique class of literature, divinely inspired.

The attitude of a faith towards its scripture is shown in a number of ways. The sacred text is often handled in a special way, both privately and in public worship. In this chapter there will be some repetition of things mentioned in the section on worship, but it would be wise when reading that section to bear in mind what is said here. The physical position of the scripture during public worship, and sometimes when it is not actually being used, is also significant. The use that is made of the book in public worship and private devotion is also important. These are aspects to be observed carefully when visiting a place of worship, especially when a service is being held. Finally, and most important, the scriptures contain teachings which are believed to come from outside man's ordinary experience. The way members of a religion react to the teaching contained in the scripture tells us most about the regard that they really have for it.

Most religions also have writings which are respected but not accorded the title 'scripture' because they are seen to be the products of human activity rather than revelation. Most commonly these are either liturgies, including credal statements, or collections of biographical material about the messengers.

ॐ The Hindu scriptures

The sacred writings of Hinduism are divided into two groups, sruti and smrti. Sruti means 'that which has been heard' and refers to writings which are believed to have come directly from God. The priests who passed them on orally for centuries trace them back to men who heard them from God himself. Smrti means remembered. Hindus believe that scriptures which fall into this category represent human recollections of God's message to mankind. Memory can be defective so these writings are not as highly regarded as the sruti texts.

The Vedas. The revealed scriptures are the Vedas, a word meaning knowledge. These are divided into two groups, the Vedas and the Upanishads, both written in Sanskrit. There are four Vedas, the most important being the Rig, or Royal, Veda. This is a collection of hymns divided into ten sections (mandalas). These were composed by the Aryans who conquered northern India somewhere

53

around 1750 BCE. Most of them, if not all, were intended for use in the sacrificial worship of the Aryans. One of the most important subjects is Agni who represents fire, an essential ingredient in sacrificial worship, for fire consumes the offerings and so takes them to the gods. The first hymn of the Rig Veda which is dedicated to Agni, reads:

> 'I extol Agni, the household priest, the divine minister of the sacrifice, the chief priest, the bestower of blessings.
> May that Agni, who is to be extolled by ancient and modern seers, conduct the gods here.
> Through Agni may one gain day by day wealth and welfare which is glorious and replete with heroic sons.
> O Agni, the sacrifice and ritual which you encompass on every side, that indeed goes to the gods.
> May Agni, the chief priest, who possesses the insight of a sage who is truthful, widely renowned, and divine, come here with the gods.
> O Agni, O Angiras ('messenger'), whatever prosperity you bring to the pious is indeed in accordance with your true function.
> O Agni, illuminator of darkness, day by day we approach you with holy thought bringing homage to you,
> Presiding at ritual functions, the brightly shining custodian of the cosmic order (rita), thriving in your own realm.
> O Agni, be easy of access to us as a father to his son.
> Join us for our wellbeing.'

(Rig Veda 1:1)

Two of the many Hindu gods

Sarasvati

Kubera

54

Among the gods who were worshipped was Indra, the warrior, another was Varuna, universal monarch who fixed the laws of the universe such as gravity, directed the rivers and fixed the course of the planets. He was also concerned about human behaviour and morality. One of the hymns to Varuna contains this verse:

> 'What sin we have ever committed against an intimate, O Varuna, against a friend or companion at any time, a brother, a neighbour, or a stranger, free us from it, O Varuna.
> If like gamblers at play we have cheated, whether in truth or without knowing, free us from our guilt, God. So may we be dear to thee, O Varuna.'

(Rig Veda 5:85)

Did the Aryans who compiled the Rig Veda believe in many gods or one? It is not easy to provide a conclusive answer but one line in the Rig Veda says:

> 'To what is one, wise men give many a title,
> They call it Agni (Fire), Yama (Death),
> Matarisvan.'

Another passage is even clearer:

> 'For an awakened soul Indra, Varuna, Agni, Yama, Aditya, Chandra – all these names represent only one basic power and spiritual reality.'

This sentence occurs in the Yajur-Veda, a collection of formulas and prayers based on the Rig Veda and intended to help the priest who officiated at sacrificial ceremonies. The many gods referred to are only different aspects of the one God. Another compilation was the Sama-Veda, a manual used by the 'singing priest' whose chanting was an important aspect of Aryan worship. Beside these three Vedas there was a fourth book called the Atharva Veda. This is later than the others and may contain material belonging to the people conquered by the Aryans.

Although many of the Aryans and their subjects found the sacrificial system administered by the Brahmin priests and sometimes by kings comforting, some Indians were not satisfied. Instead they preferred to meditate upon the teachings of Gurus, some of whom were Brahmins, though caste divisions had not yet become as rigid as they were later. The right to give spiritual guidance does not yet seem to have been regarded as the exclusive prerogative of the Brahmins. The purpose of meditating upon the teaching of a Guru was to gain such spiritual enlightenment that the soul (atman) attained liberation and did not have to be reborn in another body.

The Upanishads. Examples of this teaching can be found in the other revealed scriptures of the Hindus, the Upanishads. Upanishad is a combination of three words, 'upa' near, 'ni' down, and 'shad' meaning to sit. Put together they suggest the idea of 'sitting down near'. Put very simply the Upanishads are the teachings learned by seekers of enlightenment who sat near their Gurus to receive their guidance.

There were many Upanishads written in Sanskrit between about 500 and 200 BCE. About thirteen of them won more respect than the others and are still studied by Hindus as well as scholars of religious studies today.

The gods of the Vedas seem to have had little importance for the teachers of the Upanishads. In fact Indra, the mighty warrior deity, is depicted in one as a rather slow student who had to serve his Guru for over a century before he became enlightened. The Upanishads are interested in working out the relationship of man's spirit (the atman) to the Spirit underlying the universe (Brahman), to which we might give the name God. Once the relationship is understood by the student, his Guru can help him achieve it. One of the Upanishads puts the situation of natural, unenlightened man particularly well:

> 'Those who do not know the field walk time and again over the treasure hidden beneath their feet and do not find it: in the same way all creatures pass through the world of Brahman day by day but do not find it for they are carried away by unreality.'

> (Chandogya Upanishad 8.3:2)

Without a Guru, a teacher who can help him see what is true and eternal, man ignorantly lives in the world, perhaps enjoying it, but failing to meet God, the treasure contained in it. Not surprisingly the great prayer of the Upanishads is:

> 'From the unreal lead me to the real, from darkness lead me to light, from death lead me to immortality.'

> (Brihadaranyaka Upanishad 1.3:28)

Sometimes books use the word 'Veda' both of the four Vedas and the Upanishads. This is because both are regarded as sacred scripture, revealed knowledge. The Upanishads contain the essence of the religious truth which can be found in the Vedic hymns.

The use of the Vedas (including the Upanishads) in worship. A visitor to a Hindu temple may find a copy of the Vedas in the building, especially in Britain, as a Hindu benefactor has donated copies to most temples. However, the book is seldom used in worship.

Instead the priest may read or chant passages from a small book or may recite them from memory. These words and most of the hymns and prayers used during services are taken from the Vedas and Upanishads. For many centuries the sacred Vedas were an oral tradition, memorised rather than written and taught by one generation of priests to another. It is not surprising, therefore, that priests still trust their memories rather than use books.

The Epics – the Mahabharata.   The world's longest poem, and one of the finest, is the Mahabharata, originally composed in Sanskrit in the ninth century BCE, but refined and added to during the next six or seven hundred years and translated into most of the world's languages. The title of the epic means 'The Great Story of the War of the Bharatas', and it may have been inspired by a fearful battle which took place at Kurukshetra, not very far from the later city of Delhi, about 900 BCE. The story which is the thread running through the Mahabharata's 200 000 verses, is—very much simplified and condensed—that of a power struggle between two royal families, both descended from King Bharata. The diagram shows the relationship of the principal characters in the poem:

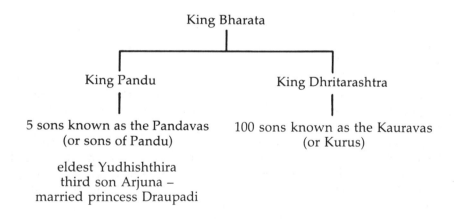

The family tree of the Pandavas

The story of the poem.   King Pandu gave up his throne to retire to the forest, so Dhritarashtra, his brother, ruled in his place. He brought up king Pandu's sons with his own. However, the Kaurava brothers became jealous of the heroism and virtue of their cousins and decided to kill them by burning down their palace. The five Pandavas, hearing of the plot, retired to the forest where they lived

57

in safety, disguised as Brahmins. Their cousins thought they had died in the fire. One of the Pandavas, Arjuna, eventually emerged from his forest retreat, won an archery contest and with it the hand of a princess, Draupadi, in marriage. He was the only man strong enough to lift and draw the bow. He also succeeded in hitting the eye of the revolving target, (a representation of a fish set on the end of a raised pole) with each of his five shots. The Kauravas were now aware that their cousins were alive. No-one else but Arjuna could have performed such a feat. They agreed to share the kingdom with them but gave them only the desolate parts. However, the Pandavas worked so hard that they soon ruled a richer kingdom than the Kauravas, whose jealousy and anger increased.

Fearing to risk a war, the Kaurava brothers decided to win the Pandava kingdom by trickery. They persuaded Yudhishthira, the eldest Pandava, to play a game of dice. The winner was to go into exile for twelve years, afterwards to return but live unrecognised, and only then would his kingdom be restored. Should he be recognised the loser would have to go into exile again. King Yudhishthira, of course, lost, and the Pandavas accepted the consequences.

When they had succeeded in passing the thirteenth year unrecognised they came forward to claim their kingdom. The Kauravas refused them even a single village and a war broke out in which Yudhishthira and the Pandavas were victorious. The epic ends with their retirement, in true Indian style, from a life of righteous action (dharma is the Hindu term) to one of meditation in the Himalayas where the five Pandavas and Draupadi await eternal bliss.

The story of the Mahabharata has been told in outline, without going into the details and digressions which the epic enjoys exploring because it plays such an important part in Indian life. The plot may sound complicated to Westerners, but this is a typical feature of Indian literature, and the listener must be attentive. It contains worldly wisdom, moral teaching, social comment and political advice, and has been drawn upon by countless story-tellers for nearly three thousand years. Few people have read the Mahabharata in its entirety, but the village story-teller, dramatists, dancers and those who produce puppet theatre (a very popular form of entertainment in India) frequently turn to the Mahabharata for inspiration.

The Ramayana. The Ramayana is more recent than the Great Epic and shorter — a mere 24 000 Sanskrit couplets. It was composed about five hundred years after the Mahabharata and claims to be the work of one man, Valmiki. Again, it is a moral tale of right and wrong, good and evil, courage and loyalty. In it Prince Rama, King of Ayodhya, loses his right to the throne and is forced to go into exile. His brother Lakshman, and his wife Sita, faithfully go with him. By trickery a demon Ravana captures Sita and takes her to his island kingdom (Sri Lanka). There she remains while Rama and Lakshman search for her in vain. Eventually it is Hanuman, king of the monkeys, who succeeds in finding her. With his army Sita is rescued and Rama returns with her, in triumph, to Ayodhya to reclaim his kingdom.

This story of womanly virtue and fidelity, male courage and kingly uprightness, is also frequently acted, danced and dramatised, as well as being told by story-tellers. It is also the victory of good over evil, Rama's defeat of Ravana, and the faithfulness of Sita which is remembered at the important festival of Dussehra, though often the goddess Durga, rather than Hanuman, is described as Rama's helper.

The Bhagavad Gita. At the beginning of this section it was suggested that the Mahabharata was a composite work, written by a number of hands over a period of six or seven centuries. One part of the epic probably produced in the second century BCE has become the most famous of all Hindu scriptures. Though it was originally written in Sanskrit, it has been translated into all the major Indian languages, as well as many European, including English. The name of these eighteen chapters which form part of the sixth book of the Mahabharata is the Bhagavad Gita, The Song of the Adorable One.

Arjuna, the son of Pandu who won the archery contest, is riding along the battle lines on the field of Kurukshetra as the armies prepare for battle. Suddenly he orders his charioteer to withdraw from the battle. The horror of fighting against his kith and kin, his cousins the Kauravas, appals him. Instead of obeying Arjuna, Krishna, his charioteer, begins first to argue with the prince and then to teach him. As the story proceeds the reader and Arjuna realise that Krishna is no mere driver of a chariot; he is God. Arjuna eventually recognises that he is not one of the many gods of popular mythology or one of the manifestations mentioned in the Rig Veda. He is the Supreme Deity who has taken human appearance to teach Arjuna the truth.

The message of the Bhagavad Gita. This is complex, but in essence it states that the highest form of worship is devotion to God as he is revealed in Krishna. Because of God's love for him and his love for God, whoever dies in the battle will live eternally, and whoever survives it will achieve the same good through worshipping this loving God. What Krishna asks is love. With this, any offering however slight, even a single flower, becomes acceptable. Without it, worship is devoid of worth. This path to bliss is open to everyone, to Brahmins, and the other higher castes, Kshatriyas like Arjuna himself, and Vaishyas, but Shudras and women may also follow it. (By this time the priests were probably teaching their hearers that only the 'twice born' castes could hope for spiritual liberation in this round of existence. Shudras and women must await rebirth into a higher caste when as men, moksha [liberation] could be attained). Interestingly, the Bhagavad Gita does not denounce caste as a social institution but it does say that it is neither an impediment to nor a guarantee of God's love.

By the end of the poem the reader has long since left the battlefield of Kurukshetra behind, but to return to that subject, the unknown author of the Bhagavad Gita brings Arjuna back to battle and he fights. However, the poem is really a commendation of the religion of personal devotion to a personal God—what is known as bhakti from a word bhaj, meaning 'devotion'—and a discouragement to those who would seek to serve God by following the path of inaction by living as recluses in the forest. Especially in modern India, struggling to feed its huge population and make democracy work, the Bhagavad Gita is regarded as the scripture of the hour, a challenge to worship God through selfless, patient, and whole-hearted service.

The Laws of Manu. Almost contemporary with the Bhagavad Gita there appeared another form of literature with a very different message, the law codes, the most famous of which is the Laws of Manu. These were not poems about men or gods, but rules governing most aspects of life, from the punishment for killing a cow —a sacred and therefore protected animal — to saying who might study the Vedas. Manu was one of the ancient rishis or wise men to whom the Vedas were revealed; he is also said to have been responsible for this volume of laws, also given to him by the gods. With regard to the role of the four castes it says:

'For the sake of the preservation of this entire creation, Purusha, the exceedingly resplendent one, assigned separate duties to the classes which had sprung from his mouth, arms, thighs and feet. Teaching, studying, performing sacrificial rites, so too making others perform sacrificial rites, and giving away and receiving gifts —these he assigned to the brahmins.
Protection of the people, giving away of wealth, performance of sacrificial rites, study, and avoiding the slavery of sensual pleasures —these are, in short, the duties of a kshatriya.
Tending of cattle, giving away wealth, performance of sacrificial

rites, study, trade and commerce, usury, and agriculture – these are the occupations of a vaishya.
The Lord has prescribed only one occupation (karma) for a shudra, namely, service without malice of even these other three classes.'

(Laws of Manu 1.87–98)

Purusha is a word for 'man'; here it refers to God, the Person from whom all beings came into existence, according to one of the Vedic hymns.

Although the Laws of Manu are smrti and not sruti, they have been the text upon which many Hindus have based every aspect of their lives. They are still very influential today though the laws of India are not derived from them. India is a secular state, a democratic republic in which everyone enjoys equal legal rights.

The story-teller has already been mentioned in this chapter. In a land where there is little need to read and write, and where a newspaper costs more than the daily wage of some of those who have paid work—and many are unemployed—the man who tells stories is a highly valued entertainer. He, and grandmother, the family story-teller, pass on the cultural traditions from one generation to another. Through watching their elders children learn what to do; through listening to the stories they learn what to believe.

The Puranas. Many of the tales are about the gods of the Vedas, though they are taken from collections of material only about one thousand years old, rather than from the Vedas themselves. Because these stories are about the distant past or even the timelessness before the existence of this world the books are called the Puranas, purana meaning 'ancient'. There are eighteen minor Puranas and eighteen major ones, the most important being the Bhagavata Purana, the Purana of the Adorable Lord. In the Purana he is not a charioteer, but a child, who often plays tricks on his parents, even stealing the milk from the butter churn, and then a young man, handsome and romantic, the lover of a beautiful girl named Radha. However, although the stories can be enjoyed as amusing tales, the thoughtful person, with insight, can perceive that Krishna is really the supreme, loving God, as Arjuna perceived the real nature of the charioteer in the Bhagavad Gita.

With the Puranas the group of scriptures known as smrti comes by an end. Since they were completed, perhaps in the twelfth century CE, Hinduism has continued to produce sacred writings, the hymns of hundreds of men and women inspired by their experience of God's love. Among these teachers are such men as Kabir, Caitanya, Ravi Das, Guru Nanak and the woman teacher Mirabai. Those who regard these people as their Gurus often

61

Shri Pramukh Swami, a Hindu guru, examines a Sanskrit text in the Bodleian library, Oxford.

consider the hymns which they composed as more important than the Vedas, for through them they, too, experience God. Recently the West has become interested in these teachings and even inspired by them. It was this influence that prompted George Harrison to write 'My sweet Lord' which begins:

'My sweet Lord
Mm my Lord
Mm my Lord.

I really wanna see you
Really wanna be with you
Really wanna see you Lord, but it takes so long—my Lord.

My sweet Lord
Mm my Lord
Mm my Lord.

I really wanna know you
Really wanna go with you
Really wanna show you Lord that it won't take long—my Lord.'

A comparable theme is expressed in the following bhajan, to use the Hindu term for these devotional songs, though at greater length, and with much poetic imagery:

'I know not how thou singest, my master! I ever listen in silent amazement.
The light of thy music illumines the world. The life-breath of thy music runs from sky to sky. The holy stream of thy music breaks through all stony obstacles and rushes on.
My heart longs to join in thy song, but vainly struggles for a voice. I would speak, but speech breaks not into song, and I cry out baffled. Ah, thou hast made my heart captive in the endless meshes of thy music, my master!'

(Anthology of Indian Literature p. 576 verse III – Tagore)

✡ The Jewish scriptures

The scriptures of the Tenakh, to give the Jewish Bible its Hebrew name, are divided into three sections, the Pentateuch, the Prophets and the Writings. The Hebrew names of these divisions are Torah, Nevi'im, and Ketubim, and from the initials of these TNK, comes the word TeNaK which may be rendered Tenakh, Tenach, or Tanach in English transliterations.

The Torah. Of the three parts the first, the Torah, traditionally called the Five Books of Moses, is the most important. Its contents are the books Genesis, Exodus, Leviticus, Numbers and Deuteronomy. Perhaps it is significant that it begins with the story of the creation of the world by the word of God, who said, 'Let there by light and there was light' (Genesis 1:3), for much of the Torah is God's word to Moses and through him to the Hebrew people, telling them how God wants them to live and to worship.

The literal meaning of Torah is 'teaching' and this is certainly an appropriate title for a group of books which teach the Jews how God works in history and creation, how they should conduct themselves towards their fellows, whether Jewish or Gentile, and how they should live in relationship to God and his world. Care for animals, 'You shall not muzzle the ox when it treads the grain' (Deuteronomy 25:4), is to be found alongside rules for observing harvest festivals (Deuteronomy 26) for example. The great affirmation of belief in one God is expressed in the Shema, the first words a Jewish child should learn and the last a Jew should utter as he passes from this life to the world to come:

> 'Hear O Israel, the Lord our God is one.
> And you shall love the Lord thy God with all they heart and with all thy soul and with all thy might.'

> (Deuteronomy 6:4–6)

The passage continues, stressing the importance of keeping these words always in mind:

> 'These words which I command you this day shall be in your heart. You shall teach them diligently to your children and shall speak of them when you sit in your house and when you walk by the way, and when you lie down and when you rise up. And you shall bind them for a sign upon your hand, and they shall be for frontlets between your eyes. And you shall write them upon the doorposts of your house and upon your gates.'

On the lintel of the outside door and of the inside rooms of a Jewish home these words can be found, placed in a small metal container called a mezuzah, which means doorpost. They are also contained in small leather cubes which a Jewish man binds to his forehead and left arm when he says his weekday morning prayers. These tefillin and the mezuzah help him to remember not only the words of the Shema, so called because the Hebrew for 'Hear O Israel' is 'Shema Israel'; they also remind him of the whole Torah, of which these teachings are the essence.

The Torah in worship.   The importance of the Torah is best and most easily seen at synagogue worship. When not in use, the scroll of the Torah is kept in the Ark, the cupboard set in the wall at the Jerusalem-facing end of the synagogue. During the service the doors are opened, the scroll is taken out with reverence and carried in procession to the lectern from which it will be read. Men will reach forward as the scroll passes them and touch it with the edge of their prayer shawls, which they will then put to their lips. To be called up to carry the scroll, to read it or to witness it being read is one of the greatest honours that can be given to a member of the congregation. Such a person, as he approaches the reading desk will say, 'Blessed is he who has given the Torah.' The scroll is normally capped by a silver crown, for the Torah is also called the 'crown of life'. When it is read the reader will not follow the words with his finger but with a Torah pointer made of wood, or more often, silver. This protects the text from finger marks but also indicates a respectful wish not to handle the scroll unnecessarily. When the portion of Torah prescribed for reading on the particular Sabbath has been completed, the scroll is put back into its covering and returned to the Ark, which is then shut.

A young Jew reads from the Torah at his Bar Mitzvah. He uses a Torah pointer to avoid unnecessarily touching the page of the sacred text.

It may seem surprising to learn that men might be called to witness the reading of the Torah rather than read it themselves. This is not because the language of the Torah is Hebrew; the men of the congregation will be able to read the Hebrew of their prayer books. It is because of the way the scroll is written. It has no punctuation and no vowels. One word runs into another. Only someone who has been specially trained can read the scroll, no matter how good his Hebrew may be. In addition, it is not precisely accurate to say that the scroll is read; it is intoned. As the scroll lacks any aid in the form of musical notation, training is necessary before one is able to do this.

There was a time when many men were capable of reading the Torah in public worship. It is still remembered as an ideal whenever a Jewish boy attains the age of thirteen and is made 'Bar Mitzvah', son of the commandment. He is carefully prepared to read a part of the Sabbath portion and in the presence of a congregation, which includes many relatives who may have travelled long distances to attend the important event, for the first time in his life he is called to offer a blessing for the Torah. From that moment onwards the duty, which until then his father had, to encourage him to obey the teachings of the Torah is his alone.

Scribes and scrolls. Great care goes into the writing of a scroll of the Torah. It must be written by hand on parchment, using ink of a special formula and with a goose quill for pen. The scribes who write copies of the Torah devote their lives to the task from the time they begin their training as young men, though they usually have other occupations besides being scribes. Should a mistake occur during the writing of a scroll the error can be erased, unless the name of God is the word that has been incorrectly written. That cannot be rubbed out, so that portion of the scroll must be buried and the section re-written. A Torah scroll that has become too worn to be used in synagogue worship is also buried, as a person who dies is buried.

The Masoretes. For centuries the earliest copies of the Torah which had survived were the texts written by the Masoretes, scholars in Babylon and Palestine who had devoted themselves to producing Biblical texts free from errors. The word Masoretes comes from a Hebrew root meaning 'to hand down'; it was their aim to pass on an accurate text of the Hebrew Bible to future generations. The Masoretes were at work during the eighth, ninth and tenth centuries. Eventually it was the text of the Palestinian Ben Asher that won universal acceptance. One old copy dating from 1008 is in the

Public Library of Leningrad. The question of the reliability of such a document has often concerned scholars. Can a text written about eleven hundred years after the last book of the Jewish Bible, the book of Daniel, be trusted? Surely changes must have been made, if only by accident. In 1947 the first of many discoveries of scrolls written before the Jewish Revolt of 66 CE was made in a cave near the Dead Sea. When these texts were examined, and they covered every book of the Hebrew Bible with the exception of Esther, they showed that the Masoretes had been remarkably successful in preserving an accurate text. The words read in the synagogue today were shown to be virtually the same as those uttered in Jerusalem two thousand years ago.

The Ark in a synagogue. The two panels between the lions of Judah and Israel represent the two tablets bearing the commandments. The line of Hebrew writing under these reads, 'Know before whom you stand'.

The Origin and development of the Torah. From the synagogue of today we must go back many centuries, beyond the Masoretes and the Dead Sea scrolls, to ask when the Torah was first written. The traditional view, still held by many Jews and some Christians, is that the Torah was revealed to Moses and written down by him in its entirety except for the last few verses of Deuteronomy, which describe his death. Those sentences were added by Joshua. Some scholars during the last two hundred years have claimed that the Torah is the result of a compilation of documents brought together over a period of something like six centuries. There may be early passages associated with the Exodus, for example the Song of Miriam (Exodus 15:21), but these were passed on by word of mouth from one generation to another. It was not until some time after the reign of King David that the earliest written documents were produced, two versions of the material now found in Genesis. In the reign of King Josiah in 621 BCE, 'a book of Torah' was found in the Temple at Jerusalem (II Kings 22). From the kinds of reform undertaken by Josiah when he had heard the book read, it is thought that this was what is now called Deuteronomy.

The book of Ezra in the Jewish Bible described the work of a priest of that name, a man who had returned from Persia to lead the population of Jerusalem. He found that they had neglected the teaching contained in Deuteronomy, and were no longer walking in the ways of the Torah. At a solemn assembly described in Nehemiah, Chapter 9, Ezra read from the Book of the Law (Torah), convinced the people that they should keep it and led them in a renewal of the covenant with God. This, it is argued, was the first reading of the Torah in the form found in the Bible. The date may have been somewhere near 458 or 397 BCE, depending on the interpretation of 'the seventh year of Artaxerxes' (Ezra 7:7). It could be the first Persian king of that name or the second.

According to this view, the Torah was a teaching not given complete to Moses during the Exodus from Egypt, but developed from fairly simple beginnings to become a sophisticated formula for everyday life, based on the belief in a God who created the world and is concerned about everything in it, plants, animals and people. Whichever view of the origin of the Torah a Jew may hold, it is the same belief in God which guides him in his approach to life.

Interpretation of the Torah. Even apparently straightforward statements are capable of more than one meaning. The Torah says, for example:

'Remember the Sabbath day, to keep it holy. Six days you shall labour and do all your work; but the seventh is a Sabbath to the

Lord your God; in it you shall not do any work, you, or your son, or your daughter, or your manservant, or your maidservant, or your cattle, or the sojourner who is within your gate.'

(Exodus 20:8–10)

A difficulty arises here over the precise definition of work. A physicist might define work as anything which creates or consumes energy. Breathing is work. A lawyer might describe work as anything for which one receives payment. The rabbi or minister conducting a service in the synagogue is working; so is the cantor who sings the service. Of course, their duties are necessary, and the worship of God is not work. However if we define work as the performance of everyday tasks which might easily be left until Saturday evening or Sunday, the Jew still has to decide what actions are really necessary. It could be argued that it would do few people harm to go a whole Sabbath without food and would do most of us good! Does it matter whether the Sabbath is kept or not? To most Jews it does; it is part of God's teaching, the Torah, given to man so that he may live as God intended him to. To ignore the Sabbath is to neglect God, even to claim that one is wiser than the God who gave the Sabbath to man. Once this happens the freedom from work is likely to be lost. The Sabbath becomes like any other day and employers ask coach drivers or shop assistants to work on the Sabbath and take Monday off instead. A famous Jew once said of the Sabbath, 'It secures a day of rest for man. It is the corner stone of all civilisation.'

The kind of discussion about the Sabbath that we have briefly undertaken has occurred throughout Jewish history with regard to the whole Torah and to the rest of the Jewish Bible. Some teachings have been considered so important that their commentaries are printed around the text in Hebrew Bibles, though not, of course, on the scrolls used in worship. Within Judaism there has always been a rich variety of belief, and in the twentieth century there are those Jews who try to keep every instruction of the Torah literally, and those who interpret it in terms of life in an industrial age far removed from the Jerusalem of Ezra or the Sinai Desert of Moses.

Behind the commentaries and the variety of interpretation permissible in Judaism lies the belief that the Torah is not a dead letter but a living word. Besides the written Torah there exists the oral Torah, its interpretation of people by faith from the time of Moses, for the Jews would remind us that Moses had the responsibility to judge and decide issues based on the Torah. The meaning of the Torah's teaching is not always clear. It has to be sought. For example, the Torah says 'An eye for an eye and a tooth for tooth'

69

(Exodus 21:24). What does this mean? That we have the right to knock out the tooth of someone who has knocked out one of ours? Can this be squared with teachings about God's mercy, love and forgiveness which are to be found in the Torah? The answer of those who taught the Torah was that the words meant that the person responsible for the injury must pay compensation to the value of harm done.

The unwritten tradition. For centuries this tradition was not written down. Teachers, who came to be called rabbis, memorised the interpretations of the Torah that had been made before their time and passed them on to their pupils. One of the most famous rabbis of all time was a man named Akiba. He began life as an ignorant shepherd and might have remained uneducated, but for the fact that he fell in love with his master's daughter. She agreed to marry him only if he would study the Torah. This he did with such enthusiasm and skill that he was the greatest teacher of Israel over a period of forty years.

After the Jewish revolt of 132 CE, led by Bar Kochba, a man some Jews thought to be the Messiah, the Emperor Hadrian forbade the study and teaching of the Torah. Rabbi Akiba continued with his work. He said, 'A fox once called the fishes in the stream to come ashore and escape from the big fish that preyed upon them. They told him that water was their life-element; if they left it they would die. If they stayed some might die but the rest would live.' Akiba continued saying, 'Torah is our element of life. Some of us may perish in the trials of these days but as long as there is Torah the people will live.' Captured by the Romans, he was executed in 135 CE by having the flesh torn from his body by red hot pincers. To his weeping disciples he said, smiling, 'Does it not say, "Thou shalt love the Lord thy God with all thy heart and with all thy soul and with all thy might?" The soul, that means my life, should I not smile, now that I may serve him with my life?' So he died, interpreting the Torah to the end.

The Mishnah. The death of Rabbi Akiba is only one martyrdom of many at this time, but perhaps it, more than any other, influenced the Jewish decision to write down the oral Torah. The result was called the Mishnah, or Review, to give the English translation. This was eventually organised into six books, each dealing with a different aspect of life. Agriculture, appointed days (festivals), marriages and divorce, civil and criminal law, Temple sacrifice and dietary laws, and ritual purification — all these were covered in volumes which reviewed the whole of Jewish religious practice.

In typically Jewish manner, the Mishnah itself became the sub-ject of great debates, many of which were taken down word by word. The whole text of the Mishnah was analysed in this way and the result was called the Gemara, the 'completion' of the Mishnah. The long process of writing down the oral Torah came to an end some time around the year 500 CE in Babylon when Rabbi Ashee and his disciple Rabina supervised the production of a revision of the Mishnah and Gemara in what came to be known as the Talmud, the 'Compendium of Learning'. From this time onward the Jews faced the future as God's people, worshipping in their synagogues and guided by the Torah in its fullness, safe from the danger of traditions and teachings being lost with a purge of its rabbis.

The Prophets (Nevi'im). The second and third parts of the Tenakh are included in the Hebrew Bible, but do not have the status of the Torah. They are regarded as words of tradition rather than words of God. Nevi'im comprises eight volumes, divided into the Former Prophets and the Latter Prophets. To the first group belong the historical books, Joshua, Judges, Samuel and Kings—the records of God's dealings with his people as he established them in Canaan, the Promised Land. The Latter Prophets are the three books which contain the teachings of Isaiah, Jeremiah and Ezekiel, the so-called major prophets, and one in which the words of the twelve 'minor' prophets have been assembled. In worship a reading from the Prophets follows the portion of Torah set for the particular Sabbath or festival, but not every part is read in the course of the year. Some sections are never read in public worship at all.

The Haftarah. The rabbis made a selection called the Haftarah, and a passage from it is chosen to match that from the Torah; for example, when the death of Jacob is read from the Torah scroll the Haftarah reading is the death of David. Unlike the Torah, the Haftarah can be read from a printed book instead of a scroll. The reading is chanted, but not with quite the same intonation as that used when the sidrah or parchah (appointed portion) of the Torah is being read.

Ketubim (Collected Writings). The third division of the Tenakh con-tains eleven books — Psalms, Proverbs, Job, Song of Songs, Ruth, Lamentations, Ecclesiastes, Esther, Daniel, Ezra and Nehemiah (in one book), and Chronicles. Five of these, known as the five scrolls, have a special place in worship.

The Song of Songs is read at Passover.

Ruth is read at Shavuot or Pentecost, the festival of the giving of the Torah.

Lamentations is read on the fast day of the month of Ab, when the fall of the Temple is remembered.

Ecclesiastes is read at Succoth.

Esther is read at Purim.

The most frequently used book of the Ketubim is the book of Psalms. Many of its phrases and sentences are to be found in the prayers of the Prayer Book, and a number of Psalms are used regularly in Sabbath worship. These and others form a major part of private devotion, and it has been the custom of many Jews to read the 150 hymns of the Psalter in their entirety on the Day of Atonement.

That the Jews are a people of the Book is well known. The significance of the Bible in Judaism can only be fully understood when we become aware of the story of its transmission and the care with which the oral Torah has been preserved. We see the willingness of Jews to die for the right to read it and teach it, the use that is made of it in worship and private study, and the importance that is attached to mastering Hebrew so that one may become a son of the Torah in practice as well as theory.

The Buddhist scriptures

What is important to Buddhists is Dharma, a word which can be translated as Reality, Truth, Law or Teaching. Finding and teaching Dharma is what is central in the life of Gautama Buddha, and he is quoted as saying that whoever has seen him has seen Dharma. It is possible to interchange with Dharma phrases like 'Buddha-word', or 'word of the Buddha'. This Buddha-word is to be found in the teaching of Gautama Buddha. It was remembered by the community of his followers (The Sangha) and eventually put into writing.

The Buddha was happy for this teaching to be translated from the dialect which he spoke (probably Magadhan) into the many other dialects and languages of the parts of India where his followers taught. It was part of his open-handedness as a teacher to use the language of the people, and translations continued after his death. This means that, by the time his words were written down, there were collections in many Indian dialects. The collection in Pali claims to be the most complete, and its three sections together are called the Pali Canon. These are the scriptures of the Theravada (Way of the Elders) or Southern School of Buddhism. Some of the contents of the Pali Canon have also survived in Sanskrit manuscripts and in the collections of scriptures of the Mahayana schools in Chinese (also translated into Japanese) and in the Tibetan canon of the Vajrayana School. The Mahayana and Vajrayana collections also contain many works which are not in the Pali Canon. These claim to be Buddha-word, and are traced back to, or set in, the time of Gautama Buddha. It is claimed that the teachings were lost or hidden for many centuries until their meaning could be properly understood.

Theravada Buddhists, and those Western scholars who are interested mainly in historical proof in such matters, are sceptical about the relationship between these late Mahayana works and Gautama. Western scholars may even say that the Pali Canon cannot contain Gautama Buddha's exact words because they were not written down for four or five centuries. Religious communities, however, have confidence in the care taken in the oral transmission of such precious teaching. Public recitation, which involves checks by people who specialise in memorising sections of the material, produces accuracy through many generations. The additional Mahayana and Vajrayana works in fact contain the development of ideas and doctrines, the seeds of which are in the Pali Canon. These Buddhists, therefore, claim for them the same spiritual source, and the status of Dharma and Buddha-word.

The Pali Canon

The scriptures known as the Pali Canon take their name from the Pali dialect in which the Dharma was brought to Sri Lanka (Ceylon) about 247 BCE. The teaching came via north-west India and traditionally was written down in Sri Lanka in the first century BCE. This written form became the scripture of the Theravadin schools in Burma, Thailand and other parts of south-east Asia. The story of the transmission up to this point is contained in the texts themselves. It begins after the death of the Buddha, about 483 BCE, when one of his followers said that now the Buddha was dead they could do what they liked. To maintain the authority of the Buddha's teaching there was a gathering of 500 senior members of the Sangha at Rajagrha, the capital of Magadha, during the next rainy season. This is called the First Council. The tradition says that Mahakasyapa presided over the assembly, which heard Ananda— one of the Buddha's closest followers—recite all the sayings he had heard. The community checked and agreed on the material; it was then thoroughly learned for transmission. Upali, another close disciple, recited all the rules which the Buddha had laid down for the Sangha. These were also agreed and memorised.

These recitations gave the community the first two of the three sections of the Pali Canon. The sayings or discourses form the Sutra Pitaka, and the Sangha rules form the Vinaya Pitaka. The third division, the Abhidharma Pitaka, is certainly rooted in the Buddha's teaching, but there is less evidence that it was fixed at this First Council. It seems to have taken longer than the other sections to reach its final form. The work of the First Council was confirmed by a Second Council at Vaisali about 386 BCE. Traditionally the material was in an authoritative oral form when it was brought to Sri Lanka, where it was written down during the second or first century BCE.

Another name for the Pali Canon is the Tripitaka. 'Tri' means three, the threefold division already mentioned. These are the Sutras, 'threads' of teaching or dialogues: the Vinaya, which means discipline or rules of conduct, and concerns the lives of the monks or nuns: and the Abhidharma, which means further or higher doctrine, and analyses the meaning of material in the other two sections. The texts were originally written on palm-leaf manuscripts and put into baskets for storage. A pitaka is a basket.

1. The Sutra Pitaka. This is a collection of dialogues. The word sutra, 'a thread', refers to those dialogues of the Buddha in which teaching is threaded together on a common theme. The word dialogue shows that there was interchange and debate. The sutras are grouped in five sections. Each of these is again sub-divided into groups of sutras and individual sutras. There are many long and short threads which fill many volumes in their English translations. Most have a precise setting, and begin with the words of Ananda as he addressed the First Council:

'Thus have I heard:

The Master was once staying near Savatthi, in the East Park at the mansion of the mother of Migara. Now at that time Vasettha and Bharadvaja were passing their probation among the brethren in order to become bhikkhus. In the evening, the Master, having arisen from his meditation, came down from the house, and was walking to and fro in the open air, in the shade of the house.
On seeing this, Vasettha told Bhara, adding, "Let us go and approach the Master and perhaps we shall have the good fortune to hear from the Master a talk on matters of doctrine." '
(*Aggana Sutta*, translated by T. Ling from *Buddha's Philosophy of Man*, p. 102)

74

The most important thing in the Sutras is the teaching. There are not only famous general summaries, such as the Four Truths and Eightfold Path, but many specific and practical sections addressed to householders or lay Buddhists.

'And which are the six ways for dissipating wealth? Drink; being in the streets late; fairs; gambling; being with bad friends and idleness . . . there are six ways of idleness: A man says, it is too cold, and does no work; he says it is too hot, and does no work; he says, it is too early . . . too late and does no work. He says, I am too hungry and does no work . . . too full and does no work. And while all that he should do remains undone he makes no money and such wealth as he has dwindles away.'

(*Sigalavada Sutta*, translated by Peggy Morgan)

Above all, the goal of the teaching is an attitude of the mind and heart, and an alertness to all of life, which is expressed in the following:

'Just as a mother would protect her only child even at the risk of her own life, even so let one cultivate a boundless heart towards all beings.
Let one's thoughts of boundless love pervade the whole world—above, below and across—without any obstruction, without hatred, without any enmity.
Whether one stands, walks, sits or lies down, as long as one is awake, one should maintain this mindfulness. This, they say, is the sublime state in this life.'
(*Metta-sutra*, translated by W. Rahula from *What the Buddha Taught*, pp. 92, 95)

'Not to do any evil, to cultivate good, to purify one's mind, this is the teaching of the Buddhas.'

(ibid.)

'Hatred is never appeased by hatred in this world; it is appeased by love. This is an eternal Law.' (Dharma)

(*Dhammapada*, ibid.)

2. The Vinaya Pitaka—The Collection of Rules of Conduct. Vinaya means discipline and this section of the canon contains the rules, and an explanation of them for the bhikkhus and bhikkhunis, or, as they are generally called, monks and nuns. The importance of the way of life of monks and nuns in Buddhism has already been discussed. The practice of ordaining them began in the lifetime of

75

Gautama Buddha and is described in this passage in the Vinaya Pitaka:

> 'I grant you, monks, this permission: Confer henceforth in the different regions and in the different countries both modes of ordination yourselves on those who desire to receive them. And you ought, monks, to confer them in this way: Let him who desires to receive ordination first have his hair and beard cut off, let him put on yellow robes, adjust his upper robe so as to cover one shoulder, salute the feet of the monks with his head, and sit down squatting; then let them raise his joined hands and tell him to say "I take my refuge in the Buddha, I take my refuge in the Dharma I take my refuge in the Sangha ... three times.... I prescribe, O monks, that the world be left and ordination given by the three times repeated declaration of taking refuge." '
>
> (*Vinaya Mahavagga*, from *Sacred Texts of the World*, ed. N. Smart and R. Hecht, pp. 255–6)

The core of the rules to be followed after ordination is in a part of the Vinaya called the Pratimoksa, which is recited at a fortnightly gathering when there is open admission of faults and penance for them. This fortnightly meeting and fast day is called the uposatha, and takes place at new moon and full moon (see Chapter Three). The Vinaya says:

> 'Let the assembly perform the uposatha and repeat the Pratimoksa.... He who has incurred a fault should declare it; if there is no fault he should keep silence.'
>
> (ibid.)

The 227 rules that follow are in eight groups, arranged according to seriousness. The most serious involve permanent expulsion from the Sangha and are:

1. Any kind of sexual intercourse.
2. Taking what is not given.
3. Taking human life or encouraging the taking of life.
4. Claiming spiritual powers which one does not have.

Other rules limit items possessed by members of the Sangha, although even these are not actually owned by them, but belong to the community. The basic items are a set of robes; a bowl for the alms round; a bed, which must not be too high and luxurious, and special substances like ghee (melted butter), oil and honey, which count as medicines. The prohibitions on lying, stirring up ill-will and eavesdropping, together with the encouragement of modesty, help the community to live in harmony and fulfil their common goal of enlightenment.

The pattern of life which the Vinaya lays down is still fundamental for Buddhists, although it is accepted that the application of rules may change in different cultural contexts. For example, a monk may need more robes in the west because of weather conditions.

3. The Abhidharma Pitaka—The Collection of the Rules of Conduct. The name of the third basket means 'higher dharma'. It is higher in the sense of being more analytic and systematic in its approach to the teaching and is probably the latest part to be drawn up and added to the Pali Canon. It contains careful summaries of material from the sutras and in addition a precise analysis of the meaning of words, passages and ideas. The Buddha used this analytical method and passed it down to his followers, who continued to develop in question and answer form the interpretation of key concepts. For example, right speech is one of the requirements of the Eightfold Path. The Abhidharma asks what 'right speech' is, and answers with four things which are later referred to as the four verbal wrong actions:

1.   Abstaining from false speech.
2.   Abstaining from slanderous speech.
3.   Abstaining from harsh speech.
4.   Abstaining from frivolous speech.

This, it says, is called right speech.
The idea of abstaining is then further analysed:

> 'that which is avoiding, desisting from, abstaining from, not committing, not doing, being guiltless of, not overstepping the limit of, destroying the causeway to the four verbal wrong actions.'
>
> (*Abhidhama Vibhaniga*, Section 2 Vol. 39 pp. 138–139 Pali Text Society)

The seven Abhidharma sections of logical and psychological analysis include one which is a description of the different types of people there are, their spiritual traits and their stage along the path to enlightenment. Since Gautama Buddha was very careful to fit his teaching to the particular needs and abilities of people, this kind of understanding is important for the continued adaptation of his teaching and the growth of the Dharma. It is an emphasis which emerges again in the Mahayana material.

Important Pali works outside the Canon

In addition to the Tripitaka, Theravada Buddhists greatly respect other works. There is, for instance, a whole tradition of commentaries which continue both the application of the Dharma in new situations and the 'higher analysis' of the Abhidharma. One famous commentator was Buddhaghosa, who came from south India to Sri Lanka in the fifth century CE and wrote commentaries on all seven parts of the Abhidharma. He also wrote a famous description of the meditation techniques of Theravada Buddhists, which has become a standard work both for study and training. It is called the Visuddhimagga, or Path of Purity. Here is one of his descriptions:

> 'A holy man will think kind thoughts about the true condition of mortal beings, and how should he want to inflict further suffering on them when they are already suffering enough from disease, death, old age and so on? If his thoughts are unkind a man may cause damage to others, or he may not; in any case his own unkind mind will be destroyed. Therefore you should strive to think of all that lives with friendliness and compassion, and not with ill-will and a desire to hurt. For whatever a man thinks about continually, to that his mind becomes inclined by the force of habit.'
>
> (ibid.)

Another famous work, probably dating from India in the second century BCE, is the Milindapanha, or Questions of King Milinda. This is an intellectual debate between the Buddhist monk Nagasena and King Milinda. Milinda's Greek name is Menander, and he ruled for a time—probably in the second century BCE—in northwest India. The work is a lively dialogue on almost all the central questions of Buddhism, such as the nature of the self and Nirvana.

> 'King Milinda said:
> "I will grant you, Nagasena, that Nirvana is absolute ease, and that nevertheless one cannot point to its form or shape, its duration or size, either by simile or explanation, by reason or by argument. But is there perhaps some quality of Nirvana which it shares with other things, and which lends itself to a metaphorical explanation?" Nagasena replies, "Its form, O king, cannot be elucidated by similes, but its qualities can. . . Nirvana shares one quality with the lotus, two with water . . . three with the jewel that grants all your wishes. . . . As the lotus is unstained by water, so is Nirvana unstained by all the defilements. As cool water allays feverish heat, so also Nirvana is cool and allays the fever of all

passions. . . . Like the jewels, Nirvana grants all one can desire, brings joy and sheds light.''

(adapted from E. Conze, *Buddhist Scriptures*, pp. 156–7)

At the end of the work Milinda asks Nagasena to accept him as a lay disciple.

IMPORTANT SCRIPTURES FROM THE TIME OF GAUTAMA BUDDHA

BCE

600	Birth of Gautama Buddha Enlightenment of Gautama Buddha	
500	Death of Gautama Buddha First Council of Rajagriha	SUTRA and VINAYA
400		fixed orally
300	Buddhism to Sri Lanka	ABHIDHARMA continued to develop
200	MILINDAPANHA	PALI TRIPITAKA
100		written down.
0	PRAJNAPARAMITA SUTRAS	

CE

100	VIMALIKIRTI NIRDESA SUTRA
200	SADDHARMAPUNDARIKA and LANKAVATARA SUTRAS
300	
400	VISUDDHIMAGGA
500	SUKHAVATI SUTRAS
600	
700	
800	
900	
1000	
1200	
1300	Buton fixed the form of the Tibetan KANJUR and TENJUR

Mahayana scriptures

The scriptures of the Mahayana and Vajrayana schools, which are in Sanskrit, Tibetan, Chinese and Japanese, overlap and include much of the material in the Pali Canon. Because it was passed down through different groups of Buddhists, this material is in a different order, and there are different readings within the texts. There are also additional sutras which have the authority of Buddha-word and provide the distinctive emphases and teachings of the different schools. These are discussed below. The two basic collections of the texts are in Tibetan and Chinese. They are both much longer than the Pali Tripitaka. The most recent edition in Japanese (which is the Chinese collection translated) is in fifty-five western-style volumes, with a supplement of another forty-five books. The title of the Chinese collection, 'Great Scripture-Store', is a much better term than the western word 'canon', which means a measuring rod or norm, and which tends to emphasise exclusion and rejection of material. Here there is a treasure-trove, a rich store of ideas and stories, which has its source in the Buddha-Nature and is skilful in helping people of all abilities and temperaments along the path to enlightenment. Certain sections are more helpful to some people than others. The following are some of the most important Mahayana works. They emerged in the period approximately 200 BCE to 200 CE.

The Vimalikirti Nirdesa Sutra: The Sutra Spoken by Vimalikirti. The Sutra begins:

> 'Thus have I heard. Once upon a time the Buddha sojourned in the Amra park at Vaisali with an assembly of 8000 great bhikkhus. With them were 32 000 bodhisattvas who were well-known for having achieved all the perfections that lead to great wisdom'
>
> (*Vimalikirti Nirdesa Sutra*, translated by C. Luk. p. 1)

> 'Thus surrounded by an incalculable number of people circumambulating to pay their respects, the Buddha was about to expound the Dharma.'
>
> (ibid., p. 5)

It is common for Mahayana sutras to set the scene at the time of Gautama Buddha with the same kind of introduction as the sutras of the Pali Canon; but the gathering is cosmic rather than historical, and describes an audience of celestial bodhisattvas as well as earthly bhikkhus.

The second chapter introduces a householder named Vimalikirti who, we are told, lives a full life in the world while using:

'countless expedient methods to teach for the benefit of living beings. . . .'

'While walking in the street he never failed to convert others (to the Dharma). When he entered a government office, he always protected others (from injustice). . . When visiting a school he enlightened the students. When entering a house of prostitution he revealed the sin of sexual intercourse. When going to a tavern he stuck to his determination (to abstain from drinking).'

(ibid, pp. 16–17)

He uses his skilful means to effect illness so that many people will visit him:

'Thus the elder Vimalikirti expounded the Dharma to all those who came to enquire after his health, urging countless visitors to seek supreme enlightenment.'

(ibid., p.19)

His life is very different from that of the monks, and he has not the status of the celestial bodhisattvas, but the sutra teaches that his skill in the Dharma is greater than theirs, though he is a layman. This is the sutra's great contribution. He says that 'meditation is not necessarily sitting', but is 'not straying from the truth while attending to worldly affairs'. The Bodhisattva of Wisdom, Manjusri, says Vimalikirti is 'a man of superior wisdom'. The discussions between Vimalikirti and the enlightened beings who come to visit him while he is sick show that, though a layman, he is himself a model bodhisattva and that reading about him will help others.

'if living beings listening to the Dharma of this sutra, believe, understand, receive, uphold, read and recite it, they will surely realise this Dharma'.

(ibid., p. 128)

'Whoever after hearing this sutra of inconceivable liberation, believes, understands, receives, keeps, reads, recites and practises this sutra his or her merits will surpass those of the former man or woman. Why? Because the enlightenment of all the buddhas originates from this Dharma, and, since enlightenment is beyond all measuring, the merit of this sutra cannot be estimated.'

(ibid., p. 129)

81

Prajnaparamita Sutras: Discourses on the perfection of wisdom. Prajna is wisdom and prajnaparamita the perfection of wisdom. Wisdom was part of the Buddhist path right from the beginning where this is summarised in three stages as sila (morality), samadhi (concentration) and panha (Pali for prajna, wisdom). In the Mahayana and Vajrayana literature the fact that this wisdom cuts through conventional truth like a vajra, a diamond or thunderbolt, is emphasised. Seeing the transcendent, the Buddha-Nature in the midst of the world involves seeing through conventional truth, even conventional Buddhist truth. Various Mahayana sutras concentrate on this wisdom. Some are named after their length, for example the Astasahasrika Prajnaparamita, or Perfection of Wisdom in 8000 lines, which emerged in the first century BCE. Its teaching was extended into 18 000; 25 000; and 100 000 lines and also condensed into 25 000 and 700 lines. The most famous shorter versions are the Vajracchedika, or Diamond Sutra, and the Hridayasutra or Heart Sutra, so called because it gives the heart or essence of the wisdom teaching. It begins, 'Homage to the Perfection of Wisdom, the lovely, the holy.'

The focus is on the understanding of the buddhas and bodhisattvas that the true nature and reality of all things is one, and can be described in the phrases 'own-being', 'suchness' or 'thatness'. The unusualness of these terms shows how far from conventional ideas this true nature is. All else can be described as 'emptiness', and once we have seen that, we can use the word

An illustrated scroll of the Diamond Sutra in Chinese.

82

'emptiness', too, to characterise truth. So the Heart Sutra continues:

> 'Avalokita, the holy lord and bodhisattva, was moving in the deep course of the wisdom which had gone beyond. He looked down from on high, he beheld but five heaps, and he saw that in their own being they were empty.'

> 'It is because of his indifference to any kind of personal attainment that a bodhisattva, through having relied on the perfection of wisdom, dwells without thought-coverings. In the absence of thought-coverings he has not been made to tremble, he has overcome what can upset, and in the end he attains to Nirvana.'
>
> (E. Conze, *Buddhist Scriptures*, pp. 162–163)

The pursuit of wisdom in the Mahayana is never a selfish one. Since all beings are united in their true nature, the bodhisattva is committed to help all of them. The Diamond Sutra summarises this in the following words:

> 'Someone who has set out in the vehicle of a Bodhisattva should think in this manner: "As many beings as there are in the universe of beings . . . all these I must lead to Nirvana, into that realm of Nirvana which leaves nothing behind." '
>
> (ibid., p. 164)

Saddharmapundarika: True Law Lotus. The title of this famous sutra is full of meaning. The lotus is a Buddhist symbol of spiritual perfection, and the law translates Dharma. This sutra gives an answer to the problem that from the second century CE, and still today, quite diverse teachings have existed which are all seen as the Dharma by different Buddhist groups. As one not limited by space and time, the Buddha teaches that upaya kausalya-skilful means have been used to help people to begin to develop spiritually. Different methods and teachings are necessary because people have different temperaments and potential. It is not a matter of which are right and which are wrong, but whether they are effective in helping people on the path to Nirvana, or to the next stage of the path. All paths lead in the same direction and in the end the paths and the goal are one. There are many allegories in the Lotus Sutra to illustrate the teaching. One of the most famous is the burning house. The burning house is samsara from which a father, the Buddha, has to rescue his sons. He uses a 'trick' to get them out, when they do not realise their danger. His device is to promise them a present if they will come. This is successful and they leave the dangerous house. Once they have emerged, like the Buddha's followers embarked upon the path, they find, not the present they were promised, but even better treasures. Another allegory, which is quoted below, shows that refuge for a time can be found in what is not ultimately real. It is necessary to point out here that these allegories and the whole sutra obviously look at Buddhist ideas and history from a Mahayana viewpoint, claiming to draw out meanings that are implicit in the early sutras, and so making explicit the full Dharma or Buddha-word. Theravada Buddhists, who believe that the material in the Pali Tripitaka is sufficient and the final authority, would obviously disagree with this emphasis.

> 'There is a steep, difficult, very bad road, five hundred yojanas in length, empty and devoid of human beings—a frightful place. There is a great multitude wishing to traverse this road to arrive at a cache of precious jewels. There is a guide, perceptive and wise, of penetrating clarity, who knows the hard road, its passable and impassable features, and who, wishing to get through these hardships, leads the multitude. The multitude being led get disgusted midway and say to the guide, "We are exhausted, and also frightened; we cannot go on. It is still a long way off, and we now wish to turn back." The guide, being a man of many skilful devices, thinks: "These wretches are to be pitied! How can they throw away a fortune in jewels and wish instead to turn back?" When he has had this thought, with his power of devising expedients he conjures up on that steep road, three hundred yojanas away, a city, then he declares to the multitude, "Have no fear! There is no need to turn back! Here is this great city. You may stop in it and do as you please. If you enter the city, you can quickly regain your composure. If you then feel able to proceed to the jewel cache, you will also be free to leave."
> At that time, the exhausted multitude, overjoyed at heart, sigh as at something they have never had before, saying, "We have escaped that bad road, and shall quickly regain our composure." Thereupon the multitude proceed to enter the conjured city, having the notion that they are saved and evincing a feeling of composure. At that time, the guide, knowing that the multitude have rested and are no longer fatigued, straightway dissolves the conjured city and says to the multitude, "Come away! The jewel cache is near. The great city of a while ago was conjured up by me for the purpose of giving you a rest, nothing more." '
>
> (*Scripture of the Lotus Blossom of the Fine Dharma*, translated by L. Hurvitz, p. 148)

Many of the Mahayana and Vajrayana sutras are connected with particular schools which find in them the inspiration and authority for their doctrines and practices. The Lotus Sutra was basic to the T'ient'ai Chinese school of the sixth century CE. The name is taken from Mount T'ient'ai in modern Chekiang. It used the Lotus Sutra to create a harmony of existing teachings, which gives the school its distinctive character. When it went to Japan in the ninth century CE it was called the Tendai school. Out of this in the thirteenth century came reform under Nichiren, and the recitation of 'Namu myo-ho-ren-ge kyo', Japanese for 'salutation to the Lotus Sutra'. This is still chanted twice daily by the twentieth-century lay Buddhist movement, which has grown from the Nichiren Shoshu, called Sokagakkai. The Lotus Sutra is also central to another Nichiren-linked lay movement, Rissho Koseikai.

The Hua-yen sect, in early seventh-century CE China and eighth-century CE Japan, focuses on the Avatamsaka Sutra. The name of the school is the name of the sutra translated into Chinese and means 'garland'. It has a reputation for being both profound and difficult, and contains a vivid section on unselfishness and the ten stages through which a bodhisattva reaches enlightenment.

'All the good deeds practised by me are for the benefit of all sentient beings, for their ultimate purification [from sin]. By the merit of these good deeds I pray that all sentient beings be released from the innumerable sufferings suffered by them in their various abodes of existence. By the turning over of these deeds I would be a haven for all beings and deliver them from their miserable existences; I would be a great beacon-light to all beings and dispel the darkness of ignorance and make the light of intelligence shine.'

(L. Stryk, ed., *World of the Buddha*, p. 276)

The Sukhavati Sutra: The Sutra of Happiness Having. This sutra describes the path of devotion to Amitabha (Chinese) or Amida (Japanese) Buddha. His name means Infinite Light, or in another Chinese variation, Amitayus, Infinite Life. If this Buddha is called upon with a faith that includes right intention and right action, then the devotee will be reborn in the place where Amida dwells. This is a paradise, a pure land, a happy land called Sukhavati-happiness-having. Calling on his name is the practice of the Pure Land school of Buddhism, which is within the Mahayana tradition. It began in China in the early sixth century CE and has blossomed in Japan since the twelfth and thirteenth centuries. Sukha is the opposite of dukkha, a word the Buddha uses for the suffering and unsatisfactoriness which characterises our life in this world. Once devotees are in the land of sukha, Amida skilfully guides them into Nirvana. The central sutra for this tradition, the Sukhavati Sutra, like other sutras mentioned, is retained in longer and shorter versions. Here is part of the description of Amida's Pure Land.

> 'That world system Sukhavati, Ananda, ... is rich in a great variety of flowers and fruits, adorned with jewel trees, which are frequented by flocks of birds with sweet voices, which the Tathagata's miraculous power has conjured up.... Such jewel trees, and clusters of banana trees and rows of palm trees, all made of precious things, grow everywhere in this Buddha field. On all sides it is ... covered with lotus flowers made of all the precious things ... and from each jewel lotus issue thirty-six hundred thousand kotis of rays. And at the end of each ray there issue thirty-six hundred thousand kotis of Buddhas, with golden-coloured bodies, and who go into countless world systems, and there demonstrate Dharma.... And all the beings who are born ... in this Buddha-field, they are all fixed on the right method of salvation, until they have won Nirvana. For this reason that world system is called the "Happy Land".'
>
> (E. Conze, *Buddhist Scriptures*, pp. 232, 235)

The Lankavatara Sutra: The Descent to Ceylon.   The setting of this sutra is a visit the Buddha traditionally made to Lanka (Ceylon). The title means Descent to the Island of Lanka and although it emerged in the first two centuries CE in connection with early Mahayana, it is a particularly important work for the Zen school within Mahayana. Bodhidharma made it central to his teaching when he founded the lineage of Ch'an masters in the fifth century CE. (Ch'an is the Chinese word for meditation; Zen is the Japanese equivalent.) The sutra emphasises inner enlightenment and the realisation that the Buddha-Nature is in all of us, is in fact our own true nature that we need to know. It is interesting to note that one aspect of the sutra's teaching is that words are not necessary for the communication of Dharma. The traditional story of the beginnings of Zen Buddhism in the Buddha's own lifetime tells of an occasion when the Buddha sat silently in front of a crowd of 1200 people who had gathered to hear him teach. He silently held up a flower. One person smiled, understood, and took the flower. This emphasis on direct, unspoken, unwritten transmission of experience is very important in Zen. It is rather paradoxical to point out in a section on the scriptures that in this tradition the written word is not set up as an authority over against experience and must be dispensed with if it is not helpful. Zen makes this point more explicitly than any other school. There is even a picture of the Sixth Patriarch tearing up a sutra.

The treasure trove of the Mahayana sutras is so extensive that we have been able to look at only a few of the most influential. As in the Theravada tradition, there are also commentaries through which the sutras are understood and taught, and systematic works by important thinkers.

The Tibetan (Vajrayana) Scriptures

The great wealth of the Mahayana sutras was added to again in Tibet, where the scriptures were organised into the Kanjur and Tenjur. These two sections were fixed by Buton, who lived from 1290 to 1354 CE. The Kanjur (translations of the Buddha-word) consisted of 100 volumes in its first printing in this form in the eighteenth century. It includes material from the Pali Canon, Mahayana sutras and Tantras (a word having the same meaning as sutra, a thread). The Tenjur (translation of teachings) comprises 225 volumes of commentaries on the Kanjur material, with additional tales and works of logic, grammar and science. Most descriptions of the Tibetan Canon stop there, but, in fact, the principle of permitting additions, which has been described, did not stop. There are collections of the orally transmitted teachings of the lamas (teachers, guru in Sanskrit). These are Buddha-word in the eyes of Tibetans. There are also termas (treasures) which are still being found. Termas were hidden by Padmasambhava, the eighth-century CE establisher of Buddhism in Tibet. They are found in mind-to-mind teaching or in physical texts when the time is right. The Tibetan Book of the Dead is one such terma, and it is still possible for termas to be found.

The use of the Scriptures

Buddhists study the scriptures to learn as much as possible about their religion. Both householders and monks should do this, but monks often have more time, and have traditionally been the experts and scholars on the texts. They teach and encourage the adults and children to know as much as possible.

Scriptures are often difficult to understand without a teacher. Buddhists emphasise the importance of living teachers for explaining the texts. These teachers know what their own teachers said, and also what is in the written commentaries. A line of interpretation is then established, which is believed to go back to

Zen monks chanting from texts of the Sutras during walking meditation.

the Buddha himself. Those texts which do not have good commentaries tend not to be used. Tibetans talk about the need for receiving a transmission, or oral preparation, before a scripture is read.

Buddhists have always been happy for the scriptures to be translated, since the Buddha and his followers taught people in their local languages. It is also important, however to keep alive a knowledge of the earliest written texts in Pali, Sanskrit, Chinese or Tibetan, so that translations can be checked. Again it is the monks who have time to study the original languages and are asked to recite texts in the original versions at worship or on special occasions like festivals, initiations and funerals.

The public recitation of texts involves many different levels of participation. Buddhists described the intellectual, aesthetic and social benefits that come from hearing a text, and say that a special connection is being made with the Dharma that it teaches, which is bound to help towards enlightenment. Any contact with sutras brings a blessing and is a way of gaining merit:

> 'If anyone in the latter age accepts and keeps, reads and recites this scripture, that person shall never again want for clothing, bedding, food and drink, or for the things to support life. . . . If there is anyone who can receive and keep, read and recite, recall properly . . . be it known that that person has seen Sakyamuni Buddha.'
>
> (*Lotus Sutra*, translated by L. Hurvitz, pp. 334, 336)

Usually only the monks know long texts by heart, but some sutras, like the Metta Sutra, are short enough to be learned by schoolchildren in Sri Lanka and used in congregational worship (see Chapter Three). Some of the long sutras, like the Sukhavati, have shortened forms, and some have a very condensed version of the teaching, as in the Heart Sutra. A sutra's teaching can be evoked in a phrase like the Japanese Nicherenite Namu-myo-ho-ren-ge-kyo (Salutation to the Lotus Sutra). The Heart Sutra is evoked in the sound 'A'. Recitation is much more than a mental skill. It involves planting the material like a seed within the heart, where it has a transforming effect upon the individual.

Texts are placed by Buddhists in shrine rooms and meditation halls in a position of honour, just below the Buddha images. The oldest copy of a text that is available is the most revered, because use has added something to it, as with an old place of worship. Old texts are also used as relics, carried in processions and enshrined in stupas for popular veneration and as a focus for pilgrimage.

89

Another popular use, which not all Buddhists approve of, is as a charm against evil.

Sutras like the Sukhavati, with its description of the Happy Land of Amida, have also inspired many paintings, which act as visual Dharma and supplement the texts. The famous Wheel of Life also presents textual teaching in visual form.

✠ The Christian Bible

The Old Testament.   The first point that must be noted about the Christian Bible is that it includes the complete Jewish Bible. To this was eventually added the New Testament, a collection of books of Christian authorship. By intention or accident, they have become something like the oral Torah in Judaism in that they often interpret the Tenakh from a Christian standpoint.

The earliest Christians had the Tenakh as their Bible. As yet its final composition had not been agreed. (This was done at the Council of Jabneh, or Jamnia in about 90 CE, but broad agreement had probably been reached by Jesus' time, sixty years earlier.) When the apostle Paul wrote to his friend and fellow missionary saying, 'All scripture is inspired by God' (II Timothy 3:16), he was referring to the Tenakh; none of the other religions Paul had yet encountered possessed a scripture. He may have been expressing the view of Christian Jews, held by some other Jews also, that the whole Bible, Torah, Nevi'im and Ketubim, was inspired by God. This was certainly the belief of Christians, apparently derived from Jesus himself. (See Mark 12:18–24, where Jesus states his belief in the resurrection of the dead. Some Jews did not accept this doctrine because it could not be found explicitly in the Torah. Jesus provides his own interpretation of a Torah passage to argue his case.)

The most important task of Paul and the Christian church was to show that Jesus, their Messiah, did correspond to the description of the Messiah found in the Tenakh. In the episode already quoted, the clash of Jesus with the Sadducees, one of the important religious groups of his day, we have seen that Jesus, like other Jews, interpreted the scriptures. It may be that he secretly explained his Messiahship in terms of such passages as Isaiah Chapter 53, for example. Some scholars suggest that his followers did this after Jesus' death. However, it is clear that whether Jesus provided a commentary upon the Tenakh as other teachers did, or whether this was done by the church, Christians were soon attempting to convince their fellow Jews as well as Gentiles that Jesus was the person promised in the Tenakh. Matthew's gospel in particular echoes with the refrain 'so that the scripture might be fulfilled'. However, Christians believed that Jesus was more than a rabbi explaining the Tenakh; they claimed that what he did was significant as well as what he taught. Both his life and teaching were the oral Torah as far as they were concerned. At this time the oral Torah was not written down. It is not surprising, then, to find that the apostles did not record the words of Jesus. They passed them on by word of mouth, in keeping with Jewish custom.

The New Testament: The letters of Paul.   Christianity's first writings, apart from the Jewish Bible, were letters sent by Paul to churches he had established in Greece and Asia Minor. In these he often reminds his readers of the teaching they had already received, (for example, I Corinthians 11:23, 15:1–3). It was not until most of Paul's letters, and maybe all of them, had been written that the first gospel was produced, about thirty years after Jesus' ministry.

The gospels: why they were written.   The questions are sometimes asked, why did Jesus not write a book of his teachings, and why did it take so long to decide to produce the gospels? The answer to the first is that Jesus as a Jewish teacher would not have thought of recording his teaching in that way. Rabbis taught disciples; they didn't write books. To a Jew of Jesus' day it would have been surprising if Jesus had written a book. The real question is what made the disciples decide to break this established tradition? They didn't. That is the most likely answer. Though the gospels of Matthew and John may somehow be associated with the disciples of those names it is very doubtful whether they were actually written by them. Mark and Luke were certainly not among the twelve disciples of Jesus' own lifetime. The gospels were probably written at the request of Christian communities at a time when the apostolic voices were disappearing, to replace the living witnesses and prevent the tradition being lost.

Early Christians' need to preserve the faith.   On 19 July 64 CE, a large area of the city of Rome was destroyed by fire. Many lives were lost and thousands of people were made homeless. Suspicion fell upon the Emperor Nero, who was known to be wanting to enlarge his palace. This might have been his way of clearing the land.

Tacitus, a Roman historian, describes Nero's response to the rumour of his guilt:

> 'Consequently, to get rid of the report, Nero fastened the guilt and inflicted the most exquisite tortures on a class hated for their abominations, called Christians by the populace. Christus, from whom the name had its origin, suffered the extreme penalty during the reign of Tiberius at the hands of one of our procurators, Pontius Pilatus, and a deadly superstition, thus checked for the moment, again broke but not only in Judaea, the first source of the evil, but also in the City, where all things hideous and shameful from every part of the world meet and become popular. Accordingly, an arrest was first made of all who confessed; then, upon their information, an immense multitude was convicted, not so much of the crime of arson, as of hatred of the human race. Mockery of every sort was added to their deaths. Covered with the skins of beasts, they were torn by dogs and perished, or were nailed to crosses, or were doomed to the flames. These served to illuminate the night when daylight failed. Nero had thrown open his gardens for the spectacle, and was exhibiting a show in the circus, while he mingled with the people in the dress of a charioteer or drove about in a chariot. Hence, even for criminals who deserved extreme and exemplary punishment, there arose a feeling of compassion; for it was not, as it seemed, for the public good, but to glut one man's cruelty, that they were being destroyed.'

(W.H.C. Frend, *The Early Church* pp. 41–42)

This is one of the earliest non-Christian accounts of Christianity. That Tacitus knew little about the faith is clear. However, the fact that he mentions it at all shows how severe Nero's action must have been. Tradition asserts that the apostles Peter and Paul were among the victims of his persecution. Although it was only confined to Rome, news of it must have spread quickly to all the Christian communities. One of their greatest anxieties must have been that the living voices of the apostles would be silenced in similar persecutions and their message lost. It was perhaps Nero's persecution that finally prompted the churches to produce the gospels.

Other reasons may also have influenced them. The Christian community was by now very widespread. Egypt, Syria, Asia Minor, Greece, Italy, Cyprus and perhaps Spain and India had their churches. The apostles couldn't be everywhere; there was a need to provide something to replace them. Local converts would have been taught the apostolic tradition, but there was always a danger of errors creeping in. A written record would go some way to preventing this happening. The churches may also have been feeling the need for some material about Jesus which could be used in worship. They had the Jewish scriptures, mostly used in their Greek translation, and they had Paul's letters; to add a Christian equivalent to the Tenakh could only seem natural. Paul's letters had also given the idea of the value of written documents to the churches. However, it was probably the shock of the Roman persecution that released the gospel-writing movement.

The four gospels. The New Testament contains four gospels, three of which are similar; the other stands a little apart from the rest. The synoptic gospels — Matthew, Mark and Luke — seem to view Jesus from the same point of view; hence the term synoptic. Their similarity can be explained by the use of Mark as a basis for the gospels of Matthew and Luke. Their differences can be accounted for by the differing interests of the writers and the communities for which they were writing. The author of John's gospel must have been exaggerating when he wrote:

> 'There is much else that Jesus did. If it were all to be recorded in detail, I suppose the whole world would not hold the books that would be written.'
>
> (John 21:25)

However, he was indicating that the authors had plenty of material from which to pick and choose, especially when the longest convenient length for a scroll was about five metres and they had to limit the amount they could write. (The book form had not yet been invented.)

The purpose of the gospels. This is not the place to discuss the motives of the various gospel authors, only to make the general point that they were trying to present Jesus to their readers who may have been non-believers, Christians, Gentiles, or Jews. Another verse from John's gospel may contain a valuable clue to their overall purpose:

> 'There were indeed many other signs that Jesus performed in the presence of his disciples, which are not recorded in this book. Those here written have been recorded that you may hold the faith that Jesus is the Christ, the Son of God, and that through this faith you may possess eternal life by his name.'
>
> (John 20:31–31)

A superficial glance at the gospel discloses the fact that they are not biographies. Only two mention Jesus' birth and childhood at all. There is a lack of balance, most of the information being about

Jesus' trial and crucifixion. The gospels are about Jesus, Messiah and Son of God, man's saviour sent by God.

The Christian Bible evolves.   Only in the fourth century, when Christians no longer lived in fear of persecution, and Christianity was favoured by such Roman emperors as Constantine, were the churches in a position to find the opportunity to discuss what ought to constitute their Bible. They already had the Tenakh, their inheritance from Judaism. They universally acknowledged the four gospels and the letters of Paul, including Hebrews, which scholars now agree was not written by him. I John, I Peter and Revelation were also acknowledged, but James, II and III John were disputed, together with II Peter. Other books such as the Epistles of Barnabas and the Didache, or 'Teaching of the Twelve Apostles' were also regarded very highly. However, they were eventually excluded from the Christian scripture because they were not accepted as being of apostolic authorship, and the five disputed works were included. It was not until 367 CE, when a theologian called Athanasius wrote a special letter to try to clear up remaining disagreements, that the New Testament's content was finally established. Even now one difference between the Bible of Roman Catholic and Protestant Christians remains. The Roman church includes certain Jewish writings called the Apocrypha, while Protestants accept only the Jewish books found in the Tenakh.

The Christian Bible is, as we have seen, divided into two sections; the first part is called the Old Testament, the second the New Testament to express the belief that Christians are members of the new covenant established with mankind through Jesus. Testament and covenant are words with much the same meaning. Agreement is the term we might be more likely to use today. At the Last Supper, Jesus took the cup of wine, and holding it in his hand, said, 'This is my blood of the covenant which is poured out for many' (Mark 14:24). Christians believe that Jesus had in mind a promise contained in Jeremiah 31:31, 'Behold the days are coming, says the Lord, when I will make a new covenant with the house of Israel and the house of Judah.' They believed that Jesus had come to establish it. Therefore, the part of the Bible written by Christians about Jesus came to be called the New Testament.

The Christian Bible in public worship.   The Christian Bible is probably used in every act of worship, with the exception of the meetings of the Society of Friends—the Quakers. In their gatherings or worship it may be read or referred to, but they believe that the spirit of God lives in every man and woman and they treasure this voice more

The Geneva Bible was originally translated in that city by a group of scholars which probably included John Knox. It is better known as the 'breeches Bible' because of its rendering of Genesis 3 : 7. The authorised version which ousted it in popularity used the word 'apron' instead. What word is used in modern translations?

than words in a Bible. In other denominations, there will almost always be a reading from one of the gospels, and often a passage from the Old Testament. In communion services part of an epistle accompanies the gospel reading, and it is in the communion service tradition that almost all the few ritual uses of the Bible occur. The congregation stands when the gospel is read. The Prayer or Mass book, which stands on the right hand side of the communion table or altar, is moved to the left for the reading of the gospel. The original purpose was to turn symbolically towards the heathen northerners so that they might hear of Jesus. The epistle was only for the ears of the believers. Sometimes the importance of the gospel is also shown by carrying the book into the midst of the congregation for the reading of the gospel. Respect is being paid to the subject of the gospel, Jesus, and not to the text. Probably the reason why Christian churches of any denomination do not appear to revere the Bible as a physical object, in the way that other faiths revere their holy books, is that they do not want people to forget that it is the living Jesus who is important—not information about him. Jesus, rather than the Bible or the church, is at the centre of Christianity. Perhaps the Eastern Orthodox church captures this idea most fully. At a point in the service called 'The Little Entrance' the clergy and other officiants pass from behind the iconostasis into the congregation carrying the Bible which represents Jesus, the 'Word made flesh'. The act symbolises the Incarnation, the coming of God into the world as the person of Jesus.

The Bible: the Word of God.   Of course the Bible as a physical object is treated with respect by Christians. In some free churches the congregation will stand when it is placed on the pulpit at the start of the service. Some people who might lie in a court of law will tell the truth because they have sworn an oath on the Bible. The Queen of England was given a Bible at her coronation in 1953 to express the hope that her laws and decisions would be guided by God. Sometimes a minister will call the Bible the 'word of God', and all Christians are expected to take its teachings into account when they are considering how they should live and what they should do. However, they should always be conscious that the Bible calls Jesus 'the word'. John's gospel says:

> 'And the Word became flesh and dwelt among us, full of grace and truth; we have beheld his glory, glory of the only Son from the Father.'

> (John 1:14)

What the Torah is to the Jews, the Buddha-word is to Buddhists, the

Qur'an to Muslims, and the Guru Granth Sahib to Sikhs, Jesus, the living word of God, is to Christians.

The Muslim scriptures

Muhammad, the last of God's prophets according to the teachings of Islam, first heard the word of God in 610 CE. He had been concerned about religious matters for a long time and would often go to a cave in a mountain outside Mecca to meditate. As we read in Chapter 1, on one of these occasions a voice spoke to him. 'Recite', it said. The word is one which can be applied to readings of scriptures during a service, so some accounts use 'Read' instead of recite. Muhammad said he could not read. Three times the voice gave the command and then Muhammad realised that he did not have to provide the words; they were being given to him. The voice was that of the angel Gabriel. The words of that first experience are those found in the Qur'an as:

> 'Recite,
> In the name of thy Lord, who created –
> Created man from a blood clot.
> Recite,
> For thy Lord is bountiful,
> Who taught by the pen,
> Taught man what he knew not.'

> (Sura 96:1–5)

The future prophet was understandably disturbed by this experience, but his wife Khadijah, her eldest cousin Waraqah for the remaining months of his life, and later his uncle Abu Talib, stood by him. Khadijah believed in the words her husband received and became the first Muslim. Wrapped in his cloak, Muhammad continued to pray in the cave on the Mount of Light, Jabal-an-Nur. Another early message was:

> 'O immantled one,
> Rise and warn;
> Thy Lord magnify,
> Thy raiment purify,
> The wrath flee,
> Give not to gain more,
> For thy Lord endure.'

> (Sura 74:1–7)

In obedience to this command he began to preach in Mecca, warning its inhabitants to worship the one God, not the many they believed in, and encouraging them to do good for its own sake, not in the hope of making a profit.

God's messages to Muhammad. The Qur'an contains many such short and terse passages. A large proportion of them are concerned with warning people of God's judgement. This is because Muhammad as a prophet was acutely aware of human failings and deeply conscious of God's desire that mankind should return to obedience. The Qur'an is a compilation of the many messages which Muhammad received from God through Gabriel with the instruction to deliver them to the Arabians, Jews, Christians, or polytheists. Muhammad could not write or read. A verse in the Qur'an describes him as 'The unlettered Prophet spoken of in the Torah and Gospel' (Sura 7: 157). Muhammad memorised what he was taught, taught the messages to those who believed him to be the Prophet of God, and they wrote down the words. No copy of the Qur'an was made during Muhammad's lifetime but many of his companions knew it by heart. It was not until a few years after his death that his companions decided to assemble the material and write it down. It is said that they compiled it from 'scraps of parchment and leather, tablets of stone, ribs of palm branches, camels' shoulder blades and ribs, pieces of board and the breasts of men'. The third Caliph, or leader of the Islamic movement, Uthman, one of the Prophet's companions, had an authoritative version of the Qur'an compiled in Medina about 650 CE, and sent copies to the main Islamic cities, which by then included Jerusalem, Damascus, Babylon and Isfahan in Persia.

The contents of the Qur'an. The word Qur'an comes from an Arabic root meaning 'recite' or 'read' and simply means 'the recitation', that is, the words revealed to the Prophet Muhammad from God through the angel Gabriel. The contents vary from short, poetical sections of great beauty to long, prosaic passages dealing with mundane, though important, matters. The shorter revelations are usually dated to the earlier years of the Prophet's ministry, between 610 and 622 CE; the longer ones may be associated with his stay in Medina after 622. In that year Muhammad found himself the leader of the city of Medina whose population had heard of his trustworthiness, and invited him to settle among them and direct their civic affairs. Not surprisingly, therefore, many of the teachings received by the Prophet during this period have to do with matters of law such as inheritance rights, usury, and the conduct of business affairs.

A guide to life. The Qur'an provides the Muslim with an almost complete guide to life. It contains doctrinal statements, exhortations to pray and keep the other Pillars of Islamic faith and practice, and is a body of teaching which instructs governments how to treat their subjects and other states, and social teachings which are the basis of law and personal conduct in Muslim societies. Here are a few examples of the Qur'an's teachings:

'God has permitted trading and forbidden taking interest.'

(Sura 2:275)

'Show kindness to your parents and to near relatives, orphans, the needy, the neighbour who is related to you as well as the neighbour who is a stranger to you, and your companion by your side and the wayfarer, and anyone who is your responsibility.'

(Sura 4:36)

'You who believe, liquor and gambling, idols and raffles, are only a work of Satan; avoid them that you may prosper.'

(Sura 5:90)

'You who believe, whenever you intend to pray, wash your faces and your hands up to the elbows, and wipe your head and wash your feet up to the ankles.'

(Sura 5:6)

'Children of Adam, wear your best clothes at every time of worship.'

(Sura 7:31)

All these examples are taken from instructions on how to pray, how to work, how to live. The teaching of the Qur'an is extremely practical in a detailed way. In this it corresponds more closely to the Jewish scriptures, and especially the Torah, than to the other sacred writings mentioned in this book. Perhaps it is best summed up in its own words:

'This Qur'an guides one to what is more straightforward and reassures believers who act honourably that they shall have great earnings. Yet we have reserved painful torment for those who refuse to believe in the hereafter.'

(Sura 17:9–10)

The reference to the hereafter is a reminder that the purpose of God as seen in the Qur'an is to teach mankind how to obey him now — it will be remembered that Islam means submission and peace — so that they may enjoy eternal peace –not only on earth but in Paradise. A few lines from the beautiful Sura 24 give some indication of the Qur'an's spiritual message:

'God is the light of heaven and earth,
His light may be compared to a niche
in which there is a lamp; the lamp
is in a glass; the glass is
just as if it were a glittering star
kindled from a blessed olive tree,
(which is) neither eastern nor western,
whose oil will almost glow though fire
has never touched it. Light upon light,
God guides whom He will to His light.
God sets up parables for mankind;
God is aware of everything.
There are houses God has permitted to be built,
Where His name is mentioned; in them
He is glorified morning and evening by men whom neither business nor trading
distract from remembering God,
keeping up prayer, and paying the welfare due.
They fear a day when their hearts and eyes will feel overcome,
unless God rewards them   *continued*

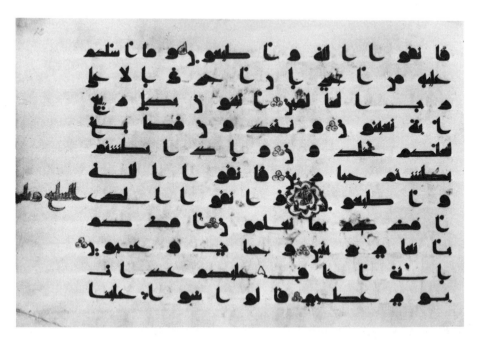

Some verses of the Qur'an written in the Kufic script almost one thousand years ago. The words are from Sura 26 : 126-136.

for the finest things they may have done,
and gives them even more out of His bounty.
God provides for whom He wills,
without any reckoning.'

(Sura 24:35–39)

The Hadith. Though the Qur'an is remarkable in the areas of life which it covers, nevertheless there is need for explanation and interpretation and for filling in some of the details. Of great help in this respect is the Hadith, or traditions describing what the Prophet did and taught. These do not have quite the force of the Qur'an, Muhammed was only a man and his words and deeds were those of a man, but he was a perfect example of a Muslim. Again, a few examples will show the wisdom of his words and how they supplement the Qur'an. The Qur'an frequently warns Muslims against ostentation; 'eat and drink, but do not be extravagant', is one of the principles (Sura 7:3;). A Hadith says, 'A wedding feast on the day after the marriage is proper, on the second day it is good, but on the third day it is pretentious and an hypocrisy'. Again the Qur'an encourages cleanliness; the instruction on washing before praying has already been noted. The Hadith goes further. 'A weekly bath is obligatory on every Muslim, he must wash his head and the whole body'. At a time when few people seem to have been concerned about hygiene this requirement is all the more remarkable.

'We have enjoined every man to look after his parents' is the word of the Qur'an (Sura 31:14). It may be that some situation arises which requires a man to choose between helping his mother or his father. The Hadith teaches, 'A man asked the holy prophet, "Who has the prior claim on my duty?" "Your mother." "And after her?" "Your mother." "And after her?" "Your mother." "And then?" "Your father and after him your kin according to their degree of kinship." ' Self respect was very important in the Prophet's eyes. Among other things he said 'eating in the street is ill-mannered.'

The Sunna. The Qur'an and the Hadith provide the basis of Islamic authority, the sunna, which is the custom by which Islamic belief and practice is regulated. How the Qur'an was to be interpreted was discussed and argued about during the early centuries of the Islamic era, and eventually principles of interpretation were evolved which hold true in modern times. The Shari'a or 'Highway' of divine command and guidance is clear and no aspect of life falls

101

outside it. There are matters which the Qur'an and the Hadith could not deal with specifically, as they did not exist. Here the principle of analogy is used to determine the correct Muslim attitude. For example, the Qur'an denounced the Arab practice of infanticide:

'Do not kill your children in dread of poverty; we shall provide for both them and you. Killing them is a serious error.'

(Sura 17:31)

By analogy this makes birth-control and abortion unlawful among Muslims. However, the Qur'an and the Hadith frequently counsel care and responsibility for the health of one's wife, so abortion is permitted to save the mother's life.

The place of the Qur'an in worship. It is possible to visit a mosque at prayer time and not see a copy of the Qur'an. However, one of its passages is always used as part of the prayers and others may be. After washing, affirming the greatness of God ('Allahu Akbar'), the Muslim then declares the intention of praying and reciting the opening Sura of the Qur'an:

'In the name of God, the merciful and the benign;
All praise is due to God, Lord of the worlds,
the merciful, the mercy-giving,
Master of the day of judgement.
Thee alone do we worship and from thee alone do we ask help.
Guide us on the straight path,
the path of those upon whom is thy favour,
not the path of those who have sought thine anger or who have
gone astray. Amen.'

It begins as all the Suras of the Qur'an do. The only exception is Sura 9, Repentance, which contains warnings against idolatry. Various translations are given of the Bismillahai'r-Rahamini'r-Rahim, the commonest perhaps being, 'in the name of God the compassionate, the merciful.' After this statement of God's nature the Muslim is then reminded that God is creator and judge as well as the source of all goodness. There is no other God to be worshipped and no other being should be given the worship due only to God. This is a warning to avoid Arabian polytheism, and also the error—which Muslims believe Christians committed—of making Jesus, a prophet, into a divine being. God is then asked to keep the praying Muslim on the right path, the way of Islam. Three examples of other verses that may be recited after 'The Opening' are given below. Each makes the same kind of point, that God is unique, the one source of life, compassion and guidance, the one who alone is worthy of worship:

> 'In the name of God, the merciful, the mercy-giving.
> Say: he is God, the one and only.
> God, the self-sufficient (upon whom everything depends).
> He begets not, nor is he begotten,
> and there is nothing which can be compared to him.'
>
> (Sura 112)

> 'In the name of God, the merciful, the mercy-giving.
> When comes the help of God, and victory, and thou (the
> Prophet) seest people enter God's religion in crowds
> then celebrate the praise of thy lord and pray for his
> forgiveness, for he is often returning (to show grace and mercy).'
>
> (Sura 110)

> 'In the name of God, the merciful, the mercy-giving,
> Time and again man is lost, except such as have faith
> and do righteous deeds, and who counsel each other to be truthful
> and who counsel each other to be patient.'
>
> (Sura 103)

The introduction to all kinds of prescribed prayer (salat) is recited in Arabic only. The English translation reads:

> 'I have turned my face only towards the Supreme being who has created the skies and the earth, and I am not one of those who ascribes a partner to God. To you be glory, and with this praise I begin this prayer. Yours is the most blessed and auspicious name; you are exalted and none other than you is worthy of worship.'

During the personal prayers (du'a) which one may make at the end of formal prayer (salat), other verses of the Qur'an may be used, of course, and it is not uncommon to enter a mosque at any time and see a Muslim studying the Qur'an prayerfully. On Friday (Jum'a), congregational prayer is obligatory for all Muslim men, and during this noon prayer a sermon (khutba) is often given, based on the Qur'an. An appropriate portion is read in Arabic, a translation may be provided, then the sermon follows in the language of the people.

Muslim respect for the Qur'an and its teaching. Muslim emphasis upon the Prophet Muhammad's illiteracy helps to stress the belief that the Qur'an is not Muhammad's book, but God's revelation. Not surprisingly, therefore, the Muslim treats the book containing the words of God with great respect. When the book is not being read it will be wrapped in cloth and kept on a shelf above all other books. Before reading it a Muslim will always wash carefully and

103

often take a bath. Sometimes when it is being read the Qur'an will be placed on a special stool so that it need not be handled more than is necessary.

However, it is the teaching in the book, and not the Qur'an as a physical object, that is the reason for the scripture's being treated with such respect. Therefore, it is a respected act of piety to learn the Qur'an by heart. Many Muslims do this when they are children and their achievement is recognised by the title 'hafiz' being attached as a prefix to their name—for example, Hafiz Ahmed Shah. Especially in the days before printing, when Qur'ans were expensive and scarce, the hafiz could perform a valuable service to the community. Blind Muslims often became hafiz and were looked after by the town or village which was grateful for their ministry. Though only a minority of Muslims become hafiz, most boys and girls attend classes at the mosque where they learn to read the Arabic Qur'an and are taught the principles of Islam. In a country like Pakistan this would be part of the child's normal education in school. In Britain the teaching has to be done in the evenings and at weekends. For a Muslim knowledge of the Qur'an is the basis of sound education and a happy life.

Islam's concern that any danger of idolatry should be avoided has already been noted. For this reason one will find no statues,

A group of Muslim boys say their prayers in a mosque.

pictures or stained glass windows in mosques. However, the aesthetic spirit of man still needs to express itself. It has done so through geometrical design and calligraphy, the exquisite ornate writings which can be seen on the walls of many mosques. The names of God, or verses from the Qur'an written in letters of gold or inlaid in marble, testify to the piety of the artist and the benefactor who built the mosque, and remind the devotee of God as he enters the mosque to offer his prayers.

This development of the art of handwriting, calligraphy, can also be seen in copies of the Qur'an, which are the Muslim equivalent of the illuminated manuscripts of medieval Europe, but differ from them in not usually having any representations of the human form on their pages—again, to avoid the danger of idolatry or associating any of God's creation with the creator.

During Ramadan, the month of fasting, one of the acts of devotion undertaken by Muslims is the reading of the Qur'an more frequently than they normally do. Towards the end of the fast, they remember the Night of Power, Lailat al-Qadr, the night when Gabriel recited to Muhammad the first passage of the Qur'an. The precise date of the revelation is not certain; in many countries the anniversary is commemorated on the night before 27 Ramadan. It is a night of vigil, during which Muslims pray and read the Qur'an bearing in mind its words:

'We sent it down on the Night of Power.
What will make you realise
what the Night of Power is?
The Night of Power is better than
a thousand months. Angels and the Spirit (Gabriel)
descend in it on their errand
with their Lord's permission;
(It means) Peace till the approach of dawn.'

(Sura 97:1-5)

This is not merely a night of remembrance; it is an occasion when Muslims attempt in faith to know the power of God, which Muhammad became aware of in the cave of Jabal-an-Nur.

The relationship of the Qur'an to the Jewish and Christian Bibles.

Sometimes Jews, Christians and Muslims are called 'children of Abraham'; or the three religions are called 'sister faiths' or the second and third are called 'daughters' of Judaism. These are all attempts to explain the relationship of Judaism, Christianity and Islam to one another. There are few pages of the Qur'an which do not contain some mention of Abraham, Moses, one of the Hebrew prophets, Jesus or his mother Mary. It would be easy to see Islam as the child of the other two religions, but this is not the Muslim view. Islam explains the similarities and differences by saying that the Hebrew and Christian scriptures are inaccurate in places. It was, therefore, necessary for God to send another prophet, Muhammad, to preach the same message as had been given to Adam, Abraham, Moses, Jesus and others, in the hope that this time it would be recorded faithfully and followed obediently. According to Muslim teaching, therefore, the Qur'an is not the last of three scriptures, dependent on the other two; it is a copy of a heavenly Qur'an, revealed to the Jewish prophets and to Jesus, but forgotten or perverted by their followers. Islam, though appearing last in time, is not regarded by Muslims as the offspring of the other two faiths, but the religion first revealed by God to Adam.

The Sikh scriptures

The Adi Granth or Guru Granth Sahib. The sacred writings of Sikhism are contained in two books, the second of which is somewhat less used and might appear less important to the casual observer. It is called the Dasam Granth and will be considered at the end of this section. We meanwhile confine our attention to the book which is the focal point of Sikh worship in the gurdwara, both in the sense that everything revolves around it—even literally, for the bride and groom walk round it clockwise four times at a wedding—and in the sense that Sikh worship is based on its contents. The book has two names, either of which may be used. The earliest title of the book was Adi Granth, meaning 'first collection or compilation'. The second is Guru Granth Sahib. For over two hundred years, from about 1499 when Guru Nanak began his ministry until the death of the tenth Guru in 1708, the Sikhs had human spiritual leaders. Shortly before his death Guru Gobind Singh conferred guruship upon the scriptures. Henceforth it became known as the Guru Granth Sahib—'sahib' is an honorific form of address rather like 'Lord' when used in the phrase 'Lord God'—but the old title never fell into disuse.

Origins and history. The origin of the Adi Granth lies in the poetic compositions of Guru Nanak. He produced many of these during the forty years of his ministry. Nine hundred and seventy-four of them are included in the Guru Granth Sahib and there may be others that were lost. At first these hymns were remembered and passed on by word of mouth. Only towards the end of the Guru's lifetime, or even after his death, were they written down. It is said that Guru Nanak was responsible for inventing the script in which the Punjabi language is written, and for this reason it is called 'gurmukhi' meaning 'pertaining to the Guru'. By the time of the third Guru, Amar Das, an official collection of his hymns, those of his predecessors, and of some Hindu and Muslim holy men existed.

The most dramatic event occurred in 1604 when Guru Arjan, the fifth leader of the Sikhs, had an authoritative collection compiled and installed it in a newly completed building in Amritsar called the Harimandir. The word means 'God's House'. On the final page of the book he wrote these words:

> 'In this platter are placed three things, truth, contentment and meditation. The nectar-bestowing name of the Lord, the support of all, has been put therein. If someone eats and relishes this food he is liberated (from rebirth). This should not be forsaken so keep it always enshrined in your mind. The world-ocean is crossed by falling at the Lord's feet. O Nanak, everything is an extension of the Lord.'

These sentences give some impression of the importance attached to the words of the book. They were the teachings of God himself, the supreme Guru; consequently they were far more important than any human Guru. To demonstrate this he, the Guru of the Sikhs always bowed in front of the book. Only two of the later Gurus composed hymns, the ninth and the tenth. The ninth, Guru Tegh Bahadur was an intensely modest man and did not add his compositions to the Adi Granth. However, his son, the tenth Guru did, but refused to include any of his own when he undertook the revision. By 1708, when the scripture was declared to be the Guru of the Sikhs, it contained the writings of six of the Gurus, twelve non-Sikhs, a number of Sikh bards at the court of Guru Arjan, whose names are not known, and three other Sikhs, Satta and Balwand, and Guru Nanak's friend and companion Mardana.

The Sikh scriptures are unusual in that they contain the writings of people who were not of the Sikh faith—Hindus, and the Muslims Kabir and Sheikh Farid. The works of these men were probably included to show the open nature of Sikhism. The Gurus never claimed that they alone possessed the truth. These works also tried to attract to Sikhism villagers who revered these North Indian holy men. It is not surprising that among the different writers some variety of language is to be found, though all are similar. But a unity of ideas exists among all the poets, and the same gurmukhi script was used by the men who wrote them down.

The contents of the Adi Granth. The Adi Granth contains no narrative passages. In this respect it is like the book of Psalms in the Bible. Most of the hymns are poems in praise of God, and exhortations to hear his voice, that of the perfect Guru speaking in one's heart. This will naturally result in the Sikh's living a responsible ethical life, with the emphasis on service to humanity in general. Many of the hymns express this social and ethical concern. The following examples may provide some idea of the message of the Guru Granth Sahib:

> 'Endless is the praise to be offered him, endless what may be said about him. Endless his actions, endless the gifts he bestows. Sight cannot reach his limit or sound a point where his voice does not reach. His will and his created universe both seem limitless. He has no end, no limit, no bounds whatsoever. Many sigh with exhaustion trying to discover his limits, but they cannot comprehend them. No one can discern the limits of the one who is infinite. However great we say he is, he is greater still. The Lord is great, his dwelling place is exalted, his name is still more exalted. If one rises to that height one may have some idea of his greatness, though it is fully known to God alone. Nanak says, grace comes only by his grace and bounty.'   (AG 5)

These lines describe the majesty of the infinite God. The next passage takes up the idea of his concern for mankind which was expressed in the last sentence:

> 'When a man is in extreme difficulties and there is no one to offer him help, when his friends turn into enemies and even his kinsfolk desert him, when all hope and support is lost, then let him remember the Lord and no harm shall befall him. The Lord is the strength of the weak; he is unborn, undying, and eternal. By the Guru's teaching we know him as the true Lord. When a man is weak with the pangs of poverty and hunger, has no money and no one to offer him consolation, when he has no one to help him in his need and all his work comes to nothing, let him remember the Supreme Lord and he will have an everlasting kingdom.' (AG 70)

As the Sikh finds strength in God and discovers him to be one who cares for mankind, so he is instructed to live an active, useful and honest life, caring for others as God cares for him:

> 'Live amid the hurly-burly of life, but remain alert. Do not covet your neighbours' possessions. Without being devoted to God's

name we cannot attain inner peace or still our inner hunger. The Guru has shown me the true way of living in the city, the real life of its shops, the inner life; our trading must be in truth, we must be moderate in everything.'   (AG 939)

The arrangement and printing of the Adi Granth.   After each of the three passages quoted above the letters 'AG' and a number have been given inside a bracket. AG stands for the words Adi Granth, and the number indicates the page of the scripture from which the quotation has been taken. In the earliest collections of the Gurus' hymns there was no uniform order or page numbering. Guru Arjan established the definitive order, following the earlier trend to put the hymns of the Gurus in sequence and then add the hymns of the non-Sikh contributors. He also arranged the collection in thirty-one sections, each set to a different kind of tune. The order in each section therefore runs: Guru Nanak, Guru Angad, Guru Amar Das, Guru Ram Das, Guru Arjan, Guru Tegh Bahadur, Kabir, Sheikh Farid, Namdev, Ravidas and then the other poets. However, as there are only one hundred and sixteen of Farid's hymns in the whole Adi Granth he, along with some others, is not represented in each section. Until the nineteenth century the Sikhs resisted the suggestion that their holy book should be printed. Partly they were of the opinion that the sacred text should only be written by hand, but much more they feared that the mass-production of the books on printing presses would result in its being sold in shops and being bought by people who might not treat it with due honour. Sikhs should not smoke and they would be very disturbed if they found their scriptures being read in a smoke-filled room. Many Sikhs would take a bath, and all Sikhs would certainly wash their hands before touching the sacred pages. Other owners of the book might well be much less respectful. Eventually, the decision to print copies of the Guru Granth Sahib was taken, and with it the decision to make each copy of identical length. Wherever there is a copy of the Adi Granth—in Amritsar, Vancouver, Bangkok or Leeds—it will have 1430 pages, and the gurmukhi form of the last passage quoted above will always be on page 939.

The first words of the Adi Granth are called the Mool Mantra, the basic verse of Sikhism. It sums up the beliefs taught by Guru Nanak:

'There is one God,
Eternal Truth is his name,
Creator of all things and the all-pervading spirit.
Fearless and without hatred,
Timeless and formless.

Beyond birth and death,
Self-enlightened.
By the grace of the Guru he is known.'

These words are also used to mark the beginning of each of the thirty-one sections of the Guru Granth Sahib.

Sikh attitudes towards the Guru Granth Sahib.   The Adi Granth is now the Guru of the Sikhs. They bow in front of it when they enter a gurdwara as they would have paid respect to the human Guru three hundred or more years ago. They turn to its pages for advice, not only in times of personal crisis, but regularly day by day.

It may come as something of a surprise to discover that only a small proportion of Sikhs own a copy of the scripture. Many instead possess a gutka, a small book containing about eighteen of the most important hymns. It is also customary for Sikhs to know by heart considerable amounts of scripture. The reason why it is fairly un-common to find a copy of the Adi Granth in a Sikh home is that the Sikhs respect the book so much. It would need to be given a room to itself. Each morning the owner would have to rise before dawn, take a bath, open the book and read it. In the evening again, he would have to find time to read the Adi Granth and meditate on its teachings. The scripture of the Sikhs is not something to be put on a shelf and read in a convenient moment.

One Sikh scholar, a man in his forties, had always wanted to own a copy of the Adi Granth but could only afford a small house just large enough for his family's needs. At last he was able to obtain a house with a spare room upstairs. This could be made into a gurdwara, which is what any room containing the holy book becomes. At much cost he furnished it with a fitted carpet, and then bought and installed a copy of the Guru Granth Sahib. He did not think of the cost—over a month's salary to furnish the room properly—or the daily obligation he had put upon himself; his only thought was that he could now meditate upon God's word 'night and day' as a true Sikh should.

The first sight that meets the eyes of anyone who enters a gurdwara is the Guru Granth Sahib. In its position of honour it is the focal point. It alone sits enthroned, while everyone else sits on the ground, and it has a canopy over it, which further demonstrates the importance of the scripture. The man or woman who sits behind the Adi Granth, facing the congregation and reading or chanting portions of the book, holds a fan of animal hairs, nylon, or peacock feathers and waves it over the book. This again shows its honoured status for such fans, called chauris, are waved over the heads of rulers and other dignitaries in India. Sikhs, heads covered and having removed their shoes, enter the room where the scripture is installed, approach the book and bow in front of it until their knees and forehead touch the ground. They make an offering of money or food to the book, as they would have done to the human Gurus long ago. Such gifts are used in the service of the community, as they were then; the Gurus never used the gifts which were made to them for their own purposes. The Sikh, without turning his back on the book, then takes his place in the congregation, being careful never to let his feet point directly at the scripture, for this, too, would be regarded as disrespectful.

The place of the Guru Granth Sahib in worship. The scripture of the Sikhs is honoured, not worshipped. The reverence paid to it is intended to remind the Sikh that its words are divine revelation. As God should be at the centre of a person's life so the Guru Granth Sahib holds the central position in Sikh worship. It is conducted in the presence of the book and the content of worship is material chanted from the book, sung by the musicians and the congregation, and explained by one of the congregation in a talk or sermon.

The Sikhs are people of their holy book to a greater degree, perhaps, than followers of the other faiths, for the scripture is also central to the wedding ceremony, is used in the naming of a child,

Reading the Guru Granth Sahib. The canopy above it and the chauri in the reader's hand indicate the respect which Sikhs have for their scriptures.

111

and consulted when decisions have to be made. A Sikh marraige is valid only when it has been solemnised in the presence of the Guru Granth Sahib and the couple has walked around it four times in a clockwise direction, while the four verses of the marriage hymn were being read. To name a child the scripture is opened at random, the first word of the verse at the top of the left hand page is read to the family, or the page is turned back if the page does not begin with a new verse. The family then chooses a name with the same initial as one of the letters of the word. Sometimes the scripture is consulted directly if the community cannot come to an agreed decision. In 1920 a group of Hindu outcastes had been admitted to the Sikh faith and wished to offer the karah parshad—a dish prepared with flour, sugar and clarified butter—which would be given to visitors at the Golden Temple in Amritsar. Some Sikhs opposed the intention, believing that they would be polluted by such an offering. Agreement could not be reached, so in a spirit of prayer the Guru Granth was opened at random. These words from page 638 were read:

> 'Upon the worthless he bestows his grace, brother, if they will serve the True Guru. Exalted is the service of the True Guru, brother, so hold the divine name in remembrance. God himself offers grace and mystic union. We are worthless sinners, brother, yet the True Guru has drawn us to that blissful union.'

The passage was regarded as a clear indication that God accepted the outcastes and their offering, so that in fact his grace made them the equals of anyone else. The community bowed to the decision of the Guru Granth Sahib.

When a Sikh family moves into a new home, or when new business premises are opened it is not unusual for a copy of the Guru Granth Sahib to be taken from the gurdwara, installed in the building and read continuously from beginning to end by a relay of people. This is known as an akhand path and takes about forty-eight hours. It is a way of seeking God's blessing. Such readings also take place in the gurdwara when the anniversary of a Guru's birth or death is being celebrated. A family which has suffered a bereavement may arrange for a reading of the Adi Granth to be held in their home, for purposes of consolation. On such occasions the reading will not be continuous, but the book will be read when most of the extended family and their friends can be present. In Britain this usually means in the evening. This reading (path) normally takes about a fortnight to complete.

The Dasam Granth. Guru Gobind Singh, the tenth and last Guru, was a prolific poet. In a lifetime of forty-two years, much of which

112

was spent planning and fighting in campaigns for independence, he composed sufficient poems to fill a book of 1428 pages. This, The Dasam Granth, or collection of the tenth Guru ('das' means ten in Punjabi) was not assembled until 1734, almost thirty years after his death. Though some of his compositions are used in Sikh ceremonies, and a number are included in the gutkas or books of hymns which many Sikhs own, he did not allow any of his verses to be inserted in the Adi Granth when a place was found for his father's hymns. Though the script of the Dasam Granth is gurmukhi throughout, the language of the poems varies. Apparently the tenth Guru was equally at home in Persian, Sanskrit or the kind of Punjabi used by the other Gurus. This makes the Dasam Granth difficult to read, and few Sikhs—and not all gurdwaras—possess a copy of the book. It is never installed in a gurdwara and never given the honour and respect with which the Adi Granth is treated.

Other important Sikh writings. One of the men who compiled the Adi Granth on the instructions of Guru Arjan was Bhai Gurdas, the nephew of Guru Amar Das. He was a poet himself, and although Guru Arjan would not allow any of his compositions to be put in the Adi Granth, his comments, together with those of one of Guru Gobind Singh's companions, Bhai Nandlal, may be used and quoted when the hymns of the Adi Granth are being explained during a Sikh service.

Scripture translations and chapter and verse divisions in the six faiths

Each of the scriptures that has been discussed in this section is available in English and in many other languages. However, the attitude towards such translations varies considerably. It is necessary to consider each in turn and at the same time we shall consider how the present-day divisions into verses came about.

Traditions about the language of the scriptures. Hindu priests would never think of using a translation of the Sanskrit Vedas in a service. They may be prepared to repeat the English form of the hymns for the benefit of visitors to the temple but there is no doubt that God should be addressed in the ancient language in which he revealed himself. Orthodox Jews hold precisely the same view. The Torah must be read in Hebrew, and the handwritten scroll used is one which lacks vowels and punctuation, unlike the printed version that the man in the pew may be using. Following in the same tradition, Muslims use only Arabic in their obligatory prayers, though they may follow the reading of the Qur'an in Arabic with a vernacular repetition of the same passage. All these traditions believe that there is something special about the language in which the scripture was given. Not only is any translation likely to be inaccurate or inadequate—just as an Englishman would deny that it is really possible to translate Shakespeare, or a German the poems of Goethe—but they also believe the language to be sacred.

Not all Hindus share the belief in the need to use Sanskrit or even the Vedas in their worship. The bhakti tradition of devotionalism often asserts that God can be worshipped by anyone in any language. Consequently it has translated the book which perhaps it regards as most sacred, the Bhagavad Gita, into many different Indian languages and it is read in these during acts of worship. The Sikhs are often thought of as belonging to the bhakti tradition by Hindus, though their view of themselves is that they are a distinct religion. However, like bhakti Hindus, they said that anyone could communicate the word of God. Guru Nanak was not a member of the priestly caste, a Brahmin, and he also taught in a tongue which the people of North India would understand, a dialect similar to Punjabi. The Adi Granth has been translated into a number of languages and though the original is used in worship the world over, occasionally English translations have been used in Britain and as time goes on and fewer British Sikhs read gurmukhi, the use of English may become more frequent.

The language of the Bible.   Not all Jews have insisted on the use of the Bible in Hebrew, either now or in the past. In fact, some three hundred years before the beginning of the Common Era, Jews living outside Palestine needed a Greek version of the Torah, as that was the tongue they spoke and read, and they no longer knew Hebrew. The story goes that the scholarly Egyptian King, Ptolemy Philadelphus (285-247 BCE), a seeker after wisdom, who even welcomed a Buddhist mission all the way from India to his court, heard of the Hebrew teachings and insisted on placing a Greek translation in his library. Accordingly, he asked the High Priest in Jerusalem to send him seventy-two scholars, six from each of the twelve Jewish tribes. These were greeted, questioned, and then taken to the island of Pharos to undertake their work in peace, in a building specially provided. The resulting Greek version came to be known as the Septuagint, the book of the seventy, even though the story mentions seventy-two. Later a Christian legend grew up around the translation. This said that the king had put the seventy-two scholars in separate rooms and prevented them from communicating with one another until the task was completed. When the translations were compared each was seen to be exactly like the others.

The purpose of this story was to express the belief that the Greek translation had been divinely inspired. No other explanation for the remarkable agreement between the texts was possible, and therefore the Greek Old Testament was as accurate as the Hebrew original and just as acceptable. Most Christians, in the first fifty years after Jesus' ministry, were Jews. From the evidence of the New Testament, a large proportion of these were Greek-speaking Jews, that is, men and women who used the Septuagint rather than the Hebrew Jewish Bible. In the New Testament they are described as 'Greeks' or 'Hellenists'. Presumably before those who believed that Jesus was the Messiah and those who did not could enter into debate, they argued which version of the Bible should form the basis of discussion—the Hebrew original or the Septuagint.

From Greek to Latin.   By the fourth century of the Common Era the Christians were using a completely Greek Bible, for the New Testament was written in Greek originally. They found themselves confronted with a problem. Whereas it was customary for all literate people to use Greek in Jesus' day, even if the mother tongue was

The oldest fragment of the New Testament known to exist is part of St. John's Gospel. It was written about 135 CE on papyrus. The photograph shows both back and front.

115

some form of Celtic (which might not have been written down) or Latin, by the fourth century Christians in Italy, and the parts of the Empire north and west of it, as well as many in North Africa, were using Latin as the oral and written language. A number of translations were made to meet their needs, but the accuracy of some of these caused concern. About the year 382 Pope Damasus asked a well-known scholar called Jerome to produce a satisfactory Latin text. This was known as the Vulgate, which meant that it was in the common or everyday speech of that time.

Rather surprisingly, the Bible may have been translated into Gothic before it became available in Latin. Bishop Ulfilas (312-380), who died shortly before Jerome began his work, was a courageous missionary who stepped outside the civilised world, from a Roman point of view, to preach to the barbarians. They were certainly not going to learn Latin. Therefore he had to translate the Bible into their tongue if he wished to succeed.

Christian attitudes. Why Christians should have a different attitude to the translation of their Scriptures from that of most Jews and Muslims to theirs, is not an easy question to answer. Clearly some Jews, even if they were in a minority and their attitude did not prevail, did believe that it was right and proper to use translations of the Tenakh in public worship. Perhaps Christianity moved in a different direction because it was excluded from stricter Jewish synagogues or left them voluntarily.

Another reason is that Christianity was a missionary faith from the beginning. So was Islam, but whereas Islam spread as a dominant culture and therefore people readily accepted Arabic, which became the language of trade and law as well as of religion, Christians belonged to an uninfluential minority for three hundred years. Like Ulfilas, if they wished to influence society, they had to use the vernacular. Gradually, Christianity aspired to dominate society and make its laws and ethics conform to Christian ideals. Latin became the religious language, with the result that the mass of the population, who spoke early English, medieval German or whatever the vernacular was, could not read the Bible for themselves. With the sixteenth-century reformation the use of the vernacular in Protestant churches encouraged the translation of the Bible into many languages. Roman Catholics, even among new converts in a country like India, insisted that worship should be in Latin until the mid-nineteen-sixties and this had the effect of discouraging Bible translation.

The trends today. Now the Roman Catholic view has changed, and members of that church are as busy in the work of Bible translation as most other Christians. Perhaps this Christian experience points to a deep-seated inclination to protect the dignity of sacred literature by confining its use to a special language. In the case of Christianity the attempt failed. In the case of Islam the sacred language often became the language of the Muslim world, replacing local dialects, especially in North Africa.

Restrictions.   One other form of protection must also be mentioned. According to strict Hindu orthodoxy, only a Brahmin may teach the words, and he may only pass on Vedic knowledge to other Brahmins, Kshatriyas, or Vaishyas, the groups which protect and provide for society. The servant classes, the Shudras and the untouchables or outcastes, were excluded from such learning. A teacher would even stop discussing the Vedas if one should pass by, lest he should overhear the sacred words. Judaism debated fiercely whether women should be taught to read the Hebrew Torah, and a woman would never touch the scrolls in the synagogue. Despite the stories in the Jewish Bible, about those who dared to touch the Ark of the Covenant and died because they were not priests (for example I Chronicles 13, 9-10, the story of Uzza), Judaism never confined the privilege of reading the Torah to men of the priestly families in the synagogue. There was a period in the Middle Ages when only Christian priests were encouraged to read the Bible. But when printing made cheap copies easily available, the Bible was one of the first books to be printed and, translated from the Latin, it quickly found its way into the hands of craftsmen and farmers as well as scholars.

In Buddhism it has tended to be the monks who read and know the scriptures, but there is no reason why others who are keen cannot do the same.

The arrangement of the Scriptures.   Most of the world's scriptures are now divided into small sections such as chapters, and into even smaller divisions such as verses. The Vedas have been divided into ten books, or mandalas, ever since they were written down. Being in poetic form, they were already in verses, though it is unlikely that anyone bothered to number them until they were printed in quite recent times. This may have been done by Western scholars, for reference purposes, rather than by Hindus (just as it is possible to find copies of Shakespeare's plays with line numberings in the margin to help students refer to the footnotes or references at the back of the book). The Bhagavad Gita seems always to have been split into eighteen parts, which now appear as chapters, but the verse numberings are a fairly modern development, though it has not been possible to discover when it happened.

As for the Bible, Rabbi Nathan divided the Tenakh into verses in 1448 in a handwritten text. Pagininus adopted the division in his Latin Bible of 1528 and divided the New Testament into chapters and verses. However, the chapter and verse structure of Christian Bibles now in use is the work of a man named Stephanus, who published a copy of the Vulgate in 1555. It must always be remembered that the original texts of both Old and New Testament books did not even separate words or sentences. They lacked any punctuation at all. Stephanus' chapters are rather arbitrary and sometimes destroy the sense of a passage. A good example of this is I Corinthians 13, which ends 'but the greatest of these is love'. Surely Paul intends the reader to continue without a pause to the sentence, 'Make love your aim'. (In fact he expected the whole of his letter to be read complete from beginning to end, and would have been surprised and perhaps annoyed if he had known that it would be used piecemeal.)

The Qur'an was revealed in sections of variable length over a period of about twenty years. These were treasured as groups of ayats or signs which were eventually built up into chapters called Suras. The word Sura can be used of a layer of stones in a wall. Muslim editions of the Qur'an divide the book into its 114 Suras but it is only copies published by non-Muslims either in Arabic or in translations which tend to divide the Suras into verses. The verse numberings normally used are those of a man called G. Fluegel, who prepared an Arabic edition in 1858. A Muslim scholar named Tabari, who knew the Qur'an by heart when he was only seven, divided the Qur'an into verses so that students could use his commentary more easily. It is this system that Muslim writers use if they print verse numbers in the margin of the text.

We come finally to the Guru Granth Sahib. Now that it is in the printed text of 1430 pages, reference to a passage by the page on which it occurs is easy. The reader then has only to scan the page to find the words he is seeking. However, Sikhs often retain the traditional method of reference. The Adi Granth is divided into thirty-one equal sections, each being given the name of an Indian musical form. Then, as mentioned above, the Gurus' compositions occur in chronological order, followed by the hymns of Kabir and others, such as Namdev and Sheikh Farid. Thus a reference reading 'Ramkali IX 6', means that the passage is to be found in the section named Ramkali, in the place where the ninth Guru's hymns are located, and in the sixth stanza. Nowadays the author might add 'AG 902' and so make easier a search that could otherwise take as long as an hour or as little as two minutes.

The story of how the world's great scriptures came to be divided into chapters and verses is a difficult one, and each religious tradition is different. It must always be remembered, however, that in every case such a breaking up of the text was undertaken not by the faithful, but by printers or scholars for reference purposes. Consequently, though this editing process may be helpful to some extent, the splitting up of a book or a Sura into verses may make it more difficult for us to read the connected and flowing thought of the writer in the way that he intended.

Questions

1. *With reference to* **two** *or more faiths describe the difference between scriptures and other important religious writings.*

2. *Which religions that you have studied refuse to allow translations of the scriptures to be used in worship? Suggest reasons why the use of translations is not approved.*

3. *What use do* **two** *of the religions make of their scriptures in worship? How is respect for the scriptures shown?*

4. *Describe the origin and growth of the scriptures of* **two** *faiths that you have studied.*

5. *Sometimes scriptures are called 'revealed books'. Refer to at least* **two** *faiths in explaining the meaning of the phrase.*

6. *Discuss a well-known passage from the sacred writings of* **two** *religions. In each case explain its importance in the religion and mention occasions when it is used.*

7. *Write out in full* **two** *of the following, then identify the religion to which each belongs, before explaining their meaning and importance: The Gayatri Mantra; The Shema; The Lord's Prayer; The Fateh; The Mool Mantra; The Three Refuges or the Four Noble Truths.*

8. *Explain the process in which* **two** *of the scriptures came to be written down. What authority do these scriptures have in their particular traditions? What makes a writing 'sacred'?*

9. *Describe the original form and language of* **two** *scriptures. Discuss the attitudes which have been taken to translating them and using translations in worship.*

TIME LINES OF SACRED WRITINGS

		HINDUISM and SIKHISM	JUDAISM
BCE	1500	● Compilation of the RIG VEDA	
	1000	● c 900 Beginning of composition of MAHABHARATA	● c 900 First strands of the TORAH written down
		● c 600–300 Composition of UPANISHADS	
	500		● 458 (or 397) EZRA Compilation of TORAH
		● c 300–200 LAWS OF MANU and BHAGAVAD GITA c 100 Composition of RAMAYANA completed	
CE	0		● 90 COUNCIL OF JAMNIA (Jewish canon fixed)
	500	● c 300 Composition of the PURANAS begins	
	1000		
		● c 1400 RIG VEDA committed to writing	
	1500	● 1499 GURU NANAK began composing hymns of Sikhism	
		● 1604 First version of SIKH SCRIPTURES (ADI GRANTH)	
		● 1706 Final recension of ADI GRANTH	
	2000	● 1708 GURU GOBIND SINGH installed ADI GRANTH as GURU	

Note: Most BCE dates can only be regarded as approximate

BUDDHISM	CHRISTIANITY	ISLAM

● c 500 onward SUTRA and VINAYA
orally fixed; ABHIDHARMA developing;
PALI TRIPITAKA written down

● c 200 MILINDAPANHA

● c 0 PRAJNAPARAMITA SUTRAS

● c 100 VIMALIKIRTI NIRDESA SUTRA

● c 200 SADDHARMAPUNDARIKA and
LANKAVATARA SUTRAS

● c 450 VISUDDHIMAGGA

● c 550 SUKHAVATI SUTRAS

● c 40–100 Books of the NEW
TESTAMENT written

● 367 ATHANASIUS listed books of NEW
TESTAMENT canon

● 404 VULGATE of JEROME completed

● 610 First revelation of QUR'AN to
Muhammad

● 632 Final revelation of QUR'AN to
Muhammad (Sura 5 v 4)

● 651 UTHMAN'S version of QUR'AN
completed

CHAPTER THREE
WORSHIP

Places of worship

Whenever we look at a great ceremonial building, whether it be the remains of Stonehenge, one of the pyramids, Westminster Abbey or the White House in Washington we should remind ourselves that however beautiful and impressive the structure may be, its true significance lies in the people who made and use it. In this section we shall be examining the places in which worship happens, but at the very beginning we need to remember that men and women worshipped God long before they built places of worship. There were no synagogues in the Sinai Desert, when Moses led his fellow Hebrews out of Egypt into Canaan. In the concentration camps of the Second World War there were no synagogues or churches, but Jews, Christians, Jehovah's Witnesses and many other prisoners still managed to pray and worship, despite the hostility of their guards. However, quite early in the history of a religion its members construct places where they may meet together to worship without interruption. The religions we are studying all have their special buildings with names which we must take the trouble to learn. First, however, we need to keep a number of general points in mind.

1. The shape of religious buildings has developed over the centuries. For example, the Roman Catholic cathedral at Liverpool is very unlike Durham cathedral, yet both are Christian churches.
2. We shall be giving most of our attention to the buildings that are in use in the twentieth century and the kinds of activity which take place in them now.
3. We shall try to concentrate on the examples which are most familiar to people living in Britain. In other parts of the world things may be different. For example, there is a small village church in Pakistan which is 'L'-shaped. Everyone sits on the earth floor, men in one leg of the 'L' and women in the other so that everyone can see the minister and the communion

table, but there is no possibility of men and women distracting one another. Religious buildings and practices, like dress, diet and language vary from country to country as well as century to century. In this example the cultural influence of Islam encouraged the separation of men and women, even in a Christian setting.

4.   Our descriptions will concentrate on the important features which are likely to be seen in any church, mosque, synagogue or temple. The place you visit may differ in detail but not in essentials. The church in Pakistan already mentioned has no pews and men and women sit apart from one another, but it does have a communion table and the white cloth which covers it has a cross marked on it. These are features found in churches worldwide, even if some have altars instead of communion tables.

Here are a few questions to keep in mind while reading the pages which follow and to consider whenever you visit a place of worship.

a.   When you enter a place of worship what is the feature that most demands your attention?
b.   Is there some focal point around which everything else seems to be arranged and to which you feel your attention being drawn?
c.   Where are the scriptures placed?
d.   Does the building face in a particular direction — perhaps towards the east or perhaps towards a city like Jerusalem or Mecca?

ॐ The Hindu temple

An old Hindu text says:

'The best places of worship are holy grounds, river banks, caves, sites of pilgrimages, the summits of mountains, confluences of rivers, sacred forests, solitary groves, the shade of the bel tree, valleys, places overgrown with tulsi plants, pasture lands, temples of Shiva without a bull, the foot of a sacred fig tree or an amalaki tree, cow sheds, islands, sanctuaries, the shore of the sea, one's own house, the abode of one's teacher, places which tend to inspire single-pointedness, lonely places free from animals.'

The list includes almost everything, so it is clearly no exaggeration to say that the chief temple of the Hindu is the universe. Some buildings create a favourable environment and atmosphere for worship.

123

Traditionally a Hindu temple is the home of a god and people visit it as one might go to see a friend. They will bow to the statue of the deity, offer flowers and incense. However, it is not necessary for someone to offer worship in a temple. Some people were not expected or allowed to go to temples in past times; they were people who ate meat or belonged to certain caste groups. According to the Indian constitution of 1951, all temples should be open to everyone.

The features of a temple.   Temples are of all kinds of shape and size. However, they have three features in common. First, there will be some object which represents the deity — a statue or some other symbol. Secondly, this will be covered by some kind of canopy. Usually this is the roof of the building, but its purpose is to cover the object respectfully, just as a parasol or umbrella is held over an important person, its function being not to shade someone from the sun, but to show him the honour his position deserves. Finally, the temple will be attended by a priest who will care for the sacred object, make offerings on behalf of those who visit the temple, and give them prasad, a gift from the deity to the worshipper, usually in the form of food.

Large temples built in past centuries had an entrance which faced the rising sun. On the open ground outside the temple there would be the statue of an animal or bird, the creature upon which the god rides in Hindu mythology. This is sometimes regarded as the temple guardian. The bull Nandi is associated with Shiva, the bird Garuda with Vishnu, and Durga rides a fierce lion.

A number of stone steps would take the worshipper into the presence of the god and its priestly attendant, probably at the end of a large hall. Above the statue its canopy would take the form of a high tower representing a mountain, which in most ancient religions is regarded as sacred.

Hindu temples in many places where Hindus have settled outside India are more than homes of the god; they are places of congregational worship. In East Africa and the Caribbean there are purpose-built temples designed on the model of classical temples in India, but they are also centres where the local Hindu community gathers. At present in Britain and other parts of Europe temples are converted churches or similar large buildings or houses. The typical prayer room has a shelf or table standing against one of the walls. On the table will be one or more statues of the deities, perhaps pictures of others, maybe a bottle containing water from the Ganges and a copy of the Bhagavad Gita. The contents of the shrine may vary from temple to temple. The statues will have a canopy above them or a symbolic representation, a pyramidical shape outlined on

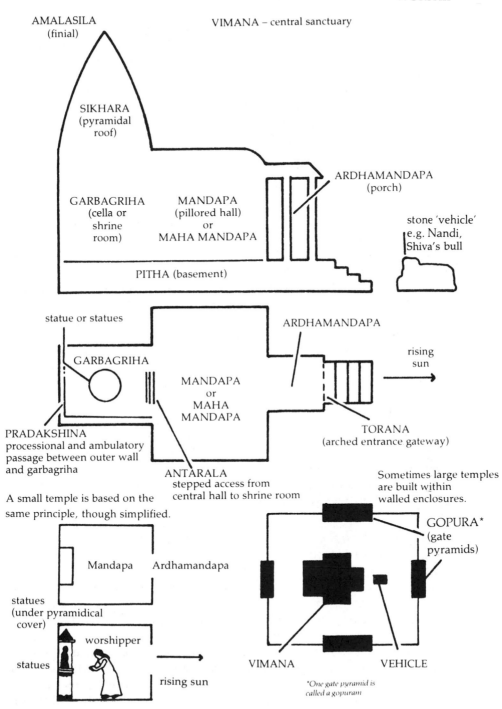

AMALASILA
(finial)

VIMANA – central sanctuary

SIKHARA
(pyramidal
roof)

GARBAGRIHA
(cella or
shrine
room)

MANDAPA
(pillored hall)
or
MAHA MANDAPA

ARDHAMANDAPA
(porch)

stone 'vehicle'
e.g. Nandi,
Shiva's bull

PITHA (basement)

statue or statues

GARBAGRIHA

MANDAPA
or
MAHA
MANDAPA

ARDHAMANDAPA

rising
sun

PRADAKSHINA
processional and ambulatory
passage between outer wall
and garbagriha

TORANA
(arched entrance gateway)

ANTARALA
stepped access from
central hall to shrine room

A small temple is based on the
same principle, though simplified.

Mandapa   Ardhamandapa

statues
(under pyramidical
cover)

worshipper

statues

rising sun

Sometimes large temples
are built within
walled enclosures.

GOPURA*
(gate
pyramids)

VIMANA   VEHICLE

*One gate pyramid is
called a gopuram

Diagram of a Hindu temple

the wall in cloth or coloured paper. On the wall or elsewhere on the shrine may be the Sanskrit letters ॐ Om, and perhaps a swastika 卐 . Om is the symbol which represents the Supreme Reality, God. The swastika says that man cannot reach the one God by his own logic directly. He must have God's help. God lies beyond his understanding and control. On the other walls there will probably be a number of pictures of other deities and perhaps of Guru Nanak, or Gandhi, one of the greatest Hindus of the twentieth century. Most Hindus believe that the soul is divine and eternal. Therefore the Sikh Gurus and a man of Gandhi's spiritual stature can be placed among the gods. Also, because Hindus tend to believe that God speaks to man through many teachers of all faiths, they can find Jesus a place of honour, though not the unique position that Christians have claimed for him.

There will be no seats in the room where services are held. All worshippers sit on the floor. Usually men sit at one side and women at the other, but to an increasing extent they now gather together as families. At times of worship a square portable fire-altar will be brought into the room and the congregation will gather around it, facing the shrine. Some members of the congregation will sit near the priest to assist him during the services; others will play musical instruments and the rest will join in the chanting and singing.

An act of worship (puja).   The congregational worship or puja which is described here combines three separate forms, arti, havan and the singing of bhajans. Each is complete in itself, but especially on a Sunday morning they are likely to be combined. Worship may take place at any time and on any day, but in Britain major services are usually held on Sunday morning when most Hindus are free to attend, and on weekday evenings.

Havan, the offering of fire.   At an agreed time the priest begins the act of worship by kindling the sacred fire. Into the portable fire-altar he and his assistants place some small pieces of wood and camphor. He then pours some liquid butter, called ghee, into the fire. As he does this he chants passages from the Vedas, and throughout the saying of these verses more wood and ghee are added to keep the fire alight.

Prayers are offered first for purity. The worshipper must be pure to approach the Holy One. Taking water in his left hand, the priest dips the tip of a finger of his right hand into it and touches his ears, nose, eyes, mouth, arms, body and legs. The other worshippers follow his example. The priest says:

An act of worship called Havan in a Hindu temple in London. A married couple share with priests in performing the ritual.

'Let my tongue have speaking power, ears have the power of hearing, the nose inhaling power and the eyes seeing power. May the arms and thighs have strength and all the limbs be full of energy.'

The priest also utters a Vedic prayer for the good of all mankind:

'Let there be good to all, let all be free from sickness, let us all see good and let none suffer. Let all be happy and fearless. Let there be sympathy for each other and success for all work. Let there be prosperity to the King (or Queen) who protects the people every day and also to the people. Let all creatures, bipeds and quadrupeds, be prosperous every day. Let there be peace among the gods and in the three worlds. Let us all and all other beings have peace everywhere. You are the creator and sustainer of the world. You encourage godliness and establish peace among the people. Whoever is my friend today, let him be in peace: whoever is my enemy, let him also be in peace. Om, shanti, shanti, shanti. (Lord God, bring peace, peace, peace.)'

Prayers are also offered to all the chief gods, who are named in turn. Havan is based upon the sacrificial worship of the Aryans.

Arti, the worship of light.   Arti is the ceremonial offering of love and devotion of the Lord. A number of symbols are used which represent the five elements from which everything is made, according to the Hindu teaching. The most obvious element is fire, for during the service a flat tray with five lights on it is waved in front of the shrine. However, incense and flowers are also offered, representing the earth, a fan is waved symbolising air, and the conch shell which is blown at the beginning of the rite is the symbol of ether; it also contains water, the fifth element.

The priest, or a member of the congregation, holds the arti tray and moves it slowly in front of the statues of the gods. The lights are also held before the pictures of the other gods and goddesses, of Guru Nanak and Jesus. A spot of red paste is put on the forehead of the statues, on the portraits of the gods and on each of the worshippers by the priest. The arti dish is then brought round to all the people in the prayer hall and each person in turn puts some money on the tray, holds his hands over the flames and then passes his hands over his forehead and hair. Thus they symbolically receive God's blessing and power. Someone else distributes a mixture of dried fuit, nuts and sugar crystals to the congregation. This is prasad, food which God gives to the worshippers as a token of his love.

The singing of Bhajans.   During arti everyone joins in the singing of hymns. One is particularly popular; it begins 'Om jai Jagdish Haré', which means 'Victory to God, Lord of the Universe'. Some of the congregation ring bells, others play tambourines, triangles and other instruments; the rest clap their hands in time to the singing.

This form of worship is one of the most popular ways of expressing devotion to God. It is possible to find Hindus singing bhajans, as these hymns are called, almost anywhere, but especially in temples dedicated to Vishnu or Shiva. Often the enthusiasm of the men and women singing them becomes so great that people start to dance.

Dance is another form of worship. It is not simply something which people do to entertain or to enjoy themselves. Before Hindus begin to dance they press the palms of their hands together and bow, a gesture of worship. Sometimes Indian dance groups, such as the Kathakali dancers, tour Britain. It must be remembered that although these performances are now given in theatres, the real home of such dances, a century ago, was the great temples of India.

Dance is used to re-enact the great myths and epics of Hinduism. Here Kathakali dancers perform scenes from the Mahabharata.

There the dancers sometimes dedicated the whole of their lives to worshipping God with their performances which were usually dramatised forms of stories from Hindu mythology.

Almost anywhere may be a place of worship. It may be offered at any time and, at least in the case of bhajans, by anyone, though only priests may offer havan. In the same way almost any act may be worship. In the great poem of devotional Hinduism, the Bhagavad Gita, God says:

> 'Whatever one offers me with true devotion—only a leaf, or a flower, a fruit, or even a little water—this I accept from a yearning soul because with a pure heart it was offered with love. Whatever you do, or eat, or give, or offer in adoration, let it be an offering to me; and whatever you suffer, suffer it for me. Give me your mind and give me your heart, give me your offerings and your adoration: thus, with your soul in harmony, and making me your supreme goal, you will in truth come to me.'

(Bhagavad Gita 9:26, 27, 34)

129

All life can be an act of puja and the aim of worship and life is eternal bliss in the presence of God.

One God or many.   Some people say Hindus believe in one God, others that they worship many. Hindus are likely to tell you that God is one, but has many names and characteristics. God exists in all life; in fact God is the life in all animals and plants. So there is Hanuman, the monkey, Agni the fire, Indra the storm and Ganga the river Ganges. Sometimes when Hindus pray they will call on Ambaji, the Divine Mother, or Ganesha, who is elephant-headed. They always pray to Ganesha before beginning any activity, from going on a journey to sitting an examination. Perhaps four thousand years ago Indians really did believe that many gods existed. Some may do still, but thoughtful Hindus will tell you that the correct teaching is that Reality, God, is one, though many names are used to describe the Supreme Being.

Private devotion.   All Hindus should begin the day by taking a bath and many will then recite the Vedic prayer:

> 'Om. O terrestrial sphere. O sphere of space. O celestial sphere.
> Let us contemplate the splendour of the solar spirit, the divine creator. May he guide our minds.'

This is the Gayatri mantra, the most sacred of all Vedic verses. The Brahmins, Kshatriyas and Vaishyas should recite it three times a day, at dawn, at midday and sunset.

From this point private devotion may vary, even among members of these castes. Some Hindus will offer prayers at shall shrines in their homes, similar to those seen in temples. Others may meditate using yoga. This is a technique involving exercises which enable the body and breath to be controlled so that full concentration of the mind may take place. In this way the soul is refreshed by being united with the Absolute.

Mala japa is another method used by Hindus. A mala is a string of beads which worshippers find helps them to concentrate. They use it when they repeat the name of God in order to experience union with the Supreme Reality. A Hindu mala has 108 beads. The person who uses it may utter the word Om or, more usually, such a name as Ram, Krishna or Ambaji. Ambaji is a goddess and the divine mother. Hindus refer to God as female as well as male, though ultimately they say that God is beyond such categories:

> 'You are woman, and you are man,
> You are the youth and the maiden too,
> You are the old man tottering on his staff.

You are born again facing all directions.

You are the blue fly and the red-eyed parrot,
the cloud pregnant with lightning.
You are the seasons and the seas,
The Beginningless, the Abiding Lord
from whom the spheres are born.'

(Svetasvatara Upanishad 4:1–4)

Private devotion also includes fasting on certain days in the month, and making pilgrimages.

The Jewish synagogue

The Exile.   In the years 597 and 587 before the Christian or Common Era (BCE), the great Babylonian king Nebuchadnezzar deported the leading members of Jewish society to Babylon. Jerusalem was left an almost deserted ruin. With the Temple priests gone, worship came to an end. It seemed that the story of the nation which had emerged from captivity in Egypt seven hundred years earlier was at an end. It appeared likely that the Jews, like the builders of Stonehenge or Troy, would simply become of interest to the archaeologist and historian. Many Jews must have despaired not only of ever seeing Jerusalem again, but of being able to worship God. They had been taught that the centre where they should worship was the Jerusalem Temple. Now it was no more, and they were living over a thousand miles away as captives. There is little cause for surprise that one of the psalms found in the Bible asks whether God can still be worshipped and provides a picture of the Jews' enemies taunting them:

'By the waters of Babylon, there we sat down and wept, when we remembered Zion.
On the willows there we hung up our lyres,
For there our captors required of us songs, and our
tormentors mirth, saying, 'Sing us one of your songs of Zion'.
How shall we sing the Lord's song in a foreign land?
If I forget you, O Jerusalem, let my right hand wither.
Let my tongue cleave to the roof of my mouth, if I do not remember you, if I do not set Jerusalem above my highest joy.'

(Psalm 137:1–6)

There is defiance as well as despair in these words, but that might not have been enough as the years passed, and a generation grew

131

up which could not remember Jerusalem.

Fortunately, one of the greatest Jewish prophets, Jeremiah, was alive at this time. He had warned his people of the coming disaster and had been imprisoned for undermining the national will to resist. Nebuchadnezzar had released him from jail, but for some reason he had been left in Jerusalem. Presumably he was regarded as having little importance. This man Jeremiah, who had warned the Jews of the fall of Jerusalem, now turned to the task of encouraging the exiles. In a letter to them he wrote:

> 'Thus says the Lord of Hosts, the God of Israel, to all the exiles that I have sent into exile from Jerusalem to Babylon: build yourselves houses and live in them; plant gardens and eat their produce. Take wives and have sons and daughters; take wives for your sons and give your daughters in marriage, that they may bear sons and daughters; multiply there and do not decrease. But seek the welfare of the city where I have sent you into exile and pray to God on its behalf, for in its welfare you will find your welfare.'
>
> (Jeremiah 29:4–8)

The readers of this letter must have been astonished to learn that it was God who had sent them into exile and amazed at the suggestion that they should pray for their captors. However, when they had had time to consider the implication of Jeremiah's words they must have realised that God was with them in the exile. After all, the prophet had said 'pray'.

The Jews in exile were not in concentration camps. On the whole they were well treated. They could meet to read letters such as that of Jeremiah. From it we learn that apparently marriage was possible and the Jews could build themselves houses. In fact, when return to Jerusalem became possible in 538 BCE, there were some Jews who preferred to stay in Babylon. Among the Jews who may have read Jeremiah's letter was a man named Ezekiel. In the Biblical book which bears his name he wrote these words:

> 'I sat in my house with the elders of Judah before me.' (Ch.8:1)
>
> '. . . certain of the elders of Israel came to enquire of the Lord and sat before me' (Ch.20:1)

In these verses we have glimpses of groups of Jews gathered together for discussion. The Greek word for 'to gather together' is 'synagein', and it may have been from such meetings as these that the synagogue came into existence. There seems no doubt that it developed during the exile in Babylon, and was one of the three features responsible for preventing the Jews from becoming extinct then and in the following two and a half thousand years. The other two features are the scriptures (Torah) and the Jewish sense of identity—the belief that they are a people with a purpose.

The first synagogues. The original meaning of synagogue was 'gathering', as we have seen. Only later did the term come to mean a place, the building where Jews gathered for worship. Perhaps the Jews in Ezekiel's home were a synagogue, though it is hardly likely that they used the word. Being Greek, it was probably coined a few hundred years later. By the time that Jerusalem was destroyed yet again, by the Romans in the year 70 of the Christian or Common Era (CE), synagogues existed in most towns or villages where there was a fairly large Jewish population. By now a rule had come into effect that where there were ten adult males there could be a synagogue. If we look back at the verses from Ezekiel we can see that its purpose was probably to ensure that such gatherings had some validity when they claimed to represent the Jewish people. It prevented a small clique of three or four men saying that they were speaking on behalf of the Jewish population of a town.

Not many changes have taken place in the appearance of the synagogue, from the earliest examples to those of the present day, though of course archaeology cannot reconstruct the past completely. Early synagogues would have had a fountain, or some kind of water supply, so that worshippers could wash the dust off their feet before entering the building where they would probably have worshipped barefooted. There would have been few seats; in large congregations many of the worshippers would have had to stand. Women probably stood behind a lattice partition, able to hear and see everything but causing no distraction from what was essentially a service conducted by men. Today, except in Reform synagogues, women and children still play no part in leading worship, but they usually sit in upstairs galleries instead of being screened off from the men. The description which follows is of the kind of synagogue that can be found in most British towns with large Jewish communities.

The synagogue today. The layout of the building is rectangular. The seats are arranged on three sides of the rectangle, facing inwards. The fourth side is the most important; it is the focal point of the synagogue. Recessed into this wall is a double door, concealed by a curtain, which opens to reveal a cupboard containing the scrolls of the Jewish Bible, written in Hebrew. The name of the cupboard is the Ark, and it is always set in the wall nearest Jerusalem. On either side of the Ark, or above it, are the Ten Commandments written in Hebrew on two plaques representing the two tablets of stone mentioned in Exodus chapter 31, verse 18. Usually only the first two words of each commandment are recorded. A tall candle-holder with seven branches stands to one side of the Ark. This is a reminder of the seven-branched candelabrum which stood in the Jerusalem Temple. It has become one of the symbols of Judaism.

Another reminder of the Temple is the lamp suspended from the roof, hanging in front of the Ark. It is in remembrance of the light that burned continually in the Temple, and indicates respect for the holiness of the scrolls. The space in front of the Ark is left open so that scrolls can be easily taken out and the congregation witness that important part of the service from wherever they are sitting, though the congregation stands as a mark of respect at that point in the service. Almost in the centre of the synagogue stands a raised platform with railings. This is the bimah. Here the man conducting worship usually stands and the scrolls are read from this platform. At the foot of the bimah, facing the Ark, is a group of seats reserved for the elders of the synagogue, the men who are elected to organise its worship and govern its affairs. To one side of the Ark, facing the congregation, stands the pulpit. This is a recent innovation, dating from only the nineteenth century or a little earlier.

The role of the synagogue in the community. Besides being a place of worship, the synagogue serves a number of functions. Its original name, beth knesset—house of assembly, and its later Greek one, are reminders that first and foremost it has always been a place where Jews could gather, a community centre. Education was a major reason for coming together. The ability to read and write has always been valued by Jews, because the scriptures have been regarded as a complete guide to correct living. Everyone should, therefore, be able to know for himself or herself what they teach and command. In the ancient world of the Greeks and Romans, Jews were often employed frequently as slaves, letter-writers, scribes and clerks. Jewish children learned to read in synagogue schools at a time when education was confined to the rich or noble in the Gentile world. The educational role of the synagogue now-adays is to teach Hebrew, the understanding of the Bible, and to transmit Jewish culture, often related to the state of Israel. Through youth clubs, sports teams, women's groups, Hebrew classes, and a variety of other activities the synagogue caters for a wide range of needs.

A house of law. Jews play as full a part in the life of the countries in which they live as they possibly can. The prayer for the Queen

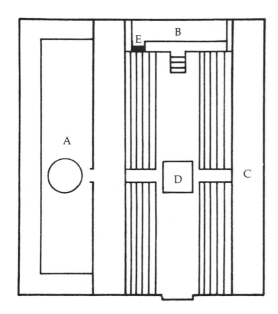

Plan of the synagogue at Capernaum, probably built in the second century CE.

A Courtyard with fountain
B Ark with Scrolls of the Law
C Gallery where women worshippers sat
D Central pulpit for scripture readings and sermons
E Seat of the rabbi or minister

Diagram of a synagogue

A Sabbath service. In orthodox synagogues women and men sit separately, women usually upstairs.

and the royal family used in the Sabbath service demonstrates their loyalty to Britain. Many Jews have died for Britain, as war memorials testify. Many Jewish people are MPs or local councillors, actively serving society in the land where they live. Nevertheless, Jews live under two laws, as might a Christian living in Pakistan or Israel, or a Muslim living in England. There is the law of the land and the code of conduct of the religion. The question of divorce can be taken as an example. British law regards marriage as a legal agreement. It must take place in the presence of approved persons and be registered. If the marriage breaks down the couple must attend a law court, where the case will be examined and a divorce granted. However, Judaism has its own rules on divorce; these differ considerably from those of Britain. Therefore, a Jew who is a true member of the Jewish community must also meet Jewish requirements before a divorce can be recognised, no matter what the law of the land says.

A commoner issue is that of licensing butchers to sell kosher meat which meets the requirements of Jewish dietary laws. The synagogue can act as a beth din, a house of law, or a court, to decide such matters. A butcher wishing to gain the court's approval would have to apply to it, open his premises to inspection, and if everything was acceptable the court would give him a certificate for display in his shop. In practice, in Britain, legal matters have now passed into the hands of rabbinical courts, but strictly speaking they are only representative of the local or national Jewish community.

Synagogues have also been used as bakeries, where the community could obtain its unleavened bread at Passover time, and sometimes as hostels for travellers. Some older synagogues have a large bath or pool, called a mikvah. When most houses had no bathrooms, and even up to the nineteen-sixties and seventies in Britain there were still some without such amenities, Jews who needed to take a ritual bath could go to the synagogue and bathe in the mikvah. Now it is rarely used and it is unusual to see one.

Arising from Judaism's first experience of being a minority religion in an alien culture, the synagogue has served the faith well for two and a half thousand years. Though the family keeps the Jewish faith and way of life alive, the synagogue is a constant reminder that each Jew is a member of a community. It was the community which created the synagogue and today it exists to serve every need of the people who live around it and meet in it.

A Sabbath service

The Sabbath begins on Friday evening, and many Jews mark it by attending a service in the synagogue before welcoming it with a ceremony in their homes. However, the main act of worship takes place on the Saturday morning, starting at about ten o'clock and lasting a little over two hours. That is the service described here. Variations occur from synagogue to synagogue, especially in Reform synagogues where men and women sit together and more of the service may be in English, but in Orthodox worship the pattern outlined here is followed closely.

When a family comes to the synagogue, the father will go into the main body of the building downstairs, while his wife will sit upstairs. Young children often decide which parent they will accompany, but those over the age of thirteen are considered adult and custom makes the decision for them. If a man enters the synagogue bareheaded he will put on his skull cap, known as a yarmulka. If he is already wearing a hat, he may keep it on or replace it with his skull cap. He will then make his way to his seat, perhaps stopping to talk to one or two friends, and will take out his prayer shawl and Daily Prayer Book from a little cupboard in the pew. Before putting on the tallith he will say a prayer and another when he has placed it over his shoulders.

The psalms. The service falls into a number of sections. First a number of psalms are read, among them 19,34,90,91,135,136,33 and 92 which is known as a song for the Sabbath Day. I Chronicles 16;8–36 is also read. Someone will lead this part of the service, but not necessarily the rabbi or minister, or the cantor—a man who sings other portions of the service in a rich, trained voice. Any man may lead the reading and each member of the congregation is expected to read the passages aloud from his prayer book.

The Shema. Secondly, the cantor sings a section reminding the Jewish people of God's many acts of redemption, especially their deliverance from Egypt. God is blessed for his faithfulness, mercy, and love, the climax being reached with the saying of the Shema. These words might be said to form the core of the service.

The Amidah. Next comes the Amidah. The word simply means 'standing'. It refers to a prayer which each member of the congregation offers silently standing facing the Ark, that is, looking towards Jerusalem. The Amidah has nineteen sections:

137

> Praise to the God of the patriarchs; praise of God's power; praise
> of God's holiness; prayers for – knowledge; forgiveness; repent-
> ance; redemption; healing of the sick; good crops; the gathering
> together of the dispersed of Israel throughout the world; righteous
> judgement; the punishment of the wicked and heretics; the reward
> of the pious; the rebuilding of Jerusalem; the restoration of the
> dynasty of David; the acceptance of prayers; thanksgiving; the
> restoration of the services in the Temple; and for peace.

As each person silently makes these petitions, one is reminded of
the responsibility which Judaism puts upon its members. No minister, rabbi, or priest says the Amidah on their behalf; everyone
must say it for himself.

The scrolls. Fourthly, after the Amidah, the doors of the Ark are
opened and the scrolls taken out to be read. The elders of the
synagogue, who sit in front of the reading dais, the bimah, and
who sometimes wear top hats to denote their position of responsibility, organise the readings. They will invite two members of the
congregation to go with them to the Ark, take out the scrolls and
carry them to the reading desk. As they carry the scrolls, members
of the congregation will press forward to touch them with their
talliths, which they will then kiss. On the bimah the scrolls will be
held up in their covers for the congregation to see, and blessings
will be offered.

The reading. Then the cover and the crown of the Torah scroll is
removed and a number of men are called up one by one to read it.
When the Torah portion has been completed the scroll is covered
again, the Haftarah scroll is unrolled and a portion read from it.
The reading is usually done by the cantor, because not only does
he have the skill to read unpunctuated Hebrew which lacks any
vowel marks, but he can also intone it in the appropriate manner.
Those given the honour of being called to the bimah will hold the
Torah pointer and follow the reading carefully. When all the readings are finished the cantor will, if the service takes place in Britain,
pray for the Queen. In Orthodox synagogues this prayer is unique
in being spoken in English; all others, as well as the readings, are
in Hebrew. Then, in Hebrew again, the cantor prays for the Queen,
the nation, and the state of Israel. After this, with more blessings
and words of praise the scrolls are returned to the Ark.

It may be at this point that the rabbi or minister speaks for the
first time in the service. Some rabbis adopt the very helpful practice
of saying a few words before the scrolls are read to summarise the
teaching contained in the lessons, but not all do. Now the rabbi

might preach a sermon.

There follows the Amidah once again, this time spoken by the cantor, the prayer for mourners — those who have lost relatives during the last eleven months—called the Kaddish, and the Aleynu, the Adoration. This is not quite the end of the service. The Hymn of Glory remains to be chanted. This is done by the cantor, or sometimes a young child, who stands in front of the open Ark to say:

> 'I will chant sweet hymns and compose songs; for my soul panteth after thee.'

He and the congregation speak alternate lines and at the end everyone together says:

> 'Thine O Lord is the greatness and the power and the glory, and the victory and the majesty: for all in heaven and in the earth is thine; thine O Lord, is the kingdom and the supremacy as head over all. Who can utter the mighty acts of the Lord, or show forth all his praise.'

The Kaddish.   The service has been extremely Biblical in nature. Not only has the Torah been read, but many psalms and other passages have been used, and many of the other prayers make use of phrases taken from the Bible. Through it the congregation has hoped to pass for a brief period of time from the world of everyday life into eternity. The Kaddish, the act of sanctification made near the end, demonstrates the dual emphasis upon praising God and seeking his blessing, so that the peace with man that God wills for mankind can become a reality. The cantor or reader begins, then the congregation follows:

> CANTOR: Magnified and sanctified be his great name throughout the world which he has created according to his will. May he establish his kingdom during your life, your days and during the life of the house of Israel, and say Amen.
> PEOPLE: Let his name be blessed for ever and to all eternity.
> CANTOR: Blessed praised and glorified, exalted, extolled and honoured, magnified and lauded be the name of the holy one, blessed be he; though he be high above all the blessings and hymns, praises and consolations, which are uttered in the world; and say Amen.
> PEOPLE: Accept our prayer in mercy and favour.
> CANTOR: May the prayers and supplications of all Israel be accepted by their father in heaven; and say Amen.
> PEOPLE: Let the name of the Lord be blessed from this time forth and for ever more.

139

CANTOR: May there be abundant peace from heaven, and life for us and for all Israel; and say Amen.
READER: My help is from the Lord, who made heaven and earth.
CANTOR: He who maketh peace in his high places, may he make peace for us and for all Israel; and say Amen.

This prayer was written long before the fall of the Temple and was originally written in Aramaic, the language of Jesus of Nazareth and all Palestinian Jews of his time. Now it is used at the end of public worship, but long ago rabbis and their followers recited it at the end of lectures and teaching sessions. Perhaps the Christian Lord's Prayer has been influenced by the Kaddish. There are similarities between the two, as there are between Jewish and Christian worship, for it was from the synagogues that Christianity spread into the Gentile world.

Private devotion in Judaism

The importance of the home.   The home has always had a vital place in Judaism. It is there that children learn the dietary traditions of their faith and the meaning of the festivals. Many of the great occasions of the Jewish year, such as Passover, are celebrated in the home rather than in the synagogue so, in a sense, these and the important saying of grace after meals might be regarded as private devotion. However, it is probably the laying of tefillin that comes to most people's minds when they think of private prayer in Judaism.

Laying the tefillin.   Every morning a man covers his head with a small skull cap, a yarmulka, puts his four-cornered fringed prayer-shawl, called a tallith, over his shoulders or also over his head and shoulders, and puts on his tefillin. This is a pair of black leather boxes which he fastens by leather thongs to his forehead and the biceps of his left arm; a left-handed person may bind them to his right arm. They contain the words of the Shema. The reason for binding these boxes to the body is to be found in the command which comes immediately after the Shema in the book of Deuteronomy. The passage is given on page 64.

The literal keeping of this commandment by Orthodox Jews shows how important they believe the words of the Shema to be. Of course, what really matters is that the beliefs in one God and love for him should fill their hearts and minds and strengthen them throughout their lives. If each day they bind them to their head and

140

their arm, there is every chance that the words will become fixed in their mind and heart. If they neglect the ritual they may soon forget the teaching as well. In a similar way the tallith reminds the Jew of the Torah. As he puts on the tallith he puts on obedience to the teachings of his faith.

Throughout his life a Jew is conscious of the long tradition of which he is an heir. As he offers his prayers three times a day, first thing in the morning, at noon and in the evening, he becomes one with such men as Daniel who, we are told, stood at the window of his house which faced towards Jerusalem and prayed even though it was forbidden by royal decree (Daniel 6:10). He faced Jerusalem because that was where the Temple stood.

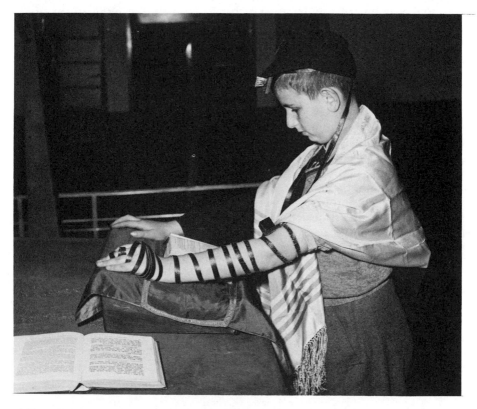

A Jewish boy wearing tefillin and prayer shawl.

141

Prayers. The prayers spoken may be taken from the Prayer Book but spontaneous praise and petition may also be made. Before putting on the tallith this prayer is said:

> 'Bless the Lord, O my soul! Lord my God, thou art very great; thou art robed in glory and majesty. Thou wrappest thyself in light as in a garment; thou spreadest the heavens like a curtain.
> I am enwrapping myself in the fringed garment in order to fulfil the command of my Creator, as it is written in the Torah: 'They shall make fringes for themselves on the corners of their garments throughout their generations'. Even as I cover myself with the tallith in this world, so may my soul deserve to be robed in a beautiful garment in the world to come, in Paradise. Amen.'

As he lays his tefillin a Jew meditates on these words:

> 'By putting on the tefillin I intend to fulfil the command of my Creator, who has commanded us to wear tefillin, as it is written in the Torah: You shall bind them as a sign on your hand, and they shall be as frontlets between your eyes. The tefillin contain four sections of the Torah which proclaim the absolute unity of God, blessed be his name, and remind us of the miracles and wonders he did for us when he brought us out from Egypt, he who has the power and the dominion over the heavenly and the earthly creatures to deal with them as he pleases. He has commanded us to wear tefillin on the arm in memory of his outstretched arm; opposite the heart, to intimate that we ought to subject our heart's desires and designs to the service of God, blessed be he; and on the head opposite the brain, to intimate that the mind which is in the brain, and all senses and faculties, ought to be subjected to his service, blessed be he. May my observance of the tefillin precept bring me long life, holy inspiration and sacred thoughts, and free me from any sinful reflection whatever. May the evil impulse never tempt us, but leave us to serve the Lord as our heart desires.'

These prayers fully bring out the symbolism of the ritual actions.

There are no rules governing the way women must pray or when they must do it. Someone once said that women don't seem to matter, to which a Jewish lady replied, 'God knew he could trust women to say their prayers. There was no need to tell then when to do it or how. But God is well aware that men are lazy — so he had to give them rules!' Women say their prayers when they can during the daily round of preserving a Jewish home. Those families which observe the Sabbath and the festivals carefully and joyfully tend to be those in which the mother takes her faith seriously.

⊕ Worship in Buddhism

Worship is recognition of worth. The word is usually associated with what is of *ultimate* worth or value, what will not change or die. So we criticise 'worshipping' a car or a pop star as mistaken.

The majority of religions call what is of ultimate value by a personal name—God—and so we have come to associate worship with the word God. But even those religions that talk about a personal God are aware that using a personal term to refer to 'ultimate reality' might be limiting. The Jewish thinker Moses Maimonides reflected that to call God a person might make him too much like men. One early Christian writer asks, 'How shall I name you then, O You who are beyond all Name?'. For many Hindus it is the supra-personal Brahman that lies behind the personal gods. Buddhists deliberately use a variety of terms for the ultimate. It is beyond personhood and conception, so the terms are quite abstract. Dharma—Truth—is one possibility, and so is the related phrase Dharma-Kaya, or Truth-Body. Nirvana describes the transcendent as a state, and Tathata, translated as 'suchness' or 'thatness', is deliberately obscure. These all emphasise otherness, but the term Tathagatha-Garbha points to a heart, or seed, of enlightenment which is within all beings.

The worth of the transcendent is acknowledged by Buddhists both with bodily actions and words. Buddhists from Theravada, Mahayana and Vajrayana schools find the words worship and prayer appropriate for what they do. Any Buddhist you meet who is doubtful about using the word 'worship' will think you are suggesting he believes in a personal God, so you will need to explain carefully what you mean by the word.

The vihara. Vihara is sometimes translated as monastery, and sometimes as temple or shrine room. Although it is a term from the Theravada tradition, most of the features of viharas are common to all the schools. In Tibetan a similar term, gompa, which means a 'place apart', or monastery, can be used for one part of it, the shrine room or even the meditation hall.

A vihara is made up of more than one building, or is a set of rooms within one house. If you visit a vihara you will probably see the following:

1. A shrine room or a temple. This contains one or more images of the Buddha. In the Theravada tradition the images are of Gautama Buddha. As a sign of honour, the images are higher than anything else in the room. There are also raised chairs or a platform for

143

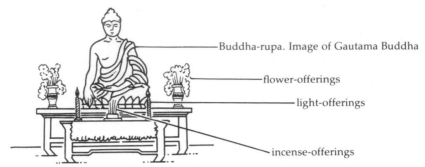

Buddha-rupa. Image of Gautama Buddha

flower-offerings

light-offerings

incense-offerings

1. The important features of a Theravadin shrine in a temple or home

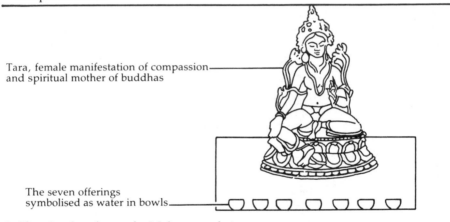

Tara, female manifestation of compassion and spiritual mother of buddhas

The seven offerings symbolised as water in bowls

2. The simplest form of a Mahayana shrine

3. A complex Mahayana shrine in Tibetan style

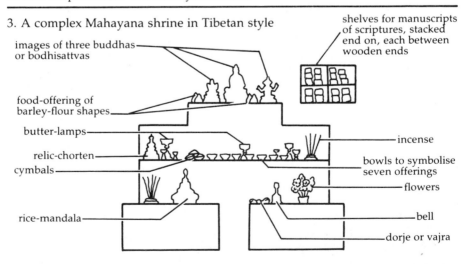

shelves for manuscripts of scriptures, stacked end on, each between wooden ends

images of three buddhas or bodhisattvas

food-offering of barley-flour shapes

butter-lamps

relic-chorten

cymbals

incense

bowls to symbolise seven offerings

flowers

rice-mandala

bell

dorje or vajra

members of the Sangha. This is practical as well as symbolic. Everyone wants to be able to see the Buddha image and to hear the monks recite the sutras or teach. The room is empty of other furniture. Buddhists traditionally sit on the floor on cushions or rugs.

The central image is often surrounded by smaller images, to give a more complicated effect than in the diagram of a Theravadin shrine. These are not essential, but are reminders of different incidents in the Buddha's life. If a member of the community or a Buddhist from another country brings an image as a gift it is given a position of honour. Shrines also contain copies of important sutras, for they too represent the Dharma.

In Mahayana shrines the images are of any of the buddhas or bodhisattvas, for example Amida or Avalokitesvara. Mahayana Buddhists emphasise the diversity of the manifestations of the Dharma-Kaya. There is also a greater variety of offerings, which are marked in the diagrams of Mahayana shrines.

The walls of shrine rooms are decorated with pictures of famous Buddha images, great stupas, centres of pilgrimage and respected meditation masters. There are also special painted wall hangings called thangkas, which Tibetans use as meditation and teaching aids. All these both inform and inspire the worshipper.

Shrines are very colourful, and every attempt is made to create a beautiful environment. Buddhists bring offerings of *flowers* to honour the Buddha. In the east these are often lotus buds, which are a symbol of spiritual purity. Artificial lotuses may be used in the west, but any flowers are acceptable. The offering of *light* is in the form of candles or night-lights, as well as the traditional coconut-oil or butter lamps. Shrine rooms are given a special fragrance with *incense*, in cone or stick form. Mahayana Buddhists add to these three offerings another four or five. These are together the gifts to an honoured guest in an Indian household. There is water for drinking, water for washing the feet, flowers, incense, light, perfumed water for a bath and food. There can also be music. All seven can be represented by bowls of water, as in the second diagram, but the food can be real, usually fruit or rice. Music can be represented by a bell, a conch shell or cymbals. There are often duplications of offerings and the perishable ones are renewed daily, and given to sentient beings, not just thrown away.

2. *A meditation room.* This is usually much less elaborate than a shrine room, although it is possible for one room to serve as a place of devotion, meditation and teaching. If there is a separate meditation room the physical atmosphere will be deliberately calm

A Theravada shrine room in England. The monk faces the laity to lead the meditation and to teach them.

and uncluttered, with space for walking as well as sitting meditation. There may be one image as a focal point, or a thangka (Tibetan wall-hanging) or a piece of calligraphy based on a sutra (typical in Zen). There may also be a seat for the meditation teacher. In Zen meditators face one another on two raised platforms.

3. *Living quarters for the monks.* These are normally part of religious buildings in Buddhism. This is why a vihara may be called both a monastery and a temple. The monks keep up a daily rhythm of practice, and the laity join them when they are able. The laity support the monks by giving food daily, or—in the west—by taking stores of food and essential items at the weekend, or giving money for others to do this. The living quarters are simple. The routine tasks of sweeping, washing and tending the vihara can be an important part of a monk's training in mindfulness, which is total attention to the worth and meaning of the present moment.

4. *The relic mound.* This has different names in different Buddhist countries. The Sanskrit term is stupa, but in Sri Lanka it is called a dagoba, a term derived from the Sanskrit phrase dhatu garbha or

146

Development of the style/form of the stupa relic mound

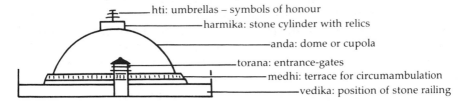

hti: umbrellas – symbols of honour
harmika: stone cylinder with relics
anda: dome or cupola
torana: entrance-gates
medhi: terrace for circumambulation
vedika: position of stone railing

The earliest development from the burial mound

The style/form typical of Sri Lanka, called a dagoba

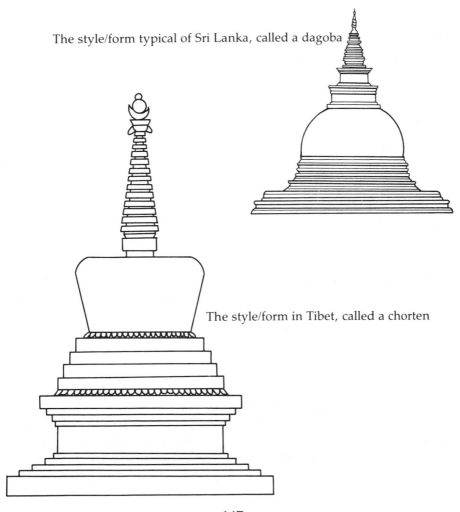

The style/form in Tibet, called a chorten

relic chamber (see page 125, the Hindu shrine room). Further east the word changes to pagoda. In Tibet the word used is chorten and another title is caitya. The shapes provides the distinctive architecture of the Buddhist world. Originally the stupa was an earth burial mound over the cremated remains of a king or great spiritual teacher. The Buddha's remains were originally placed in eight stupas, but in Ashoka's time they were subdivided and 84 000 new stupas built. This increase has continued with the spread of Buddhism. Each stupa should contain some sort of relic, if not of the Buddha himself, then of another great Buddhist saint or an ancient sutra (scripture). Chapter Five describes some famous stupas. A vihara might have a small reliquary stupa in the shrine room or one outside which is a building in its own right. It symbolises the presence of the Buddha and Dharma and is venerated in the same way as a Buddha image.

5. *Natural features.* These can include a tree grown from a shoot of the sacred *Bodhi Tree* under which Gautama Buddha attained enlightenment. Over the centuries cuttings have been taken from the original tree at Bodh Gaya, or its descendants, to famous places like Anuradhapura in Sri Lanka and to many local centres. It too, like a stupa, is a reminder of Dharma, and of the enlightenment to which all beings are moving.

Many viharas have a *lotus pond*. The lotus is one of the central symbols of Buddhism. Great beings, like the buddhas and bodhisattvas, are called 'lotus-born'. Their spiritual attainment is like the purity of the lotus flower, which grows on a long stem out of the muddy water and is not touched by the water. Even if there is no lotus pond, a garden full of flowers and shrubs is a living reminder of the cycle of life, with its birth and death, and of a harmony which includes man, and which needs his attention and co-operation but not his dominance. If there is no outdoor space with natural features that can help in meditation, then the flowers in the shrine room can be used. To watch a flower go from full-blown glory to a heap of dust illustrates very well that 'death is inherent in all compound things'.

Another feature is the *Zen garden*, which can look very different from the kinds of garden mentioned above. It is commonly made of raked sand and rocks and looks very bare. Simplicity, and seeing the world uncluttered by what is unnecessary, is important. Looking at such a garden (see diagram) reminds a Buddhist both of the expanses of the ocean and the ranges of the earth's mountains. He sees common forms underlying all life, and notices how his mind deals with the forms he sees.

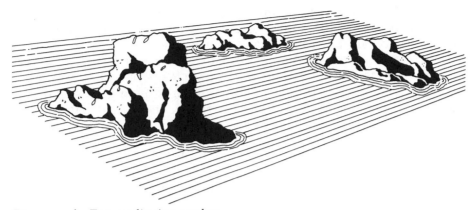

Diagram of a Zen meditation garden

When does a Buddhist visit a temple?   The monks who live at a temple site will use its shrine and meditation rooms daily, for meditation, chanting the scriptures and devotion. Lay people will come when they can. In all religions some people are more devout than others. In villages and towns in traditional Buddhist countries some people will go to the temple every day as well as on fortnightly uposatha days. The word uposatha means entering the vihara to stay. The days are at the new and full moons, but quarter days are also observed, so a weekly gathering is quite normal and suitable for western Buddhists. It is not obligatory for a Buddhist to take part in group worship or meditation, so he can have a shrine or meditation room at home. At a large festival like Wesak, described in Chapter Five, everyone will, however, try to go to the vihara. In the west festivals are often celebrated on the nearest Sunday, so that most people are free from work.

What do Buddhists do at a temple?   In India, where Buddhism began, and in the countries in which it thrived in its classical forms, people show respect for a sacred place, and often for the inside of their homes, by removing their shoes before going inside. This tradition is preserved in the west and many people feel that it is practical as well as symbolic. Shoes bring dust and dirt into the clean and often carpeted area of the shrine room, where people will sit on the floor and prostrate themselves. So the first thing Buddhists do at the door of a shrine or meditation room is to take

149

off their shoes. When they enter, the peace and influential power that seem to come from the beautiful Buddha images affect their mood and create an atmosphere of attentiveness and calm. The second act of respect is some kind of prostration. This involves putting the hands together in the Indian gesture of greeting and bowing, either from the waist or from a kneeling position, or moving from standing to a full prostration. The joined hands may move from forehead to lips to chest, to symbolise that body, speech and mind are involved in the offering of service and respect. This is called the prostration with the five limbs. The movements are repeated three times for Buddha, Dharma and Sangha, the three 'jewels', 'precious things' or 'refuges' outlined in Chapter One.

Japanese family visiting a temple. They are paying their respects, with their hands together in the traditional way.

Offerings, prayers and devotions. The description of the shrine room earlier in the chapter mentions some of the offerings that Buddhists make. Flowers, light and incense are the most common in the Theravada tradition and are accompanied by words such as the following:

'Reverencing the Buddha we offer *flowers*,
Flowers that today are fresh and sweetly blooming.
Flowers that tomorrow are faded and fallen.
Our bodies too like flowers will pass away.

Reverencing the Buddha we offer *candles*.
To Him who is the light, we offer light.
From his greater lamp a lesser lamp we light within us.
The lamp of Bodhi shining within our hearts.

Reverencing the Buddha we offer *incense*,
Incense whose fragrance pervades the air.
The fragrance of the perfect life, sweeter than incense,
Spreads in all directions throughout the world.

Mahayana Buddhists talk about a sevenfold devotion, for which they use the Indian term puja, discussed in the section on Hindu worship, page 126. In this set of devotions praise, offerings and worship are all bound together. Puja is made up of the following seven parts:

1. The prostrations. These are an act of honour and self-surrender to the transcendent in the form of the buddhas and bodhisattvas represented on the shrine.

2. The seven or eight offerings. These were described earlier in the chapter and are sometimes symbolised in bowls of water.

3. Confession. The next stage is to confess any unhelpful or unwholesome thoughts or actions and request the buddhas and bodhisattvas for help in the future. Here are some words which might be used:

'The sin that has been done by me
Through despising mother and father,
Through not understanding the Buddhas,
And through not understanding the good.

The sin of deed, word and thought
The threefold wickedness that I have done
All that will I confess
Standing before the Buddhas.'

151

4. The sense of joy.   This follows the experience of release produced by confession and the worshippers become aware of the goodness of the buddhas and bodhisattvas and are reminded of their example.

5. The petitioning.   Next the buddhas and bodhisattvas are asked, or petitioned, to 'turn the Wheel of the Dharma', which is the Buddhist expression for teaching and a phrase often used for the Buddha's first sermon.

6. Asking the buddhas and bodhisattvas to remain active in the world.   This is for the sake of all sentient beings. As Buddhists think about their unselfish ideal they might renew their Bodhisattva vow, which is mentioned in Chapter One. Here is one form of that vow:

> 'Living beings are without number: I vow to row them to the other shore. (Nirvana)
> Defilements are without number: I vow to remove them from myself.
> The teachings are immeasurable: I vow to study and practise them.
> The way is very long: I vow to arrive in the end.'

7. The giving away of merit.   Any merit that has been made at this puja is dedicated to the good of all beings. This ensures that religious actions are never done in pride or selfishness.

> 'My own self and my pleasures, my righteous past, present and future, may I sacrifice without regard, in order to achieve the welfare of all beings.'

While they are in the shrine room, and in the symbolic presence of all the buddhas and bodhisattvas, Buddhists also frequently make or renew the five vows taken by all Buddhist laymen. These are listed in Chapter One.

Congregational or community worship

This is not obligatory for Buddhists, although they recognise that the support of other people can be helpful for meditation and worship. Traditionally at a temple monks perform the rituals, while people watch and listen. As many of the prayers are said in their original languages it is difficult for ordinary people to participate completely. However, lay Buddhists are now becoming more involved in teaching and organising Buddhist groups, and the ordinary language of the people is being used. This is seen to be entirely in keeping with the spirit of Buddhism and a practice encouraged by Gautama Buddha. Here are three examples of congregational worship.

1. *A Buddhist Litany for Peace.*   Here is an extract from such a litany used by the Venerable Thich Nhat Hahn at an ecumenical gathering in Canterbury in 1976.

'As we are together, praying for peace, let us be truly with each other.
silence
Let us pay attention to our breathing.
silence
Let us be at peace in our bodies and our minds.
silence
Let us be aware of the source of all being common to us all and to all living things.
silence
Evoking the presence of the Great Compassion, let us fill our hearts with our own compassion—towards ourselves and towards all living beings.
silence
Let us pray that we ourselves cease to be the cause of suffering to each other.
silence
Let us plead with ourselves to live in a way which will not deprive other beings of air, water, food, shelter or the chance to live.
silence
With humility, with awareness of the existence of life, and the sufferings that are going on around us, let us pray for the establishment of peace in our hearts and on the earth.'

2. *A celebration of the festival of Wesak.*   Here is the programme for an English University's Buddhist Society's celebration of the occasion:

Puja—Three Refuges and Five Precepts
Reading of passages from the Sutras
Ten minutes' meditation
Talk by a venerable Bhikkhu from Burma
Talk by an English lay Buddhist leader
Chanting Sutra on mindfulness

This was followed by tea and a programme of films and slides on Buddhism. The room was prepared in a 'western' style with rows of chairs facing a table on which there was a Buddha image, surrounded by flowers, candles and incense which people had offered on arrival. The guests sat on either side of the table, facing the congregation. The puja began with everyone standing together and saying the Three Refuges and the Five Precepts. The passages that were read from the sutras reminded everyone of some important parts of the Buddha's teaching. For ten minutes there was 'sitting meditation'. People either stayed on their chairs or took up more traditional positions on the floor. The two speakers talked about the theme of the festival and the group listened to a bhikkhu chant in Pali the sutra on mindfulness. This blending of traditional features and what is appropriate for a western group is typical of the way Buddhism is developing.

3. A form of liturgy recently developed in Sri Lanka. Here a bhikkhu leads, and begins with prostration and the words, 'Homage to the Blessed, Worthy, the Fully Enlightened Buddha.' The group then 'take refuge' and repeat the first eight of the Ten Precepts. They then proclaim together the worthiness of the Buddha and his place in their hearts. The Buddha image, or rather the enlightenment which it symbolises, is honoured with light, flowers and incense. The following words focus the thoughts of the devotees:

'To see the Lord Buddha's image is consolation to the eyes;
To bow before the Lord Buddha is consolation to the mind;
To take the path the Lord took is consolation for becoming.
In life there is trouble every day.
And to death we approach ever a little closer;
Only doing good is at least some palliative;
Nirvana it is that is the comfort for us all.

They end with the words 'May all beings be happy. Sadhu (good)!' A congregational recitation of the Metta Sutra follows. This part of the liturgy is rounded off with the words:

'If one habitually makes salutation and always waits on one's elders four things increase; length of life, good looks, happiness and strength. By this you may successfully achieve long life, healthy heaven and finally Nirvana. Sadhu!'

After this there is a long sermon by the bhikkhu leading the liturgy. 'Chanting the Sutras' is mentioned in two of the above examples. It can be done either by a bhikkhu or a whole congregation. For the most part the scriptures are in the original language, Pali, Sanskrit or Tibetan, but there is no real reason why good translations should not be used instead. Short texts like the Metta Sutra or the Mangala Sutra quoted below are favourites.

'Not to associate with fools, to associate with the wise,
To honour those who are worthy of honour—this is the highest blessing.

Supporting one's father and mother, cherishing wife and children,
Peaceful occupations—this is the highest blessing.

Reverence, humility, contentment, gratitude,
The opportune hearing of Dharma—this is the highest blessing.

Patience, obedience, seeing holy men,
Taking part in religious discussions at proper times—this is the highest blessing.

Self-control, holy life, perception of the Noble Truths,
The realisation of Nirvana—this is the highest blessing.'

(Mangala Sutra)

The daily routine at home

This is a matter of choice for individual Buddhists. Most try to have a shelf, recess or room in which to place a Buddha image or picture. This place, and their actions there, will be a simpler version of those given for the shrine room. A Buddha image is never just an ornament and should be on a top shelf, or in the highest room in the house. The best time for devotion is the early morning when everything is quiet and the day can begin with thoughts of the Dharma. But daily-life practices are not restricted to shrine rooms. The following words can be said on waking. 'May all beings awake from ignorance.' Dressing can be linked with 'May all beings dress in the clothes of morality.' There are Buddhist prayers or blessings that can be said before meals, and a blessing ceremony for a new house, but the most important thing for a Buddhist in daily life is to be mindful in every situation.

Prayer beads and prayer wheels

Both are used by Buddhists. Prayer beads are called malas and are made up of 108 beads like the Hindu and Sikh counterparts. The number 108 is pre-Buddhist and goes back into ancient Indian astrology, which is referred to again in the section on the Japanese New Year Festival. Buddhists can make their own prayer beads out of available material, but many of the bought ones are bone or wood. Those who go to Bodh Gaya on pilgrimage can bring back

Hand prayer-wheel used by Tibetan Buddhists. It contains the mantra 'Aum mani padme hum'. Turning the wheel is like saying the mantra.

prayer beads made of pipal nuts or seeds from the Bodhi Tree there.

Prayer beads are a kind of 'spiritual abacus' on which a Buddhist can count a set number of prostrations or mantras as they are completed. Prostrations have already been described. Mantras are words or phrases, often from the scriptures, which are used as tools for thinking and focusing one's thoughts. Teachers often recommend a certain number of prostrations or mantras, usually in multiples of ten. The extra beads on a mala then make sure that more, rather than fewer, mantras have been said. There are often one or two 'tails' attached to the beads, which are used to record the completed rounds. Because 108 beads can be noisy, or get tangled during prostrations, Buddhists often use a quarter-sized one of 27 beads. There are often larger or different coloured beads at number 1, 7 and 21. This is a means of remembering the Buddha, Dharma and Sangha during the practice. Beads may have a symbol attached, like the vajra which stands for wisdom.

Some Buddhists talk about turning the circle of beads as analogous to 'Turning the Wheel of the Dharma'. This is a movement of centrifugal force (moving outwards) in which loving-kindness is sent circling outwards to all parts of the world. The circle is also symbolic of Nirvana.

Prayer wheels are, particularly in Tibet, a way of 'Turning the Wheel of the Dharma'. Written on the outside or inside of prayer wheels is the mantra 'Aum mani padme, hum'. They can be called 'mani wheels'. One Tibetan Buddhist explained that this mantra springs to the lips of Tibetans as a response to all kinds of life-situations. For instance they may see a new grave, or pick up a creature from the ground, or see a sick person. It is rather like a blessing, or saying, 'God bless' if you are a Christian. A more literal translation is 'Hail (aum) to the diamond jewel (mani) of Nirvana in the wisdom and compassion (padme—the lotus which symbolises these) of samsara. Welcome (hum).' The four words condense the meaning. The mantra is associated both with hand wheels and large drum prayer wheels, and is also put on prayer flags. The wind, or water or a human hand can set the mantra in motion without a word being spoken.

Meditation

It is this word that most people associate with Buddhism. It has already been mentioned in connection with the meditation room in a vihara and in Buddhists' experience of a garden. It says in the peace litany, 'Let us pay attention to our breathing,' and 'Let us be at peace with our bodies and our minds.'

The heart of Buddhist meditation is mindfulness, a total alertness to the present moment and its significance. To be mindful one has to let every distraction drop away. At first this means finding a quiet place, but with practice it is possible to be completely quiet even in a crowd or near traffic. Relaxing the body and making an effort to concentrate on the rising and falling of the breath soon reveals how restless our minds are. They are like pools of water, stirred up and muddy with activity. We need to let the ripples subside and the mud settle so that we can see the bottom of a clear pool. Minds are like monkeys swinging from branch to branch or from thought to thought. We become aware of the content of our minds as a rapid succession of thoughts which reveal our desires, hates and delusions. To be aware of these, and see them for what they are and then let them go, is part of the purpose of meditation. It opens a door to the inner life, helps us to see what is true and to be valued and creates peace.

> 'The purpose of the holy life does not consist in acquiring honour or fame ... but that unshakable deliverance of the heart—that indeed is the object of the holy life.'

Peace is not just an absence of noise or activity, but has a quality all its own. For the Buddhist this quality is close to Nirvana itself. In the end it is not a withdrawal from the world, but the finding of a calm base from which to help the world. There are two main types of meditation. Samatha means calm, and is the stability and concentration of a peaceful mind. Vipassana means insight, and develops the ability of the concentrated mind to see reality—things as they really are. The goal is the alleviation of the unsatisfactoriness of samsara for all beings, which is Nirvana itself.

✠ Christian places of worship

The building in which Christians worship is called a church. Sometimes the word 'chapel' has been preferred, mostly by non-conformists in Wales and northern England. These were people who refused to use the *Book of Common Prayer* of the Church of England or accept its teaching, and they worshipped in houses, barns or in the open air, often in the face of severe persecution. In parts of Wales it is still possible to be asked, 'Are you church or chapel?' Chapel is also used to describe places of worship inside a castle or stately home, like the Royal Chapel in Windsor Castle. It may even be the name of a special place of worship within a larger church—for example, King Henry's Chapel in Westminster Abbey. Here, the single word 'church' will be used throughout to describe all kinds of Christian buildings for worship.

Christianity began as a movement inside Judaism. Its first members were Jews. Like other Jews, they worshipped in the Temple at Jerusalem, in synagogues, and in their own homes. (See the section on Jewish worship.) Some synagogues may have become Christian churches if all their members converted to the new religion and accepted Jesus as the Messiah. However, it was not until 260 or 261 CE that the Christians were legally allowed to own property. In 260 Gallienus succeeded his father Valerian as Emperor. The change of Emperor was accompanied by a change of heart or policy. Gallienus issued an order that Christians should have their cemeteries and other properties restored to them. They had been confiscated by Valerian, but, as Christianity was an illegal religion, the Christians had in any case, no right to own buildings. The Edict of Gallienus, as the order was called, gave Christians legal rights for the first time, though, paradoxically it was still illegal to be a Christian.

The catacombs. The first known places of Christian worship to have survived into modern times are the catacombs. These were caves, long mine-shafts and underground quarries lying beneath the north-east and southern parts of the city of Rome. They were used as burial places. In one of them, where the martyr St. Priscilla was buried, the stone coffin may have served as an altar and the platform behind it as the place where the priest stood. In the catacomb of Sant'Agnese, there is a stone seat set at the centre of the rear wall and a bench or either side. The seat was probably used by the bishop presiding at the communion service and the benches by the priests. In another catacomb, a basin large enough for immersion, supplied with water from a spring has been found at the foot of a staircase. Apparently this was a baptistry. Christian symbols, a dove, the fish, the Chi-Rho ✳ monogram of Christ, anchors and olive branches, have been found on the walls. One wall painting portrays the Last Supper. The catacomb churches were not very large, but small congregations could have squeezed into them.

Early churches.   The earliest church in Britain was found some years ago at the Roman villa of Lullingstone in Kent. This was a room with Christian symbols painted on the plaster of the walls. Had it not been for these being preserved, the archaeologists would have had no reason to suspect that they had found a church. One or two buildings have been described as churches simply because of their rectangular shape with a semi-circular bulge at one end, their lack of statues and altars, and their east-facing position. None of these features provides conclusive proof, and even if they all occur together there must still be an element of doubt.

Eventually a church design did emerge which was that of a rectangle with a semi-circular bulge which was always at the eastern end. This is called an apse. One early church with this plan was the ancient church of St. Peter in Rome. It was probably built on the site of St. Peter's grave. The present church of St. Peter stands on the same spot.

Christian worship

The first thing that strikes anyone trying to study Christian worship is its variety. Every denomination has its own form of worship and even between churches of the same denomination there may be differences. A glance at the notice-boards of two or three Anglican churches is likely to show that the main service in one is Parish Communion using the liturgy on the *Alternative Service Book* in (ASB), 1980, in another Matins, and in a third, a Communion service at 8.00 a.m. using the *Book of Common Prayer*. Perhaps only two general comments can be made with any certainty about Christian worship: first, that it takes place on

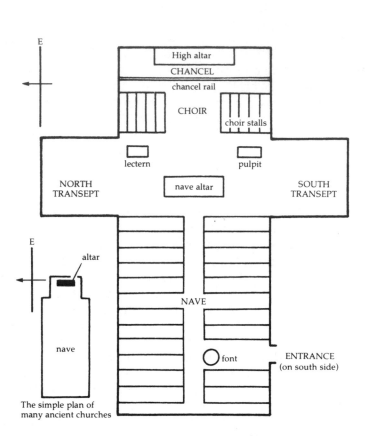

E

High altar

CHANCEL

chancel rail

CHOIR

choir stalls

lectern

pulpit

NORTH
TRANSEPT

nave altar

SOUTH
TRANSEPT

E

altar

NAVE

nave

font

ENTRANCE
(on south side)

The simple plan of
many ancient churches

The church was cross-shaped. However, the most important features from a practical point of view were the choir and the nave in which the congregation sat. By the late Middle Ages, therefore, many churches resembled, by accident, ancient churches, though they were much larger. These had a small area where the altar was placed and a slightly larger one where the congregation stood.

The original design did not allow for a pulpit or an organ. The pulpit, being small in Roman Catholic or Anglican churches, could easily be accommodated (usually against a pillar), though often it cannot be seen by some members of the congregation, and the choir cannot easily hear the sermon. The organ was sometimes put in a loft between the nave and the choir, in a gallery at the west end of the church or among the choir stalls.

Diagram of traditional medieval style church as used in the twentieth century

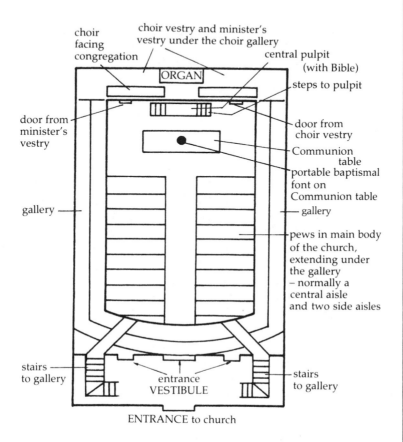

choir facing congregation

choir vestry and minister's vestry under the choir gallery

central pulpit (with Bible)

ORGAN

steps to pulpit

door from minister's vestry

door from choir vestry

Communion table

portable baptismal font on Communion table

gallery

gallery

pews in main body of the church, extending under the gallery – normally a central aisle and two side aisles

stairs to gallery

entrance VESTIBULE

stairs to gallery

ENTRANCE to church

By the nineteenth century the nonconformist or free denominations were building churches which conformed to a basic design. The focal point was the elevated pulpit in front of which was a far less noticeable Communion table. The problem of where the organ should be placed, which perplexed many Anglican churches, was solved by putting it and the choir in a gallery behind the minister.

Late twentieth-century nonconformist churches are often a blend of the plans on pages 116 and 117.

Diagram of a nonconformist church or chapel

Sunday, and secondly that it is offered to God through Jesus his son.

The significance of Sunday. Sunday is important to Christians for three reasons. They are all hinted at in the following verse of a hymn by John Ellerton, who lived from 1826 to 1893:

> 'This is the first of days;
> Send forth thy quickening breath;
> And wake dead souls to love and praise,
> the vanquisher of death.'

Sunday is the first day of the week. On that day, according to the story in the first chapter of the Bible, God said, 'Let there be light', and began the work of creation. Few Christians take the Genesis account literally, but they do believe that the world is the result of God's creative power. On Sunday they remember this. It was also on the first day of the week that the crucified Jesus rose from the dead at Easter. Seven weeks later the disciples experienced the Holy Spirit, on the first Whit Sunday (Acts 2). The first day of the week may have been chosen to distinguish Christian from Jew, in the same way that Muslims later took Friday as their weekly holy day to mark a difference between themselves and their Jewish and Christian neighbours. By the end of the first century of the Christian era Christians were calling the day which we now refer to as Sunday 'the Lord's day' (Revelation 1:10), though some Christians continued to keep Saturday as the Sabbath, and Seventh Day Adventists still do this in the twentieth century.

God through Jesus. Jesus is, of course, the focal point of Christianity. He is the 'Son of God', the 'Word made flesh' (John 1:14), according to Christian belief. In other words, he is God. Therefore in worship Christians approach God through Jesus. This is not because they cannot worship God directly; they do in fact worship him directly because Jesus is God. When the Christian ends a prayer with the phrase 'through Jesus Christ our Lord', he is reminding himself of the way he has come to know God. As people of other faiths know God through the Torah, the Qur'an, the Guru Granth Sahib, or Krishna, Christians know him through Jesus. He is the medium of revelation.

The variety of Christian worship. This has a number of explanations. One is the fact that Jesus' earthly ministry was very brief and came to an end before the community numbered more than a few hundred at most. Though his disciples asked him about prayer and he taught them the Lord's Prayer, there is no evidence that Jesus encouraged his followers to forsake worshipping in the synagogue and the Temple. His own custom was to attend Sabbath service in the synagogue (Luke 4:16), and throughout the story of the Acts of the Apostles, Peter, Paul and the other members of the early Christian community are to be found in the Temple.

A second, and perhaps important reason, is to be found in the nature of Christianity. Jesus describes himself as 'the way, the truth and the life', in John's gospel (John 14:6). He gave his disciples no rules other than the two which he selected from his Jewish heritage, 'You shall love the Lord your God with all your heart, with all your strength and with all your mind; and your neighbour as yourself.' (Luke 10:27, see also Deuteronomy 6:5 and Leviticus 19:18). The kind of discipleship Jesus seems to have demanded was one which offered his friends his companionship and then expected them to work things out for themselves. When they stopped worshipping in the Temple at Jerusalem and the synagogues the Christians had few teachings of Jesus to turn to for guidance. They had only the model of Judaism, from which they also obtained their first scriptures.

There is a third reason for the immense variety that is to be found in Christian worship—the many divisions of the church. By the fifth century after the ministry of Jesus a form of worship had developed which in broad outline was the same in every part of Western Europe. The order of service, or the liturgy of the Mass that is contained in a Roman Catholic Missal or part of the Prayer Book Communion service of the Church of England is based on it. However, in the sixteenth century Western Christendom split into many fragments. The main issue was one of authority: who should be at the head of the church? Many continued to accept the Roman Catholic teaching that the Pope was Christ's vicar or representative, citing the words of Jesus to Simon Peter, 'You are Peter, on this rock I will build my church' (Matthew 16:18). Those who disagreed turned to other forms of authority, the Bible, the Holy Spirit, the gathered community of believers, quoting such verses of the New Testament as 'Where two or three are gathered together in my name I am present in their midst' (Matthew 18:20, see I Corinthians 5:4). They rejected Roman Catholic teaching about the communion service, that the bread and wine contained the real presence of Jesus when they had been consecrated, and began to hold different forms of services. Once the authority of the Roman church had been rejected, Christians interpreted the Bible in many different ways and devised new liturgies.

Some forms of Christian worship

If you entered a Christian church anywhere in the world on a Sunday morning you would discover one of two kinds of service taking place. One would be sacramental, the other non-sacramental, sometimes called 'the service of the word'. That means that one would be centred upon the Last Supper and the other would not. We shall begin by considering the contents and purpose of non-sacramental acts of worship.

Order of service. The main ingredients of these services are hymns, readings from the Bible, prayers and a sermon. A fairly typical order of service is the following:

> *Opening sentences*, some words from the Bible, setting the theme of the service or inviting the congregation to concentrate its mind on God.
>
> *Hymn*
>
> *Prayer and Lord's Prayer*
>
> *Old Testament reading*
>
> *Hymn*, or perhaps a psalm from the Old Testament
>
> *New Testament reading*
>
> *Hymn*
>
> *Prayer*, longer than the first prayer and often having petition as its main purpose – that is, seeking God's guidance and asking for the welfare of the sick, hungry, bereaved, . . . any people anywhere who stand in the need of the assurance of God's love.
>
> *Hymn*
>
> *Sermon*, usually based on a Biblical text, often from one of the two readings or 'lessons', as they are commonly called.
>
> *Hymn*
>
> *Blessing*, a prayer commending the congregation and the world to God's care. One of the most frequently used is, 'May the blessing of God Almighty, the Father the Son, and the Holy Spirit be upon you (or us) all, now and for evermore, Amen.'

Those who conduct the services often spend a considerable time over their preparation, and not all of it is given to thinking about the sermon. Ministers attempt to choose hymns to suit the theme.

164

They may begin and end with a hymn of praise to God. Between the lessons they may have a hymn about the Bible, and before the prayer use a hymn which helps the congregation to prepare for the important act of praying on behalf of all mankind.

The Bible in worship. The Bible is at the centre of this kind of service. The lessons are read from it; the sermon probably explains one of its teachings and may contain Biblical quotations and allusions; the hymns have usually been inspired by the Bible. Biblical reference can be found in many of the prayers and the most famous of all, the Lord's Prayer, comes from Matthew's gospel, Chapter 6 verses 9 to 13 (see also Luke 11:2–4), though the best-known version is not found in any of the Bible translations which are in use now. It comes from the Prayer Book:

'Our Father, which art in heaven, hallowed be thy name. Thy kingdom come. Thy will be done, in earth, as it is in heaven. Give us this day our daily bread. And forgive us our trespasses. As we forgive them that trespass against us. And lead us not into temptation. But deliver us from evil. For thine is the kingdom, the power and the glory. For ever and ever. Amen.'

This form might be compared with the words of the *Alternative Service Book*:

Our Father in heaven,
hallowed be your name,
your kingdom come,
your will be done,
on earth as in heaven.
Give us today our daily bread.
Forgive us our sins
as we forgive those who sin
against us.
Lead us not into temptation
but deliver us from evil.

For the kingdom, the power and
the glory are yours
now and for ever. Amen

The Prayer Book whose full title is *The Book of Common Prayer*, also contains the most famous non-sacramental liturgies, the orders of service for morning and evening prayer, called Matins and Evensong respectively. Although some Anglican churches have replaced Matins with Parish Communion and hold no evening service

165

at all on Sundays, it is nevertheless laid down as the duty of the parish clergyman to conduct both services, not only on Sunday but on every day of the week. One of the key ideas of Christian worship is that the community's offering of reverence and praise to God also represents an offering of worship on behalf of all mankind. The clergyman prays for himself and for everyone in his parish as he reads Matins or Evensong.

The Bible in different denominations. The importance of the Bible in Christian services has already been noted. Often this is emphasised by the way that the Bible is used. For example, in the Church of Scotland, Baptist, Methodist or United Reformed churches and others, it is sometimes carried into the pulpit before the service begins. The congregation may well stand as a mark of respect. Here, the Bible, containing the word of God, is being used symbolically to remind the worshippers of God's presence. Whoever reads the lesson may introduce it with such a sentence as 'Hear the word of God as it is written in . . .', and then go on to announce

South Indian Christians in Vellore celebrating the sacrament of Holy Communion.

the book and chapter which is about to be read. The reading may be concluded with another sentence, for example, 'May God bless to us this reading from his word and to his name be the praise and the glory, Amen.'

In Anglican and Roman Catholic churches the Bible stands on a separate reading desk, or lectern, not on the pulpit, from which the sermon is preached. This again shows the importance of the Bible, but perhaps indicates that the sermon is not thought to be as necessary as it is in nonconformist churches. Where the Bible is placed in the pulpit it usually means that the church attaches great importance to 'the preaching of the word', and believes that the Bible should not only be read, but should also be explained to the congregation. When the notices of the coming week's events are given out in these churches, the congregation may be told, 'The preacher next Sunday will be . . .' This suggests that the sermon based on the Bible is the most important part of the service. At other churches the congregation may be told, 'the Celebrant at Mass next Sunday will be . . .', or 'next Sunday's morning service will be conducted by . . .' These are little clues that often help the visitor to discover where the particular church places the emphasis — on the Bible or the sacrament of Holy Communion.

Sacramental worship

A sign of love. A sacrament is 'a visible form of invisible grace'. Such was the definition of St. Augustine of Hippo, a great Christian thinker who lived from 354 to 430. What he meant was this. A man gives a woman a ring when he marries her. This is a token of love and of their promise to share life together. The love cannot be seen but the ring can. It is the visible form which their love takes. In the same way a sacrament is a visible form of God's grace. The word grace is harder to explain; perhaps 'undeserved love' is the simplest phrase that can be suggested.

Some Christians think of the parable of the prodigal son when they try to understand the word grace (Luke 15). In this story, which Jesus told, a man had two sons. One of them, the younger, asked his father to give him the share of his father's wealth that would have been his when his father died. He then left home for a life of pleasure and 'riotous living'. When his money had been squandered and he was almost starving he decided to return to his father and throw himself on his mercy. The father saw him approaching, ran to meet him, embraced him, and received him back into the family. This is grace. Love shown to the undeserving, shown simply because that is what God is like. A sacrament is a sign of this love. It is like the embrace, the clothes, and the meal given by the father to his wastrel son. They assured the son that his father's words of forgiveness were real.

The Roman Catholic church recognises seven sacraments: Baptism, Confirmation, the Eucharist, Penance, Unction, Holy Orders and Matrimony. The Eastern Orthodox church recognises the same seven, but calls them 'mysteries'. Most Protestant denominations accept only two—Baptism and the Eucharist—which are specifically mentioned in the New Testament, though most Christians hold the view that anything done in the service of God can in some sense be a means of grace. The Christian poet George Herbert said that anything done 'for thy sake', that is for Jesus, even if it be scrubbing floors, could become a way of knowing God. In this section on Christian worship attention will be confined to Baptism and the Eucharist as they form part of worship.

The Eucharist

This sacrament is called by many names. 'Eucharist' means thanksgiving, and is derived from the account of the Last Supper given in Luke's gospel. The words 'gave thanks' occur a number of times (Luke 22:14–19). The earliest written record of this meal is to be found in St. Paul's first letter to the Christians of Corinth, a coastal town near Athens. He had heard that the congregation was celebrating the Lord's Supper, as he called it, unworthily. They were perhaps using it as an opportunity to get drunk and eat greedily, not caring if the poorer members were hungry. He reminded them that in his meal Jesus was present in the bread and wine; therefore they must behave respectfully. He wrote:

> 'For this tradition which I handed on to you came to me from the Lord himself: that the Lord Jesus, on the night of his arrest, took bread and, after giving thanks to God, broke it and said; "This is my body which is given for you; do this as a memorial to me." In the same way, he took the cup after supper, and said "This cup is the new covenant sealed by my blood. Whenever you drink it, do this as a memorial of me." For every time you eat this bread and drink the cup, you proclaim the death of the Lord, until he comes.'
> (I Corinthians 11:23–26)

Every service of Holy Communion, Mass, Eucharist, Lord's Supper, Breaking of Bread, or whatever name the church uses, is based on those words, which St. Paul claimed had been handed on to him and were the faithful tradition of what happened in the upper room of a house in Jerusalem on the evening before Jesus was crucified. Probably the words of Paul's letter have been used by Christians ever since his own times. Eventually liturgies emerged, but it is most unlikely that there was ever a time when Christians had one form of Communion service which was used everywhere. Even in the Middle Ages, there were slight variations from diocese to diocese and in different countries. However, in those parts of Europe and Africa acknowledging the Pope as leader of the church, the Mass, in Latin, became the main Christian service. It was held daily. The custom grew up that priests should say Mass every day, whether anyone else was present or not.

In the early centuries after the ministry of Jesus, only baptised Christians were allowed to be present at the Eucharist. Those who were preparing for baptism or considering whether to become Christians had to leave before the prayer of blessing was offered over the bread and wine. The service was held in the morning of the Lord's Day, before dawn, partly because this was a time when it was safest for Christians to be about the streets, partly because many of them were slaves and would have to work throughout the rest of the day. Another reason was that it was early, while it was still dark, that the first person to see the risen Jesus met him in the garden where he had been buried. Since those times it has been the custom of many churches to hold the service of Holy Communion in the morning, not before dawn perhaps, but sometimes at 7.00 or 8.00 a.m. winter or summer.

The order of service found in a Roman Catholic missal, or in one of the later, modern English liturgies, still resembles the ancient forms of service.

The Mass was divided into two main parts, 'the Mass of the catechumens', the name given to those who were undergoing catechism, that is preparation for baptism, and the Mass of the faithful, those who were baptised members of the church. The first section of the Mass ended after the reading of a passage from the gospels. When they had heard it the unbaptised left and the doors of the church were closed. In those times the Lord's Prayer seems to have been taught to converts shortly before baptism. It was used in the second part of the Mass, not the first. Nowadays, there is no secrecy attached to it; probably most Christians can never remember being taught it. They learnt it at their mother's knee, or picked it up with other customs when they began to go to church with their parents.

In English Roman Catholic churches today the Mass is celebrated in the English language, not in Latin, and the order is as follows: *The Introductory Rite.* This includes a confession of sin and the saying, or often singing, of the Gloria, an ancient text which began

Receiving the Blessed Sacrament during a Roman Catholic Mass.

in Latin with the words, 'Gloria in excelsis deo'. In English it reads:

'Glory to God in the highest
and peace to his people on earth.
Lord God, heavenly king,
almighty God and Father,
we worship you, we give you thanks,
we praise you for your glory.
Lord Jesus Christ, only Son of the Father,
Lord God, Lamb of God,
you take away the sin of the world:
have mercy upon us;
you are seated at the right hand of the Father:
receive our prayer.
For you alone are the Holy One,
you alone are the Lord,
you alone are the Most High,
Jesus Christ,
with the Holy Spirit,
in the glory of God the Father. Amen.'

The Liturgy of the Word.   This comprises three readings from the Bible. One is from the Old Testament, and two are from the New Testament, one passage being taken from the letters or the Acts of the Apostles, and the last reading from one of the gospels. A brief sermon usually follows the gospel. This part of the service ends with the congregation standing to say the creed together. This is a statement of fundamental Christian belief. The Nicene Creed, dating from 325 when Constantine the Great convened a council of the church at Nicaea, near Constantinople, may be used, or the Apostles' Creed, an expression of faith used by the Christians of Rome.

The Liturgy of the Eucharist.   This contains the words of Jesus at the Last Supper. The priest takes the bread and the wine which have been placed on the altar, offers them to God, and consecrates them with a prayer. He takes a piece of the host, that is the bread, and places it in the chalice while the congregation says or sings the Agnus Dei, a hymn to the Lamb of God:

'Lamb of God, you take away the sins of the world:
have mercy upon us.
Lamb of God, you take away the sins of the world:
grant us peace.'

The priest then raises the host and says:

'This is the lamb of God who takes away the sin of the world.
Happy are those who are called to his supper.'

These words show that the death of Jesus is regarded as a sacrifice, hence the name 'host' from a Latin word 'hostia' meaning sacrificial victim. The congregation then comes forward to receive the consecrated host, which the priest places in their mouths.

The Concluding Rite. This very simple but important rite is an act of thanksgiving for Jesus' death and love received in the host and the whole act of worship, and an expression of rededication to God's service. One of the prayers that may be used reads:

> 'Jesus, my saviour, I thank you for the privilege granted to me this day to receive your body and blood. I know that this favour comes to me through your kindness and love. I thank you for the institution of the holy eucharist. You have come to me in spite of my ingratitude in the past. Jesus, I thank you.'

Other forms of Communion service. The order of service of Holy Communion found in the Anglican *Book of Common Prayer* similar to the English translation of the Roman Catholic Mass. Recently, both churches have been attempting to produce liturgies in modern English and there is now very close agreement in the words used at the two services. However, the visitor to a nonconformist church may discover many differences. First, the name of the service may be Holy Communion, or simply Communion Service. As we have seen, The Lord's Supper, or Breaking of Bread are other names used. The service will be held much less frequently, perhaps once a month, quarterly, or even annually—certainly not every Sunday. Often it will form an addition to the morning or evening service, being placed after the sermon. Instead of a priest standing at an altar, there will be a minister standing or sitting behind a table and probably accompanied by members of the congregation. Instead of going to the table the congregation may remain seated while the minister's assistants bring them small pieces of bread on individual metal plates and wine in individual glasses. In the Church of England, and some other churches, everyone drinks from the same chalice. While Roman Catholic custom in some countries is to give the chalice only to priest, monks and nuns—though everyone receives the host—a movement exists towards communion in both kinds.

The meaning of the Eucharist. Jesus said, 'This is my body which is given for you. . . This is my blood which is shed for you. Do this in remembrance of me.' And St. Paul added, 'In this way you proclaim the Lord's death until he comes.' From these words Christians have worked out what they consider the meaning of the

Eucharist to be. Roman Catholic Christians, for example, take the words of Jesus literally, believing that when the priest has consecrated the host it is the real body of Jesus. Some Christians go to the other extreme and argue that the Communion service is a memorial of the Last Supper. It reminds them that they are one with Jesus and his disciples in faith, but the bread and wine remain unchanged. No words of consecration are used, the service re-enacts a simple farewell meal. For the Society of Friends, also known as the Quakers, and the Salvation Army even this is too much. They repudiate sacraments altogether. Most Christians, however, feel that Jesus' command, 'Do this in remembrance of me,' and the fact that Christians have taken the words seriously ever since they were uttered, require them to celebrate the Supper of the Lord.

While there may be much disagreement on many aspects of the Eucharist, and some variation in ritual, there is more unity on the meaning of the sacrament. It reminds Christians of their discipleship; in faith they, like the first disciples, are with Jesus in the upper room. It reminds Christians that Jesus' death was for them and for all mankind, 'This is my body which is given for you.' They also remember that St. Paul called Christians 'the body of Christ'. Those who share the Lord's Supper must share in his willingness to sacrifice themselves in the service of their fellow human beings. St. Paul said, 'In this way you proclaim the Lord's death until he comes.' Once again, there are many views on the meaning of the reference to Jesus' 'coming'. Some believe he comes in the bread and wine. Some emphasise his continuous presence in the Holy Spirit. Others think more of some final event in history. All Christians believe that God will one day be acknowledged as sovereign by men. The Communion service reminds them that the last act in the drama of Jesus' work remains to be carried out.

Whatever the way in which different Christians receive Communion, whether they sit or kneel, they all bring the same kinds of belief to the service. For a few moments they step out of the world of time into the eternal presence of God, afterwards returning to the tasks Jesus has given them to do on his behalf, refreshed by his presence.

Baptism

The second sacrament accepted by all Christians — except the Society of Friends and the Salvation Army — is baptism. It is the rite of initiation by which people enter the Christian church. For this reason the font containing the water used in baptism is found near the door of the church.

Immersion in water is no new practice. Members of Jesus' Jewish faith took a bath to remove the ritual pollution caused by contact with dead bodies. It was a way of expressing repentance for one's sins, and for converts to Judaism a bath was part of their initiation into the Jewish faith. The New Testament assumes that readers are aware of the rite of baptism. Nowhere is it explained. In John's gospel, the writer mentions the fact that Jesus' disciples, as well as John the Baptist, baptised people, but he does not dwell on it (John 4:2). At the end of Matthew's gospel are the completely unheralded and unexplained words of Jesus, 'Go into all the world and make disciples of all nations, baptising them in the name of the Father, and of the Son, and of the Holy Spirit. And be assured, I am always with you, to the end of time.' (Matthew 28:20).

In early Christian times.   The Acts of the Apostles contains the account of how the Jewish treasurer of the Queen of Ethiopia became a Christian and was baptised (Acts 8:26–40). An evangelist named Philip heard him reading the Isaiah scroll as he rode by in his chariot and entered into conversation with him. The treasurer invited Philip to join him in his chariot and the two went on their bumpy way, reading and talking. Philip explained the passage from Isaiah Chapter 53 in terms of the Messiahship of Jesus, and the treasurer expressed the desire to become a Christian. 'Here is water, what is to prevent me being baptised?' he asked. Without any delay Philip baptised him. Baptism in the earliest days of Christianity was as simple and as swift as that. Someone would confess faith in Jesus, recognising all that this might involve — for Christians were no more popular than Jesus had been with the Jewish and Roman authorities — and baptism followed immediately. A note of reservation creeps into another baptism story in Acts, but that is because the man was a Gentile, not a Jew, and St. Peter was not sure that such people could become Christians (Acts 10). However, the apostle eventually realised that sincere faith was all that mattered and the centurion was baptised. Clearly, at this time only believers, and perhaps their families, were baptised, and the rite was not an act which conferred something; it confirmed faith. It is important to note these facts, because as the Christian movement became popular and won many converts, baptismal practices changed.

The most important change may have taken place only a hundred years after Jesus' ministry. This was the introduction of a long period of preparation for baptism. It was no longer possible to stop the chariot and be baptised in the nearest river; it was necess-

174

ary to undergo a course of teaching and training that might last as long as three years. One reason for this change was certainly the development of ideas about Jesus which were contrary to the teachings of the apostles. There were some who called themselves Christians, but rejected the divinity of Jesus. Another group went to the other extreme and denied his manhood. He was pure spirit, they argued. He never died on the cross; Simon of Cyrene or someone else was crucified in his place. Gods cannot die. With such a variety of opinions about, it was considered necessary to teach people the apostolic message carefully and accurately before baptising them. Another reason for the long period of training may have been to test the sincerity of the converts. There have always been those enthusiasts who join a movement for a few weeks and then leave. The church gained no credit from lapsed Christians whose weakness and perhaps immoral way of life brought it into disrepute.

The washing away of sin. Christianity has always taught that the act of baptism, if it is undertaken in good faith and with sincerity, removes the guilt of past sins. The Nicene creed contains the sentence, 'We believe in one baptism for the forgiveness of sins.' St. Paul wrote, 'We died to sin, how can we live in it any longer? Have you forgotten that when we were baptised into union with Christ Jesus we were baptised into his death? By baptism we were buried with him and lay dead, in order that as Christ was raised from the dead in the splendour of the father, so we might also set our feet upon the new path of life.' (Romans 6:2–4)

A tendency grew up to take the idea that baptism washes away past sins so literally that converts put off their baptism until old age. Deathbed baptisms became quite common. A person might be a practising and sincere Christian for fifty years, yet only be baptised a few moments before dying. This custom of deferred baptism is obviously contrary to anything found in the New Testament, but once it had gained a hold it was only slowly discontinued. Church leaders might describe baptism as joining the Christian army, to fight the world, the flesh and the devil, but worldly wisdom and to some extent the story of Jesus forgiving the dying thief (Luke 23:40–43), might have seemed to favour deferment. A last-minute absolution for the sins of a lifetime seemed to guarantee a blissful eternity.

Infant baptism. Eventually the custom of baptising infants prevailed, except in missionary areas where the Christian gospel was being preached for the first time. In such lands baptism continued to be dependent on a personal confession of faith. Most denomi-

175

nations practise infant baptism nowadays, but there are many Christians who have some doubts about the wisdom of doing so. They argue that it is meaningless to the baby and that unless the parents are serious in their intention to bring up the child as a Christian, as they have promised, more harm than good has been done. People have been encouraged to make light of a sacrament that should have great significance. Consequently, some Anglican Christians, and also members of other denominations, prefer to hold a service of blessing in which the baby is offered to God and the parents give thanks for the child's birth, asking that they may care for this gift from God responsibly. It is usually the people who regard baptism as a serious matter who make use of the service of blessing, preferring to defer baptism until a believer can make his or her own vows as an adult. Some less conscientious people still take their children to be baptised, but may have no very firm intention of keeping the promises made during the service.

One group of Christians has asked the question 'Did the early church baptise infants?' and has come to the conclusion that it did not. Therefore, they only baptise people on confession of belief in Jesus as saviour and lord. Not surprisingly, the denomination that is best-known for holding this view is known by the name 'Baptist'. Keeping as close as possible to the practice of early Christianity, as they understand it, they immerse the person who is being baptised completely, whereas other Christians only sprinkle water on the baby and make the sign of the cross on the person's forehead. Most Baptist churches have a baptistry concealed beneath the floor of the church. It looks rather like a small swimming pool. In countries with warm climates, Baptists still follow the custom of the early church by baptising believers in the running water of a river or stream.

To the question of whether the New Testament supports the baptism of infants or not, no clear reply can be given, and the Bible here, as on many other issues, gives no answer. In the Acts of the Apostles, the conversion of a jailer is recorded (Acts 16:16–34). It ends with these words, 'He and his whole family are baptised. He brought them (Paul and Silas) into his house, set out a meal, and rejoiced with his whole household in his new found faith in God.' What is meant by the word 'household' in these sentences? The jailer's wife and slaves, or his children as well, including, perhaps, a baby?

Baptismal services. From New Testament times until the reign of the Emperor Constantine in the fourth century it is impossible to say that the rite of baptism was conducted in the same way everywhere in the Christian world. What is more, the evidence is so scrappy that it is only possible to give an imperfect and incomplete picture of what actually happened.

Sometimes running water was used, but often water from a font was poured over the candidates head three times, once for each person of the Trinity, Father, Son and Holy Spirit. The fonts were often octagonal in shape, as a reminder that Jesus rose on the 'eighth day' (I Peter 3:20). Anointing and exorcism were often part of the rite, as the candidate vowed to 'relinquish the devil and all his works'. In the North African churches after baptism the new member of the church was given milk and honey to drink to symbolise entry into the promised land (see Exodus 3:8). Easter and Pentecost were popular times for baptising converts who had completed their course of catechism. On these occasions, in particular, the church remembered the resurrection of Jesus and the outpouring of the Holy Spirit.

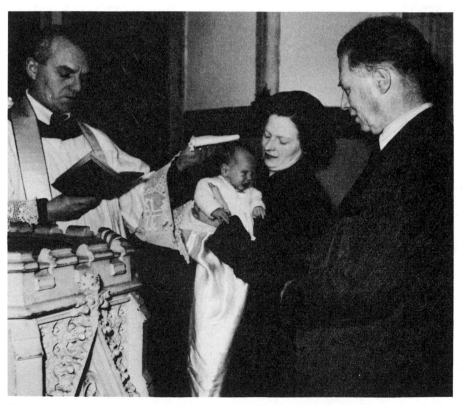

'In the name of the Father, and of the Son and of the Holy Spirit'—a baby is baptised in an Anglican church.

Nowadays, the service of baptism may take place in church in the afternoon when only the clergyman, parents, relatives and friends are present to witness the ceremony, but it is increasingly likely that it will be part of another service. It may be inserted in the parish Eucharist between the gospel and the consecration, in place of the sermon. The Church of Scotland, and many English free churches include it in the normal morning act of worship. The reason for including baptisms in other services is the realisation that the baby or adult who is being baptised is becoming part of the church, the Christian family. The ceremony which brings that person into the family should be witnessed by the whole church.

Church of Scotland baptism today. Here are two descriptions of baptism, out of the many which could be included. The first took place as part of morning worship in the Church of Scotland.

During a hymn one of the women in the congregation left her seat and went out of the door at the back of the church to a little room beyond. She reappeared, followed by the mother, who carried the baby, then came the father and their two daughters, holding their father's hands. The small procession went to the front pew of the church where they were joined by a few other members of the congregation. The minister had come down from the pulpit and was waiting to welcome them with a friendly smile. When the hymn had ended he spoke to the congregation. He told them that the parents wanted their new daughter to be baptised into the family of Christians and that he would perform the rite on behalf of the church.

The parents were asked if they believed in God, the Father, in his son, Jesus Christ, and in the Holy Spirit, to which they answered 'Yes'. They and the congregation promised to bring up the baby in the Christian faith. Then, while the father held the baby, the minister sprinkled water on her head, from the small wooden font standing on the communion table, as her two sisters watched closely. 'Ann, I baptise you in the name of the Father, and of the Son, and of the Holy Spirit,' he said. A prayer of thanksgiving for the baby was offered, and a prayer for her family. A blessing followed, and the congregation, which had been standing for most of the baptism, joined in the final hymn of the morning service.

Anglican baptism. The second example is much more elaborate, and is the description of an Anglican baptismal service which took place during parish communion. That morning Peter was the only person being baptised. Some Sundays there were five or six baptisms, and occasionally a whole family was baptised, parents first, followed by each of the children until the youngest was received. A large stone medieval font stood at the west end of the church, just inside the main entrance, but because he wanted everyone to be able to see the baptism the vicar used a portable font carried by a server. During the hymn after the gospel, the vicar, preceded by a man carrying the cross, a boy carrying the font, and another boy carrying the service book, walked from the chancel into the nave of the church where Peter's mother was sitting with him in her arms. With his family were some friends who were acting as 'godparents', two men and one woman for a boy, two women and a man for a girl. They are expected to make sure that a child is brought up in the Christian faith. Godparents were very important a few centuries ago when the death rate was higher and there was a fairly strong possibility that they might have to take an orphan godchild into their home.

When the procession had stopped the vicar asked the family and godparents to stand at his side, took the baby from his mother and then asked them a number of questions: 'Do you believe and trust in God the Father who made the world? Do you believe and trust in his Son Jesus Christ, who redeemed mankind? Do you believe and trust in his Holy Spirit, who sanctified the people of God?' To each of these the parents and godparents replied, 'I believe and trust in him.' The vicar then poured water from the font over the baby's forehead, saying, 'I baptise you in the name of the Father, and of the Son, and of the Holy Spirit, Amen'. He then asked the whole congregation to stand and join him in saying some words as he gave a lighted candle to the father. Turning to the baby, he said:

'Receive this light.
This is to show you have passed from darkness to light.'

Then everyone added:

'Shine as a light in the world, to the glory of God the Father.'

After the Lord's Prayer and other prayers that part of the service ended. As Peter had remained quiet throughout his baptism and showed signs of going to sleep his family remained in church for the rest of the service.

The meaning of baptism. The significance of the sacrament of baptism has been touched upon a number of times in the preceding paragraphs. Now we must conclude this section listing and examining the many meanings.

Baptism is an act of spiritual cleansing. An Old Testament passage which may be used in Anglican baptism services reads:

'Thus says the Lord God: I will sprinkle clean water upon you and you shall be clean from all your uncleannesses.'

(Ezekiel 36:25)

Baptism is an act of renunciation. The parents who bring their children to be baptised may be asked, 'Do you repent you of your sins? Do you renounce evil?' For later in the service they are told that it is their duty to bring up their children to repent of sin and renounce evil for themselves. Where mature people are being baptised the responsibility for these things is laid directly upon them. In some liturgies, though not many that are in use nowadays, an act of exorcism combined the notions of spiritual cleansing and renunciation. *The Alternative Service Book* of the Church of England asks those who bring children for baptism to answer these questions for themselves and the children:

'Do you turn to Christ?
Answer: I turn to Christ.
Do you repent of your sins?
Answer: I repent of my sins.
Do you renounce evil?
Answer: I renounce evil.'

At the base of the font in the church of St Mary, Astbury, Cheshire, are the words, 'A fountain for sin and all uncleanness'.

Baptism is also an act of renewal. The words of Ezekiel quoted above continue, 'A new heart I will give you, and a new spirit will I put within you.' St Paul linked the ideas of renunciation and renewal when he wrote these words to Christians living in Rome:

'Shall we persist in sin so that there may be all the more grace? No, no! We died to sin: how can we live in sin any longer? Have you forgotten that when we were baptised into union with Christ Jesus we were baptised into his death? By baptism we were buried with him, and lay dead, in order that, as Christ was raised from the dead in the splendour of the father, so also we might set our feet upon the new path of life.'

(Romans 6:1–4)

Clearly, baptism was intended to be a kind of Easter Day experience. Through faith the candidate experienced Jesus here and now and was assured that after his own bodily death he would rise to eternal life in Christ.

Baptism was also a new way of expressing spiritual equality.

180

How could the Jew, having the same religion as Jesus, the richest spiritual heritage in the Western world, become a fellow member with 'pagans' and Gentiles in the Christian community? How could the slave-owner join the church to which his slave might already belong without losing face? These issues must have caused many problems to church leaders. Gentile slave-owners, as well as the majority of Jews, must have refused to become members of a faith which said that Jesus had died for all humanity, (Romans 5:18), and that nothing but belief in Jesus counted for anything as far as salvation was concerned. St. Paul declared baptism to be the one rite necessary for everyone:

> 'Christ is like a single body with its many limbs and organs, which, many as they are, together make up one body. For indeed, we were all brought into one body by baptism, in the one spirit, whether we are Jews or Greeks, slaves or freemen, and that holy spirit was poured out for us all to drink.'
>
> (I Corinthians 12:12–13)

Baptism, then, means that in the presence of God everyone is equal, that there is one church, one faith, one Lord, and that the only way to become a Christian is through baptism. For this reason baptism is a sacrament which cannot be repeated. If someone is baptised in the name of the Father, the Son and the Holy Spirit in a Methodist church as a baby, and wishes to join another denomination many years later, the validity of his baptism will be recognised. Baptism is also the one sacrament which can be performed by anyone — a nurse in hospital, an air hostess, or the captain of a ship at sea. Of course they would only baptise a child on the request of the parents, and probably because there was a likelihood of the baby's dying before a clergyman could be found.

Baptism is the sacrament by which the past is renounced, life in Christ is begun, and one becomes a member of the body of Christ, the church. However, two highly respected Christian bodies, the Salvation Army and the Society of Friends, do not practise the rite of baptism at all. Salvationists reject infant baptism because they believe a person must choose for himself, and the young child is clearly incapable of doing this. They think that the emphasis often put upon the ritual might obscure the fact that baptism is an act of inner spiritual renewal performed by the Holy Spirit, not by a clergyman or church. For the same reason — their stress upon the inwardness of religion — Quakers, too, have no baptism.

Confirmation

In the early days of the church, especially those recorded in the

181

New Testament, baptism meant 'putting on Christ'. When infant baptism became widespread, the need arose for a service in which the person who had been baptised as an infant could reaffirm for himself or herself the undertakings made earlier by proxy. This became known as the rite of 'confirmation'. It is usually conducted by a bishop. In denominations which have no bishops, such as the United Reformed Church and some others, an act of 'church membership' takes the place of confirmation.

Whatever the name and form of the rite, the essential content and purpose is the same. The promises made on the infant's behalf are made again publicly by the young man or woman, who is now of an age to understand them and profess his or her beliefs. God is asked to grant his gift of the Holy Spirit, so that henceforth he or she may be a full member of the Christian church, the body of Christ. One Anglican prayer expresses the idea thus:

> 'Defend, O Lord, these thy servants with thy heavenly grace, that they may continue thine forever, and daily increase in thy Holy Spirit more and more, until they come unto thy everlasting kingdom.'

The candidates listening to this prayer would be kneeling in front of a bishop who would have placed his hands on their heads and said, 'Confirm, O Lord, thy servant with thy Holy Spirit.' Candidates in another denomination might have been given the right hand of fellowship—that is, have shaken hands with the minister —though the custom of the laying on of hands is now being adopted by some congregations in the United Reformed Church.

As a postscript, it is necessary to add that fewer children are being baptised as infants and, therefore, it is increasingly the practice to combine baptism and confirmation in a single service for the admission of new church members. Thus, it has come about by chance and changing circumstances that the ways of the early church are being restored.

Finding out more about Christianity

Christianity is so complex and varied that the information covered in this section can only be an outline. Those who are interested can discover more by visiting churches, observing acts of worship, and having discussions with ministers. If an opportunity arises to talk to clergymen about worship and church organisation, these are some of the questions that might be asked.

a.   What is the main Sunday service?

b. Who may celebrate the Eucharist?

c. How frequently is there a service of Holy Communion – weekly, daily, monthly. . . . . .?

d. What is the meaning and purpose of the Eucharist?

e. Are babies baptised?

f. What is the meaning and purpose of baptism?

g. Are there any positions or activities in your denomination which are not open to those who have not been baptised?

h. Are there any activities which only the clergy can perform?

i. Do you have a confirmation or church membership ceremony? If so, what is the normal age of candidates and what is the purpose of the act?

j. Do men and women have equal status in your denomination?

k. What do you think has been the distinctive contribution of your denomination to Christianity in the past?

l. What do you consider to be the distinctive contributions which your denomination is making to Christianity today?

m. How is your denomination organised and governed?

You should always try to discover whether your speaker is expressing his own opinions or the beliefs and teachings of his denomination. In the long run it is the latter which are most important.

Christian private devotion. Christianity places a strong emphasis on personal belief. Strictly speaking, no-one is a Christian by birth— only by baptism. That ought to mean that becoming a Christian is a matter of personal decision, not following in one's father's footsteps. As Christianity became the established religion in many countries it was natural for children to be taken to church and to accept their parents' example without much thought. Nevertheless, baptism, confirmation or whatever rites are used when one is made a full member of the church, are constant reminders of the personal nature of the Christian religion.

Prayer. It may seem surprising, therefore, that Jesus gave his disciples very little guidance about private devotion. He simply told them to pray in a quiet place, 'in secret'—that is, where they would

183

not be interrupted and would not be tempted to show off by praying in public places (see Matthew 6:1–18). Apart from this, Jesus only gave them what we know as the Lord's Prayer to be a model. Perhaps he thought that they would continue to pray in the manner to which they were accustomed as Jews. He may also have wanted his followers to realise that prayers can be said anywhere at any time. There is no need for special preparations—simply go into a room by yourself, shut the door, and pray to your Father, who is there in the secret place. Consequently, there are many ways in which Christians pray privately to God and there is always the danger of neglect. Some might wish that Jesus had given more guidance and told them how often to pray and when, but Jesus apparently respected his disciples so much that he made them fully responsible. His only command was 'pray'.

There is a long tradition of parents encouraging their children to kneel at the side of their beds to say their prayers before going to sleep. The child may say the Lord's Prayer and one, which asks God to bless various relatives, ends 'Make me a good boy (or girl)'. There is also a long tradition of family prayers, but amidst the pressures and pleasures of twentieth-century life this custom is kept today by relatively few families. The Bible is the most commonly used aid to private devotion. Many Christians read a passage each day, guided by a set of notes published by such organisations as the British and Foreign Bible Society or the Scripture Union. Others may also use a Missal, *The Book of Common Prayer*, *The Alternative Service Book*, or a classical book of private devotion such as *Of the Imitation of Christ*, by Thomas à Kempis. Forms of meditation based on yoga and the Christian mystical tradition have become popular in recent years.

Retreat.   To deepen their spiritual life some Christians spend a few days, perhaps a weekend, at a local or national centre where they will receive help and instruction and can give their full attention to prayer and reflection. This is called 'going on retreat'. By turning away from the daily concerns of the world, for as little as a day or as long as a week, the Christian is inwardly refreshed, renewed and enabled to take a full place again in the life of the church and society.

Lenten devotions.   At Lent, the forty-day period between Shrove Tuesday and Easter, all Christians are expected to commit themselves more seriously than usual to their devotions. It is hoped that by sharing to some extent in the hardships faced by Jesus they will receive a greater appreciation of his love and so become more faithful disciples. Fasting — of a very mild nature compared with the severity of Ramadan, the Muslim month of fasting, or the Jewish Day of Atonement — is sometimes practised by Christians during Lent, but often observance consists of attending special services and giving more time to prayer.

Private devotion.   This is always difficult to write about, because it is something which people keep very much to themselves and prefer not to discuss. However, it is probably correct to say that Christians in this century have often neglected such devotion. They have been more eager to feed the hungry and heal the sick than to say prayers or meditate. A trend in the opposite direction may now be starting, but whether the reason is that Christians feel a need to discover the inwardness of religion or that they despair of solving the world's social problems is not easy to say. Jesus seems to have encouraged personal piety and social action. His followers, on the other hand, have often found it difficult to keep the balance between the two, sometimes expecting priests and monks to do the praying while the laity do the building and digging.

The mosque

The building used by Muslims in their worship is called a mosque. This word comes from 'masjid' which is derived from an Arabic verb meaning 'to prostrate oneself'. A mosque is a place where Muslims bow before God to affirm their obedience to his will. During Muhammad's early days as a prophet in Mecca there was no mosque. He and his companions prayed almost anywhere, in the narrow streets, in the Prophet's house, at the Ka'ba, the large cube-shaped building in the town centre. Muhammad's simple teaching was, 'Wherever the hour of prayer overtakes you, you shall perform the prayer. That place is a mosque.' Clearly, he wanted his companions to realise that prayer was more important than any building.

It is said that the first mosque in Medina was built at the place where Muhammad's camel chose to stop when the Prophet went to the city in 622 CE, though an earlier one had been built outside the city. Muhammad's house stood in the mosque's courtyard. It is clear that it was open to Jews and Christians as well as Muslims and was a meeting place and social centre, as well as a place of prayer, where the Prophet preached and taught the faith of Islam. People might eat and sleep in the mosque — practices which have since become very rare, though occasionally they still provide refreshment and shelter for the traveller.

The features of a mosque.   Mosques today are generally rectangular in shape. The walls define the sacred area which should only be entered by people who have removed their shoes. At the entrance or in the courtyard, if the mosque is a large one, there will be a place for washing. In a village in India or Pakistan it may only be a hand pump; in a larger mosque it may be a fine ornamental fountain. In Britain there is often a small washroom with a row of sinks, set at a fairly low level so that worshippers can wash their feet as well as their hands and faces before saying their prayers.

Minaret and muezzin.   Mosques in Muslim countries have at least one high tower, called a minaret, from which one of the community can call Muslims to prayer five times a day. The minaret and its muezzin, the man who summons the faithful to prayer, serve the same purpose as the belltower and bells of Christian churches. Once, when worshippers had no watches, it was necessary to remind them that it was time for worship; now the bells are simply part of Sunday life. The muezzin's importance remains, however, because Muslim prayer times are fixed by the sun and change daily. Remembering them is a task left to the muezzin.

The qibla wall.   A mosque need not be a covered building. Wayside mosques in hot countries are merely enclosed rectangles. However, even these will have one wall which differs from the other three. It may be higher. It may have a small indentation or niche in it. In some way the stranger's attention will be attracted to this wall. It is called the qibla wall, from a word meaning 'direction'. It tells the Muslim where Mecca is, for it has been carefully built to lie in the direction of Mecca, the city which the Muslim must face to say his prayers. The niche in the qibla wall is known as the mihrab. It indicates the precise direction of Mecca and the prayer leader will stand in front of it when he leads the congregation in worship. In Mecca the mihrab points in the direction of the Ka'ba and, even more precisely, to the part of the Ka'ba between the water-spout for draining away rain water and the north-west corner. In the great mosque of Lahore, in Pakistan, or in Delhi, or the Blue Mosque at Isfahan, Persia, the qibla wall has become a covered colonnade and the mihrab a majestic ornamental arch.

A plain interior.   Many mosques are completely covered with a roof, often crowned by a dome, which symbolises the universe, and

An imam, with other Muslims stands outside the Regent's Park mosque, London.
Note the symbol of the crescent on the dome and minaret.

helps to magnify the voice of the imam. The main room of the building, the one where prayers are offered, may be carpeted and lines may be marked on the floor to help the congregation to assemble in neat rows. The building may look very plain. It will have no stained glass windows or pictures, no statues or other decorations—merely, perhaps, elaborate Arabic inscriptions, so artistically produced that few Muslims may now be able to read them without training. A comparison might be made with the Gothic script which used to be found at the top of the front page of some daily prayers and can still be seen in some German books. Muslims believe that statues might encourage idolatry.

God alone is to be worshipped and he is pure spirit. It is impossible to produce any likeness of him and it is wrong to try. Many Muslims also believe that to draw, paint or make a sculpture of any human, animal or even plant form is to imitate the work of God as creator. This should be avoided, as there is always the possibility that the person who begins by copying God's handiwork may come to think of himself as being as great as God. Muslim artistic effort has been largely devoted to architecture, expecially the beautiful mosques built to the glory of God. Calligraphy is also a highly developed art. The beautiful handwritten characters are used to present the Qur'an — God's greatest gift to man — with a skill and artistry worthy of such a holy book, and at the same time to remind Muslims of its importance in their faith. In Muslim homes, or mosques in Britain made from converted houses or churches, plaques of such calligraphy are often used to show the qibla, the direction of Mecca.

The pulpit. The final feature one is likely to see in a mosque is the pulpit from which addresses are given on Fridays and other special occasions. This is called the minbar by Muslims, and it is usually to be found in front of the qibla wall and to one side of the mihrab. Sometimes it may be quite imposing, standing at the top of a flight of stairs, but often it will be no more than a raised platform just high enough to enable the speaker to be seen by everyone in the congregation.

Muslim worship. 'Prayer is the essence of worship' (Muhammad). Worship for the Muslim really means praying. Sermons, festival celebrations and the pilgrimage to Mecca can all be regarded as worship, as can the whole of life, but praying five times a day is the normal act of worship. There are many rules and instructions guiding the Muslim so that prayers may be properly offered. However, there is a story which reminds us that sincere devotion in

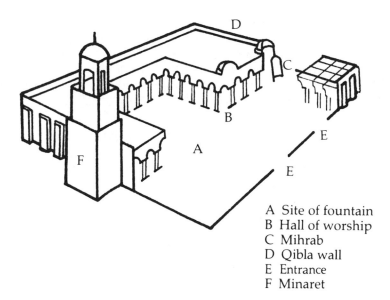

A Site of fountain
B Hall of worship
C Mihrab
D Qibla wall
E Entrance
F Minaret

Diagram of a mosque

prayer is far more important than facing in the right direction and saying certain words at the right time. When Muhammad had taught his companions to wash before praying, to find a clean place, to turn towards the Ka'ba and to pray at certain times, one of them asked, 'What if we cannot wash?' 'Clean yourselves with sand,' came the reply. 'And if we cannot find a clean place. . .?' So the questions went on and the Prophet replied to each. At last he halted the questioner by saying, 'If you cannot wash or clean yourself, if you don't know the direction of the Ka'ba or when it is time for prayer, nevertheless say your prayers.' However, for most Muslims it is possible to prepare for prayers according to the Prophet's instructions.

Times of prayer. Each of the occasions for daily prayer has a name related to the time of day when it is to be offered. They are:

morning (fajr)	after dawn – it can be made until sunrise;
noonday (zuhr)	as soon as the sun has passed its zenith and until an object throws a shadow twice its length this prayer may be said;

189

mid afternoon ('asr)	from the end of the zuhr prayer until the sun sets, but preferably before it loses its brilliance;
sunset (maghrib)	between sunset and the end of twilight;
night ('isha)	any time during the hours of darkness, but preferably before midnight.

A number of points emerge from this list. First, the times are all related to the place of the sun in the sky and assume that the believer is living in a country like Arabia where the sun can usually be seen and where there is not much change in the times of day between summer and winter. It comes as a surprise to a visitor from Britain that sunrise in India or Pakistan is somewhere near 6.00 a.m., and sunset not long after 6.00 p.m. summer and winter. In a northern country like Britain Muslim prayers vary considerably throughout the year. In summer the noon prayers can take place about 2.00 p.m.

Although the idea of praying five times a day might seem a hard discipline to people who have grown lazy and only say their prayers when they go to church on Sunday, there are two concessions to human weakness in the prayer times. First, they are related to times of day when to pray is most convenient — immediately upon getting up; during the heat of the day when people in the hotter lands of the world take a necessary siesta; at the end of the working day; after the evening meal; and just before going to sleep. Secondly, though the formal Muslim prayers take only a few minutes, each period of prayer lasts for about two hours, so that those who are busy at the moment when the muezzin calls them to prayer have a period of grace in which to complete what they are doing and still say their prayers.

The frequency of prayer, five times daily, and the sensible timing of prayer show that Islam regards prayer as important and something to be encouraged and made possible for everyone. It is not merely for very pious people with time to spare. A few other examples can be given, which also serve to show the importance of prayer. In a Muslim country such as Pakistan it is not unusual to see a large arrow at railway stations, rather like a weather vane but fixed so that it points towards Mecca. Its purpose is to indicate the qibla to travellers wishing to say their prayers. It is a common sight to see a man kneeling on the platform saying his prayers, perhaps using a clean handkerchief as a prayer carpet. In these countries one can frequently see a group of jute mats placed on the ground behind a roadside café, ready for travellers to use when they break their journey.

Many Muslims, no matter how tired or thirsty and hungry they may be, will first pray and then refresh themselves. Factories often have a mosque as one of the complex of buildings so that workers may say their prayers, especially at noon on Friday, which may not be a rest day but is the Muslim day corresponding to the Christian Sunday or the Jewish Sabbath. In Britain a Muslim bus conductor may quietly say his prayers on the top deck of the bus while it is standing at the terminus. Because British holidays, like Sunday or Christmas, are still determined by the Christian tradition, members of other faiths sometimes find it difficult to fulfil their religious obligations. This is particularly true of Muslims, whose religious practices are so much a part of their daily lives.

Prayer at home.   A Muslim, as we have seen, may pray anywhere, though there are one or two guiding principles to be observed. It is said that the Prophet preferred to pray in an enclosed space, though he did pray in the street when necessary. Muslims, therefore, will pray in the house or in the garden, if they cannot go to the mosque, which is the place primarily intended for prayer. For many reasons, they may have to pray at home. Most families possess prayer carpets which they will lay down for this purpose. The carpets often have a picture of the Ka'ba or the mosque at Medina woven in them. If one is uncertain of the qibla it is possible to buy a compass with special marking, so that the direction of Mecca can be worked out anywhere in the world. Whether a Muslim prays at home or in the mosque, the form of prayer and the preparations are the same.

The call to prayer.   This is made by the muezzin. It is like a chant, often very musical and extremely beautiful. The first muezzin was a negro slave named Bilal, a man who had been tortured for his faith and might have died, had not one of Muhammad's companions, Abu Bakr, bought him from his owner and released him. The companions of the Prophet said, 'The Jews summon people to worship by blowing a horn. The Christians ring a bell. What shall we do? Muhammad turned to Bilal and instructed him to form his hands into a trumpet and shout.

The words of the call (in Arabic its name is adhan or azan, a word sometimes applied also to the muezzin) are:

Allahu Akbar/Allahu Akbar ....God is most great, God is
most great,
Allahu Akbar/Allahu Akbar ....God is most great, God is
most great,

191

Ashhadu an la ilaha Allah .....I bear witness that there is
Ashhadu an la ilaha Allah ..... none worthy of worship but
God (repeated twice)
Ashhadu anna Muhammadan
Rasoolullah ....I bear witness that
Ashhadu anna Muhammadan Muhammad is the Prophet of
Rasoolullah God (repeated twice)
Hayya 'alas salah ....Come to prayer,
Hayya 'alas salah ....Come to prayer,
Hayya 'alal falah ....Come to success,
Hayya 'alal falah ....Come to success,
Allahu Akbar ....God is most great,
Allahu Akbar ....God is most great,
La ilah ill Allah ....There is no deity but God.

To the call for the morning prayer are added the words:

Assalatu khayrun minan
nawm ....Prayer is better than sleep.
(This is also repeated twice)

Preparation for prayer. The sound of these Arabic words coming across the village rooftops from the minaret of the mosque is very impressive, especially in the quiet of the early morning. Upon hearing them the Muslim should prepare for prayer by ritual washing as laid down by the Qur'an in Suras 4:43 and 5:6. First the right hand is washed to the wrist and then the left. Next the mouth and throat by gargling so that the organ which will be used to address God is clean. Then the nose and face are cleansed. After this the arms up to the elbow, right arm first. The hands are then passed over the head from the forehead to the neck. The ears are cleansed next and finally the feet up to the ankles, again the right one first. If the body is dirty—perhaps after working in a factory or down a mine—washing should be replaced by taking a bath.

This act of cleansing, wudu, serves a number of purposes. Muslims believe that the body can become impure and this ritual removes impurity if it is properly, that is sincerely, performed.

It is not simply a matter of being dirty. The rite is connected with the idea of being defiled. Sleeping is believed to make a person impure, so even if a Muslim has a bath before going to bed, he should wash again before saying his morning prayers. In this way he makes himself fit to stand before God who is holy. Cold water is often used for wudu. This helps to make the worshipper alert. He goes to his prayers fresh and clear-headed, not half asleep. Finally, although the act may take only two minutes, it helps turn the mind from whatever the Muslim has been doing and concentrate it on God instead. In a few minutes he is going to do the most important thing a human being can do, that is to speak with God. Prayer must be performed thoughtfully, not casually. To the question, 'Why prepare for prayer in this way and not some other?' the Muslim replies that this is the form laid down by God in the Qur'an. The instructions are to be found in Sura 4:43 and Sura 5:6.

The imam. When several Muslims pray together they usually ask one of their number to stand in front of the rest and lead the prayers. He is their imam. Anyone may be chosen to do this. When the imam is standing in his place the muezzin, who is now just behind him, repeats this azan, though not as loudly as the first time, of course. The rest of the congregation stands shoulder-to-shoulder in lines behind the imam, with everyone facing Mecca.

Prayer positions. In the course of saying his prayers, the Muslim stands, kneels and touches the ground with his forehead. Some of these actions, can be seen on page 194, together with English versions of the Arabic which every Muslim uses, whatever his nationality. They are based on the tradition followed by the Prophet Muhammad, who provides Muslims with their best example. First, in Position 1, the intention of praying is expressed. The concentration of the body and mind begun during the ablutions is completed. In Position 2 the important opening verses of the Qur'an are recited:

'In the name of God, the merciful, the mercy-giving.
Praise be to God, lord of the Universe, the merciful and mercy-giving. Ruler of the day of judgement.
You alone we worship and from you alone we seek help.
Guide us along the straight road, the road of those you have favoured, not the path of those who have sought your anger, or who have gone astray. Amen.'

The emphasis upon God's greatness and words in praise of God dominate the rest of the prayers until Position 8. Then, sitting on his heels, the worshipper prays first for the Prophet and all Muslims and turning first to the right and then to the left, gives the Muslim greeting and blessing to those who are praying with him and to all mankind, 'Assalamu 'allaykum wa rahmatullah,' 'Peace be upon you and the mercy of God.'

Salat, which is the name given to formal prayer, is always the same. Each completion of the words and actions is called a rakat. Two rakats are made in the morning prayer, four at noon, afternoon and night, and three for the sunset prayer.

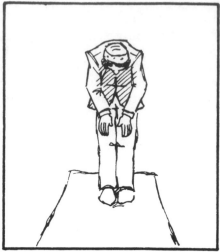

The full sequence of prayer involves twelve positions, starting with the Declaration of Intent. From the standing posture the worshipper proceeds to the bending, stands once again and there follow two sitting postures alternating with two prostrations and two salams in a kneeling position. The pictures above show Position 2: 'God is very great'; Position 4: Bending – Praise of God's majesty; Position 6 and 8: First and Second Prostrations and Position 11: Second salam – 'Peace and mercy to you'.

The sequence of prayer positions in Islam

Friday prayer. On Friday, the Muslim holy day, the noonday prayer is one which all men should attend, unless sickness or travelling
prevents them. In large towns this will take place at the main
mosque where the gathering may be so large that some men have
to pray in the street outside. On these occasions the Prophet used
to deliver a sermon (khutba) and now the imam or another learned
member of the congregation imitates his example. Traditionally the
khutba was preached in Arabic, but it is becoming increasingly the
custom to use the everyday language spoken by the congregation,
along with the obligatory Arabic introduction. For most Muslims
living in Britain this means Urdu, a language used by Muslims in
the Indo-Pakistan subcontinent.

Women and worship in Islam. With the coming of Islam, Arab
women were given a dignity which contrasted with their previous
humiliating status as mere chattels to be bought and sold at will.
Muhammad realised the importance of the wife and mother; from
her the family is provided with an example. The Prophet encouraged women to pray, and during his lifetime they formed part of
the mosque congregation, though their attendance at the mosque
to say prayers was not obligatory. Some mosques reserved a special
area for women, where they could join in the prayers without
distracting the men or being distracted by them. As time passed it
became less common for the women to attend the mosque and in
some countries not only did the custom fall into neglect, but they
were even forbidden to enter them. Although Islam does not teach
that a woman must go to the mosque, it does command her to
pray. Normally she will do this at home at a moment when it is
convenient to put her domestic tasks on one side. She may pray
alone or with other members of her family. In every detail she prays
as the menfolk do, first of all washing and then facing towards
Mecca.

The purpose of prayer in Islam. The Muslim prays first of all because
God has instructed him to pray. Prayer is one of the five Pillars of
Islam and is frequently mentioned in the Qur'an. Secondly, he
prays in order to praise and glorify God:

> 'Glory be to God when you reach evening and when you arise in
> the morning. Praise belongs to him in heaven and on earth; Glorify
> him in the late afternoon and when you enter the noon hour.'

(Qur'an 30:18)

God does not need the praise of man but it is a man's duty and
the condition that God has laid down if man is to receive God's

195

blessing. It is rather like saying that God has given man water to drink. If man refuses to drink God is not harmed in any way, but man goes thirsty. Those who do obey God by offering him their prayers receive refreshment. That is a third reason for praying:

> 'He brings forth the living from the dead and brings forth the dead from the living, and he revives the earth after its death. Thus shall you be brought forth again.'

> (Qur'an 30:19)

This passage promises refreshment now and also a joyful resurrection to Paradise for those who faithfully keep God in mind throughout their lives on earth. Such a person can also expect material blessings:

> 'Believers will succeed, those who are reverent in their prayers.'

> (Qur'an 23:1–2)

Prosperity in this world is certainly a fourth reason for praying, but its importance must be kept in proportion. To remember God, to keep him firmly in mind is the main reason why, five times a day, at the most important moments of a person's daily routine, prayers are made. Perhaps this verse sums it up:

> 'Remember me, I shall remember you! Thank me, do not be ungrateful to me. You who believe, seek help through patience and prayer.'

> (Qur'an 2:152–3)

Wherever the Muslim may be—at home, at work, in the course of a journey or in the mosque — he will offer prayers in Arabic, facing the Ka'ba at Mecca, in the tradition established by Muhammad. As he speaks the words passed down to him by generations of his forebears, the Muslim feels himself to be part of a worldwide brotherhood which has existed for almost fourteen hundred years.

Other uses of mosques.   As has been stated, the mosque is a place where the Muslim can come away from the everyday world and pray to God in peace, without interruption. During its long history it has also served other purposes. Muhammad used the mosque in Medina as his headquarters. Discussions about the government of Medina took place there. For some time he met Jews and Christians in the mosque and argued about religion with them. People sometimes ate and slept in mosques if they were travelling. As time passed, the mosque became regarded as a sacred building in which such things should not be allowed, though it is still possible to find

An Islamic school in Nelson, Lancashire.

some mosques which provide shelter for travellers. Sometimes Jewish and Christian unbelievers and also women were excluded from mosques, though again not everywhere.

The mosque has never been only a house of prayer. It usually gives Islamic education to young children. In the evening especially, boys and girls can be seen sitting barefoot on the floor, learning to read from copies of the Qur'an. These rest on benches in front of them. They read, or rather chant, the words aloud and their teacher tries to check their pronunciation of Arabic words. This is not an easy task, as the children may be at different stages and he has to try to hear each child, despite the noise made by the rest. Once the children can read the Qur'an in Arabic some may go further and attempt to commit it to memory. This is regarded as a fine achievement, and those men and women who accomplish the feat are given the title 'Hafiz' in front of their name.

In a country like Britain, a mosque is often a building with many rooms. Besides being a place of prayer and education, it may also be the community centre to which Muslims come from

197

considerable distances, especially on Sundays, when most of them do not have to go to work. Weddings may be celebrated there which in warmer countries would be held in the open air. Part of the building may be used by the imam, the teacher and leader of the religious community, as a home for himself and his family.

Muslim private devotion.   Because Islam lays down so carefully the times of the five daily prayers and the form they should take, there is a tendency for non-Muslims to think that private devotion has no place in Islam. Nothing could be further from the truth. Besides the prescribed prayers, usually referred to as 'salat', there is du'a, the cry of the heart. To draw a clear-cut distinction between the two would be wrong, for at the end of salat the Muslim is encouraged to sit back on his heels, still kneeling and petition God directly in the language in which he feels most at home. At this point Urdu, or English, may be used, rather than Arabic.

It is also difficult to separate salat from du'a, because it is always permissible for the prayer times to be observed in the home rather than in the mosque, though men should at least attend the mosque for noon prayers on Friday. For women, salat is generally a form of private devotion, because it is performed in the home, perhaps with other women of the family and the children, but often alone. Just as salat needs no prayer leader, so du'a can be said at any time. The words of Muhammad to his daughter apply to all Muslims, 'O Fatima, daughter of Muhammad, I shall be of no help to you before Allah'.

Du'a comes most naturally at the end of salat. The worshipper raises the hands, palms upwards to about the level of the chin, and petitions God on his own behalf and for others, remembering such verses from the Qur'an as:

> 'If my servants ask about me, I am near, and I answer the call of the caller if he calls upon me.'

> (Sura 2:183)

However, many Muslims are aware that Muhammad, near to despair, once cried to God :

> 'O Lord, I make my complaint unto thee of my helplessness and my insignificance before mankind. But thou art the Lord of the poor and feeble, and thou art my Lord. Into whose hands wilt thou abandon me?'

As the need comes, so may they pray. At the end of du'a, if the palms have been stretched out to God they will be wiped over the face in a gesture symbolising the receipt of God's blessing.

The subha. Muslims may also use a kind of rosary. It is called a subha in Arabic or a tasbi (sometimes tasbir) in Turkish and related languages. These come from words meaning to praise, for the subha is an instrument for counting the wonderful names of God used in praising him. Islam speaks of God as having a hundred names. Besides being known as Allah, which simply means 'the God' in Arabic, the supreme being is also known as the Compassionate, the Merciful, the Holy One, the Loving One, the Truth, and the Eternal. In all there are a hundred names, so on the subha there a hundred beads of wood, bone, or other materials strung together. As each bead is passed through the hand, the user meditates upon one of the names of God. The subha is, therefore, an aid to concentration and to keeping a tally of the praises offered to God. By uttering God's names the believer comes to be more aware of the presence and inner reality of God who is nearer to us than our jugular vein (Sura 50:16). Elsewhere in the Qur'an occurs this verse:

> 'Hast thou not seen that God knows whatever is in the heaven and whatsoever is on the earth? Three men do not confer secretly together but he is the fourth, neither five but he is the sixth, neither fewer than that or more, but he is with them wherever they may be.'

> (Sura 58:7)

Through thinking of God with or without the aid of the subha the Muslim can become aware of the presence whose nearness is assured in these words.

In the mosque, in the home, sometimes as they walk down the street, Muslims can be seen passing the beads of the subha through their fingers and bearing a silent witness to the belief that there is no place where God is not to be found. Frequently the Qur'an is used as a help to private devotion. Often it will be put on a lectern no higher than a stool and the reader will kneel in front of it, oblivious to whatever is taking place around him as he studies and muses upon the sacred teachings of the scripture. However, the use of the subha or the reading of the Qur'an is not a substitute for the faithful saying of prayers five times a day. It is an additional act of piety.

The Sikh gurdwara

Wherever there is a Sikh community, however small it may be, one is likely to find a gurdwara. It may be in a village in East Africa or India, it may be a large and imposing building in Delhi or it may be a converted terrace house in one of the large industrial towns of Britain. Strictly speaking, a gurdwara is any room in which a copy of the Sikh scriptures is installed. Many homes contain a gurdwara because Sikhs who can accommodate it properly, that is by giving it a room of its own, often keep a copy of the Guru Granth Sahib in an upstairs room of their home, to be read every day.

The first Sikh communities came into existence about 1521 when Guru Nanak came to the end of his preaching journeys and settled in Kartarpur, where he remained until his death in 1539. Many of his followers must have joined him there and stayed with him, enjoying his company every day. But there must have been other Sikhs who were able to visit him only rarely. Guru Nanak put his teaching into poetic form, and these followers must have memorised his songs or hymns and sung them when they met together for worship. Sikhism is a congregational religion. Guru Nanak and his successors often spoke of the importance of the sangat, the congregation of believers. In one of the hymns he said:

'Man becomes good in good company, it helps him to pursue virtue and cleanses him of vices.'

(AG 414)

In another he went even further:

'The company of those who cherish the true Lord who is within, turns mortals into godly people.'

(AG 228)

Guru Nanak wrote at least 974 hymns of varying lengths, and some of the other Gurus matched or exceeded this tremendous output. Before long it was necessary to provide written copies of these religious songs; it may have been done even before Guru Nanak died. From Sikh congregations probably meeting daily to sing God's praises the gurdwara began.

The first gurdwaras. In 1604 the fifth Guru, Arjan, made an official collection of his own hymns, those of his predecessors, and some compositions of non-Sikhs like the Muslims, Kabir and Sheikh Farid, and the Hindus Ravidas, Beni and Ramanand. The Guru installed this book in a newly constructed building in Amritsar, the Harimandir, or 'house of God', and bowed before it, thus showing that the teaching was more important than his own person. Handwritten copies of the book were distributed to Sikh communities to be used by them in worship. These places came to be known as gurdwaras not long after this time and they have been called by that name ever since. The word means literally, 'The Guru's door';

the best translation is 'God's house', for the true Guru is God himself, the one from whom the ten Gurus received their enlightenment and message. Previously the buildings or rooms used by Sikhs for worship had been called dharmsalas. In India this name is given to any place where rest and accommodation may be found by travellers. Perhaps Sikhs used it to signify that the dharmsala was a place of spiritual refreshment and comfort.

In 1708 the last of the ten Gurus died. His final significant act was to install the book containing the scriptures as Guru. God, speaking through the teachings of the Guru Granth Sahib, was now to be the only teacher of the Sikhs. The gurdwara in its internal details emphasises this.

The appearance of the gurdwara. The external appearance of a gurdwara is unimportant and without significance. Many, especially those associated with the ten Gurus, such as that marking the place where Guru Tegh Bahadur died, or where Guru Gobind Singh was born, are elaborate and majestic, but many village gurdwaras do not catch the eye. In Britain, terraced houses, former churches, and at least one day school have been converted into gurdwaras. In Huddersfield and Bradford, purpose-built gurdwaras have been constructed. One feature, common to all gurdwaras the world over, distinguishes them from other buildings. This is the Sikh flag, the nishan sahib, comprising a double-edged sword, two scimitar-like swords, and a circle, on a saffron background. The two-edged sword, the khanda, is a symbol of the teaching that Sikhs must be prepared to fight for the truth with the weapons of the spirit and, if need be, using physical force. The cutting swords, known as kirpans, represent the spiritual and temporal powers which the Gurus wielded. The chakra or circle has many meanings for Indians. It reminds the Sikh that God is one and that he is inseparably united with God through his faith. Another symbol which may be seen outside many gurdwaras is one formed by two Punjabi letters,

ik oankar, ੧ ੴ, meaning 'God is the one being or eternal reality'.

The Guru Granth Sahib. Inside the gurdwara, the attention of even the most casual observer is immediately drawn to the Guru Granth Sahib under its canopy. The Gurus of the sixteenth and seventeenth centuries would sit in a special place from which they would teach their followers. Someone would stand behind the Guru holding a large fan or parasol over his head, not to shelter him from the sun but as a way of showing respect. Now the scripture is enthroned and is itself a Guru and has a canopy over it for the same reason.

When the scripture is not being read, the book should be covered with a piece of silk cloth called a romalla.

In some gurdwaras the Guru Granth Sahib is put in a special room at night and ceremonially placed on its dais early in the morning. At Amritsar, the scripture is put on a palanquin and carried in procession by a number of bearers from the Golden Temple—where it is read continuously during the day—to the place where it is kept at night. The two names used by Sikhs for the dais are significant. One is palki, which sounds like palanquin and has the same meaning; the other is takht, meaning throne.

The Guru Granth Sahib may stand in any position in the gurdwara. There is no requirement that it should be at the east end, facing Amritsar, or pointing in any other direction. Usually it will stand opposite the main entrance, simply for the sake of convenience. It will be set a little way away from the wall so that the reader can pass round to the back of it easily, but also, as we have seen, to enable marriage parties to walk round it ceremonially.

There is only one other feature common to all gurdwaras: there are no seats. The congregation sits on the floor at the foot of the Guru Granth Sahib. The lack of seating serves two purposes. It deliberately emphasises the unique status of the scripture which is raised up on its throne and it demonstrates very clearly the equality of all those who sit in its presence. Kings or queens, prime ministers or presidents, all are the equal of the youngest child or the poorest peasant before the Guru Granth Sahib.

The role of the gurdwara. The main function of the gurdwara is to be a place where Sikhs can assemble to meditate upon the words of the Guru Granth Sahib and to sing God's praise. The Guru Granth Sahib was composed with both these objects in mind. However, the gurdwara also serves a number of other purposes. In India travellers can find temporary accommodation there. The hungry can obtain a free meal in its kitchen. Clinics and dispensaries often operate in its precincts. In Britain it is the social centre of the Sikh community. Sometimes gatherings will be arranged, such as youth clubs or a weekday afternoon women's meeting for worship. At other times friends will sit in one of its rooms to enjoy an informal chat. The gurdwara plays an essential educational role in Britain. The children of Asian parents are growing up with English, not Urdu, Punjabi or some other Indian language, as their mother tongue. Their mothers and fathers are anxious that if they lose the language they will lose their culture. Therefore Sikh parents send their children to the gurdwara to learn Punjabi, to acquire the skill

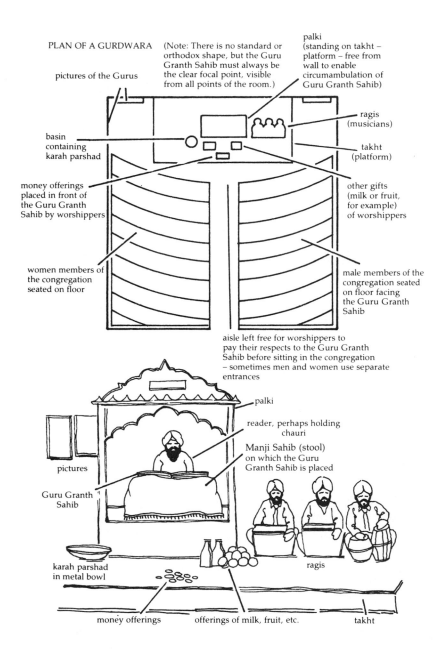

PLAN OF A GURDWARA (Note: There is no standard or orthodox shape, but the Guru Granth Sahib must always be the clear focal point, visible from all points of the room.)

pictures of the Gurus

palki (standing on takht – platform – free from wall to enable circumambulation of Guru Granth Sahib)

ragis (musicians)

basin containing karah parshad

takht (platform)

money offerings placed in front of the Guru Granth Sahib by worshippers

other gifts (milk or fruit, for example) of worshippers

women members of the congregation seated on floor

male members of the congregation seated on floor facing the Guru Granth Sahib

aisle left free for worshippers to pay their respects to the Guru Granth Sahib before sitting in the congregation – sometimes men and women use separate entrances

palki

reader, perhaps holding chauri

Manji Sahib (stool) on which the Guru Granth Sahib is placed

pictures

Guru Granth Sahib

karah parshad in metal bowl

ragis

money offerings

offerings of milk, fruit, etc.

takht

Diagram of a gurdwara

203

of reading the Guru Granth Sahib properly, to be taught the doctrines of Sikhism, and to be helped to take their place as adult members of the community.

Perhaps the changed social role of the gurdwara in Britain can most easily be seen with regard to weddings and funerals. In the Punjab, where the weather is usually predictable, weddings often take place in the open air, perhaps on the flat roof of a house, possibly in the bride's home, anywhere where a copy of the scripture, which may have been carried in procession from the gurdwara, has been installed. In Britain weddings generally take place in the gurdwara, often during the Sunday service. In the Punjab funerals are normally conducted at the cremation ground on the day after the person has died. British Sikhs usually hold a service in the gurdwara, before taking the body to the crematorium, though the coffin is not taken into the room where the service is held, in front of the Guru Granth, but left in the entrance hall or put in a side room.

Sikh worship. In the days of the first ten Gurus worship must often have taken place in their presence and been led by them. It would have consisted of singing the hymns they had composed and listening to their teachings. Nowadays Sikh worship is faithful to the same principles. The hymns of the Guru Granth Sahib are sung by the congregation and someone explains their meaning in lectures or sermons. Just as the early Sikhs would visit Guru Nanak whenever they could, and those who lived near him probably worshipped with him daily, early in the morning and in the evening when their day's work was done, so Sikhs today offer prayers in the gurdwara at any time of day. However, in Britain, because Sunday is a public holiday, this has become the occasion when most Sikhs go to the gurdwara, though many still worship there on weekday evenings. Sikhs have no fixed holy day, so they can easily accommodate themselves to the customs of the land in which they are living.

Worship does not usually begin at a stated time. Early in the morning the Guru Granth Sahib will be installed on the manji and a verse read at random from it. Gradually the room will begin to fill. A group of musicians will sit near the scripture and sing verses from the book. Perhaps someone will read, or rather intone or chant, the hymn, then the musicians will sing it, encouraging the congregation to join them. Finally someone may explain the significance of the passage. This may be done by anyone, the reader, a musician, some member of the congregation, or a visitor from India or from another gurdwara. After one hymn will come another, possibly by a different groups of musicians. Some British gurdwaras train their young people in the singing of the gurbani, as the scripture is often called, and a group of them, playing guitars as well as the traditional hand drums and harmonium, may lead a section of the worship. The language of worship is Punjabi because this is the language of the scripture and of most Sikhs. There is nothing, however, to prevent the use of other languages. There have been services in English in Britain, but Punjabi will remain the language of Sikh worship, even in Britain and the USA, for many years to come.

Throughout the act of worship men, women and children will continually enter and leave the room. Each person who enters the room approaches the Guru Granth Sahib, bows and kneels in front of it until the head touches the floor, and makes an offering of money; a romalla, or food to be used in the kitchen of the gurdwara, may be offered as well. After paying respect to the teachings of God which the scripture contains, the worshipper will sit on the floor in the congregation. Usually men sit on one side in front of the Guru Granth Sahib, and women sit on the other, with a narrow

A Sikh congregation offering the prayer Ardas in front of the Guru Granth Sahib at the end of an act of worship.

passage left between them. Everyone in the gurdwara but the smaller children will wear a head covering. As the women enter the building they pull their muslin scarves over their hair, and those men and boys who are not wearing turbans will tie handkerchieves on their heads. No one wears shoes. Removing shoes on entering a place of worship is an ancient and widespread custom. Moses did it when he became aware of being in God's presence at the burning bush (Exodus Chapter 3). Covering the head is also a feature of many religions—see St. Paul's teaching in I Corinthians chapter II, for example. Sikhs follow these customs because for them coming into the presence of the Guru Granth Sahib is coming into the presence of God.

Ardas. The rather informal service may last anything from one hour to four or five. Its end is marked by the one set prayer and the one ritual act which characterises all Sikh ceremonies. The first is a prayer known as Ardas. After the congregation have been sitting for the earlier part of the service, they stand as one of their members comes between them and the scripture and, facing the Guru Granth Sahib, addresses God on behalf of the assembly.

The prayer is in three parts. First the Sikhs are told to remember God and the ten Gurus, then to keep the teachings of the Guru Granth Sahib with the same fidelity as that shown by famous Sikhs of the past. Thirdly, God's blessing is sought upon the Sikh community and the whole of mankind. At the end of this section specific prayers are made, perhaps for a couple who have been married during the service, for the sick or in memory of a member who has recently died. Sometimes there may be a thanksgiving for a member's examination success or a wedding anniversary.

During Ardas a member of the congregation lifts the cover of a container and puts the blade of his kirpan, a short sword, into a heated mixture inside it. This is karah parshad, made of flour or semolina, butter, sugar and water. After Ardas the congregation sits and a number of people distribute karah parshad to everyone while the gurdwara secretary reads the notices. Everyone, including non-Sikh visitors will be given a small portion of karah parshad which they will eat with their right hand. By eating together Sikhs wish to demonstrate that all are equal before God, and to ensure that no one goes away from his presence hungry. The meal also symbolises the belief that God's nature is to bless mankind. The sweet food is chosen with that meaning in mind.

Langar. After worship on a Sunday, or especially if the anniversary of a Guru's birth or death is being commemorated, a full meal will be served in the dining room of the gurdwara. This is called langar, the 'free kitchen' which has been an important aspect of Sikhism since the days of Guru Nanak. It has the same meaning as the sharing of karah parshad. Occasionally langar expands from the dining hall of the gurdwaras to the street outside. In the month of May or June, Sikhs remember the death of their fifth leader, Guru Arjan. Even in England the weather is sometimes sunny and warm, so langar is held in the open air. Passers-by may find themselves offered a glass of squash or an orange by Sikhs inviting them to share in the celebrations. In India it is quite common for Christians, Hindus, Muslims and Sikhs to enjoy one another's festivals.

Private devotion. Sikhs are encouraged to regard themselves as members of the local Sikh community, the sangat, and the world-wide brotherhood of Sikhs, the Panth. They should, therefore, worship together frequently. However, emphasis is also placed on the belief that God is present in every human being, Guru Nanak said:

> 'The one God pervades every place. He alone dwells in every soul.'

> (AG 433)

The discovery of God within the soul comes as the result of faith and the practice of meditation. In Sikhism this is called Nam simran, or calling God to mind. The idea is that the more one thinks about God and the more acutely and deeply one becomes aware of him, the more one will be filled with his presence. Gradually self-centredness will be replaced by God-centredness.

A verse of the fourth Guru describes the morning devotions of a Sikh:

> 'He who calls himself a Sikh of the great Sat Guru (God), should rise early in the morning and meditate on God's name. He should rise early, take a bath, and make an effort to wash himself in the Pool of Nectar (God). By repeating God's name according to the Guru's instruction, all evil deeds and mistakes will be washed away. Afterwards, at sunrise, he should sing the gurbani and throughout the busy day he should discipline his mind to live in God's presence. The Guru's disciple (Sikh), who contemplates God with every breath and each morsel of food, becomes pleasing to the Guru's mind.'

> (AG 305)

So the Sikh should rise from his bed before dawn and take a bath which symbolises the washing of the soul in God himself. At sunrise he should repeat the thirty-eight verses of the Japji, composed by Guru Nanak, the tenth Guru's hymn with a similar name, the Jap, and some other verses of this Guru, his swayyas. Some Sikhs will follow their private meditation by joining with other Sikhs in a gurdwara service. In the evening, a Sikh should meditate on two other hymns, Rahiras which means the 'Holy Path'; this is recited at dusk, and Sohilla, the vesper hymn, before going to bed. Some Sikhs use a mala or rosary made of cotton to aid them in their meditation. The mala has 108 knots, and these are passed through the fingers one by one, as the devotee repeats the word 'Waheguru', Wonderful Lord. This is perhaps the most popular name of God used by Sikhs.

A family which owns a copy of the Guru Granth Sahib, and therefore has a gurdwara in its house, will hold family prayers in its presence. The pressures of life in Britain may prevent them sitting together in the morning. Perhaps the father leaves for work at seven o'clock and the children must get ready for school. Nevertheless, the family will gather together every evening to listen to scripture passages being read and to say the evening prayers. It is such families that are most successfully transmitting the Sikh way of life to children born in Britain.

Questions

1. Describe the buildings used for worship in **two** different religions. Explain the significance of their main features.

2. Compare the importance of public worship with that of private devotion in **two** of the religions you have studied.

3. Why does it seem important that people should worship in special buildings and at set times? Refer both to public worship and private devotion in your answer.

4. What place does private devotion have in **two** of the faiths you have studied?

5. Is private devotion subordinate to the regular act of worship? Discuss this in relation to any religion you have studied.

6. Which of the following symbolic acts of worship are characteristic of more than one religion? Washing; covering the head; removing footwear; prostration; recitation. Explain their significance.

7. Describe with examples how places of worship have been adapted to the conditions of life in countries far different from those where the religions began.

8. In what ways do the Jewish Sabbath and the Christian Sunday differ? In what respects are they similar?

9. Describe **two** places of worship from different religions, explaining how their plans and furnishings are influenced by beliefs and practices.

10. What uses are **two** of the religious buildings that you have studied put to besides being a place of worship?

11. How important do women seem to be in the devotional life of **two** religions which you have studied?

12. Sometimes a building like a church or mosque is said to preach 'a sermon in stones'. What might you learn about a religion by visiting one of its places of worship? What more might you learn by attending an act of worship?

A Christian church in Uganda. The architecture of the building has clearly been influenced by European traditions.

CHAPTER FOUR
PILGRIMAGE

'Who would true valour see,
Let him come hither;
One here will constant be,
Come wind come weather;
There's no discouragement
Shall make him once relent
His first avowed intent
To be a pilgrim.'

This is the first verse of one of the most famous of Christian hymns. It is to be found in the best-known Christian book to have been written in the English language, *Pilgrim's Progress* (1678), the work of a tinker's son called John Bunyan. Although the author was in prison when he wrote these words, he could still view the whole of his life as a pilgrimage, a journey undertaken on behalf of God, a form of devotion, an act of worship.

Some Muslims have shared this view, believing that men and women of true piety perform the pilgrimage to Mecca, the Hajj, by the way they live even if they never leave their own village, just as surely as the person who travels to the holy city. The story is told of a man who saved up for many years and was about to undertake the journey from Persia to Mecca with some of his friends. He noticed a poor man who was so hungry that he was cooking a chicken which had died a natural death. The pilgrim gave his money to the poor man, and told his friends that because he felt unwell he would have to delay his journey. They went on to Mecca while he sadly remained at home. When they returned they congratulated him on completing the Hajj. 'But I never went,' he said. 'We saw you many times,' his friends replied. 'We had a vision in which Allah told us that you had made the most wonderful pilgrimage.'

The nature and meaning of pilgrimage

. True pilgrimage is a matter of the heart and mind just as much as undertaking a difficult journey. Those who visit holy places may go searching for a sense of peace with God and unity with other members of their faith. They may equally well be inspired by a deep faith which they already possess to visit a centre of pilgrimage. Each of the six religions examined in this book attaches some importance to pilgrimage, some more than others. For the Hindu and Buddhist there are many pilgrimages, to Benares, to the source of the river Ganges, to the peaks of mountains and to the shrines of holy men and women. For the Muslim there is one pilgrimage which must be undertaken, the Hajj, to Mecca and places round it. This journey is a pillar of Islam, as important as prayer or the belief in one God. Pilgrimages are not obligatory for Christians and Jews, and many Buddhists and Sikhs would deny that pilgrimage has a place in their religion. Nevertheless, many of the faithful visit Lourdes, Rome, Jerusalem, Masada, Bodh Gaya, or Amritsar, not merely as tourists, but something more.

Pilgrimages and the holy places to which the sacred journey is made often provide in some sense a meeting point between heaven and earth. The place visited usually has some historical significance in the religion. The time of the pilgrimage may be significant too —perhaps the anniversary of the great event. The combination of the two may help the pilgrim to feel that he has passed into God's presence. He is no longer standing in the hot sun at the mouth of a cave near Mecca. He is one in spirit with Muhammad, the Messenger of God, who in that cave received the revelation of the Qur'an. The student who would understand the true meaning of pilgrimage must try to appreciate the feelings and thoughts of those for whom the journey may be the experience of a lifetime.

ॐ Hindu pilgrimage

Some books will give the number of Hindu pilgrimages as fifty-eight, others say 64 000. One thing, however, is clear: the most famous pilgrimage in the world may be the Muslim Hajj, but those performed by Hindus attract enormous support. India sometimes seems to be a country where everyone is on the move. Many of the travellers are making visits to holy places as pilgrims. The kinds of place which are regarded as holy are the banks of rivers, rivers themselves, mountains, coasts and seashores. Such locations seem to have become very significant in Hinduism. Where earth and sky, land and sea meet, where two rivers converge, there a place of pilgrimage is likely to be found.

Famous centres of pilgrimage: Benares.   The most famous centres are usually associated also with stories of the gods. Benares is the most famous of all. The city is situated on the bank of the holiest of rivers, the Ganges, at the point where it is joined by its minor tributary the Varuna, from which the city gets another of its names, Varansi. It is also called Kashi, 'resplendent' because of its temples and religious importance. The town is especially sacred to the god Shiva, who is said to have lived there as an ascetic. It also has associations with the god Rama, and every year in the October-November period of the Dussehra festival the story of the Ramayana is enacted in a thirty-day cycle. It ends with Rama entering the city to claim his throne.

Benares is also visited by the Jains, a small but influential religious group, Buddhists, and to a lesser extent Sikhs, for it is believed that one of the great Jain teachers was born there and that Buddha and Guru Nanak preached there. To die in Benares and have one's ashes thrown into the Ganges is said to bring purification and deliverance from rebirth, even to the most evil of people, but the teachers insist that repentance and faith are also necessary. Pilgrims who return home often take a bottle of Ganges water with them and these can sometimes be seen on shrines in Hindu temples and homes in Britain.

Hardwar.   At the head of the Ganges, where the river leaves the hills and enters the plain of north India, Hardwar is another centre where the ashes of the dead are committed to the river. The name of the city means 'the Lord's gate'. Both at Benares and Hardwar many priests are to be found teaching and studying, and Hindu families will visit them to ask them to perform ceremonies on behalf of their relatives and to record births, marriages and deaths. They will also be consulted for horoscopes.

Vrindaban.   This city on the river Jumna has sometimes been called the Bethlehem of India, for it is regarded as the birthplace of Krishna. The whole district is associated with incidents in his childhood and youth, and there is a special route around the city which pilgrims follow. Sometimes pilgrims to Vrindaban will proceed to Dwarka, a small town on the far western coast of India where Krishna had his palace. It was from Dwarka that he left the world.

Rameshwaram.   Situated in the south of India opposite Sri Lanka,

☐ Place with religious significance for all Hindus in India, attracting many pilgrims

● Place with significance for Hindus of a particular region or sect

Note: Places of pilgrimage are keyed, where
appropriate, by the initial of the principal deity or
form of worship, i.e.

(V) Vaisnava   (S) Saiva
(D) Sakta (Mother Goddess or Devī)

A popular pilgrimage(*tīrtha yātrā*) taking about ten
weeks, mainly by train, involving a round tour of
India

Places of Hindu pilgrimage in India

213

Rameshwaram is sacred to both Vishnu and Shiva. Here Rama, an incarnation of Vishnu, landed with his wife Sita when she had been saved from the demon Ravana. Through killing Ravana's soldiers Rama had become impure, so to purge the pollution and offer thanks he and Sita built a shrine to Shiva and worshipped him at Rameshwaram.

At Puri in Orissa there is one of the most famous of Hindu temples, dedicated to Jagganath, that is to Vishnu, the Master or Lord of the Universe. A statue of Krishna is taken from the temple and paraded round the streets of the town on a huge cart pulled by the people of Puri and enthusiastic pilgrims. The size of the statue on its vehicle is so great that it has given the word 'juggernaut' to the English language.

Besides these examples of well-known national and regional shrines there are many local places of pilgrimage, visited regularly by inhabitants of the region in which they are situated. These may be visited at any time or at particular times of the year, just like the major centres. The most sacred times are obviously the festivals. Holi in spring, or Janamashtami, the birthday of Krishna, in summer, are good times to go to Vrindaban, where he was born. It is said that on spring evenings the faithful may be given a vision of the young man playing his flute to the dancing cow girls. The day before each new moon is sacred to Shiva and his consort Parvati, but to visit a Shaivite pilgrimage centre just before the new moon of January-February is particularly auspicious, for this is Mahashivaratri, the great night of Shiva.

The reasons for pilgrimage. These probably vary from person to person. Some pilgrims seek the feeling of satisfaction that is achieved when a promise has been fulfilled or a kindness done, especially if it has entailed some cost in the form of effort or self-sacrifice. The pilgrim who journeys up one side of the Ganges and down the other, from sea to source and back, may be exhausted when the exercise has been accomplished, but there is the enjoyment of success, of having done what you set out to do. Such a person is sure that the experience will have a lasting value, in this life and beyond. He may express this belief in phrases like 'acquiring merit', or 'gaining good karma', that is building up a balance of good actions to weigh against bad deeds that have been committed. Perhaps he will be visiting the holy places related to Krishna, as did a family from Calcutta who travelled to Vrindaban. The man had taken time from work — with his employer's approval — and was travelling with his wife, two children and recently widowed mother. The journey was being made to comfort his mother and benefit his father and other ancestors, for Hindus have a strong belief in the continuity of life. Those who have not achieved spiritual enlightenment are reborn, and a bond still unites the living and the so-called dead. Children can render kindness to parents and other ancestors who have died by performing rituals on their behalf.

The family from Calcutta was travelling by normal public transport, but some pilgrims use tour buses and go in organised parties, while others still walk every inch of the way. It is possible to witness some pilgrims crawling to shrines, measuring their length in the dusty road, and it is quite common to see them going round the outside of the temple which is their destination on hands and knees. This act of circling, undertaken with the right shoulder towards the sacred place, is called pradakshina.

From the steps on the river bank Hindu pilgrims bathe in the Ganges at Benares.

215

The value of pilgrimage.   In the eyes of those who make the pilgrimage, its value is determined by a number of factors – the importance of the shrine, the distance being travelled, the means of transport used, the purpose for which it was undertaken, and the time of year. To visit Dwarka at Janamashtami, Krishna's birthday, and to go on foot from Delhi, would be better than to make the journey by car from a village a few miles away, at some other time of year. However, no one works out the mathematics of all this; that would be to lose sight of the whole purpose of pilgrimage which is to serve God; whether the effort be great or small he will accept it in the spirit with which it is offered.

Pilgrimage also has a levelling effect in a number of ways. Poor women and men of low caste may travel the same road as Brahmins. At the temple of Jagganath at Orissa, for the time they are there, all barriers of caste disappear. In the Ganges at Benares all receive equal cleansing. The differences between those who worship God in the form of Shiva and those who call God Krishna or Durga also vanish, for no one would think of passing by a place of pilgrimage because it was associated with God under some other name. On a journey to a great shrine one will pass many minor, local ones, and worship will be offered at them all.

The following passage about the battlefield of Kurukshetra, already mentioned on page 59, holy to Vishnu who appeared there as Krishna, Arjuna's charioteer, conveys many ideas about the purpose and worth of pilgrimage. Though it was written many centuries ago, the beliefs expressed in it will still be shared by those Hindus who still go on pilgrimages:

'Originally this place was the holy lake of Brahma. Then it was called Rama's pool. Ploughed by the seer Kuru, it was named Kurukshetra, or Kuru's field. Carrying holy water, the holy Sarasvati now flows deep underneath the middle of this field.

Listening to the instructions of the wise seer Markandeya, that river entered Kurukshetra in a continuous stream. After reaching Rantuka, the Sarasvati flooded Kurukshetra with her holy waters and swept off towards the west, where there are a thousand sacred fords frequented by seers. These I shall celebrate, by the grace of the supreme lord. The memory of those shrines brings merit, the sight of them destroys evil; bathing at them brings release even for wicked men. Those who call to mind the sacred fords, those who please the gods there, those who bathe in them and those who have faith in them gain the supreme goal. Whoever remembers Kurukshetra no matter whether he is clean or unclean, is purified both inside and out. Whoever utters these words, "I shall go to Kurukshetra! I shall live in Kurukshetra!" is released from all evils. Whoever lives on the bank of the Sarasvati, bathing in its waters, shall gain the knowledge of Brahman, without a doubt. Gods, seers and perfected ones frequent this place of the Kurus. Whoever visits it continually sees Brahman within himself. Even criminals with a fickle human nature, if they control themselves out of a desire for release and frequent this place, are freed from the impurities which have accrued to them in many previous lifetimes, and witness a spotless deity eternally dwelling in the heart. Men who continually attend the altar of Brahman, the holy field of Kurukshetra, and lake Sannihita, gain the ultimate goal. For in time, even planets, constellations and stars may fall from the sky, but those who die in Kurukshetra will never fall at all. A man who goes there filled with faith and who bathes in the great pool Sthanu, wins whatever his heart desires; of this there is no doubt. A man should practise self-control, circumambulate the lake, go to Rantuka to seek forgiveness again and again, bathe in the Sarasvati, offer flowers and incense and food to the god, and recite the following: "By your grace, I shall make a pilgrimage to whatever sacred fords, forest and rivers there may be. Make my way ever clear!" '

(from *The Vamana Saromahatmya*, quoted in *A Reader in the Sanskrit Puranas*, ed. C. Dimmitt & J. A. B. Buitenen, Philadelphia 1978, pp. 328–9.)

✡ Pilgrimage in Judaism

There is no obligation upon Jews to make a pilgrimage to any holy place associated with their religion. However, in recent years, since the establishment of the independent state of Israel in 1947, there has been a growing tendency among Jews to visit that country. For many the journey to Israel, even for a holiday, might be regarded as a pilgrimage in itself.

In Israel the pilgrimage may take on a number of aspects. For some, especially the young, it may become a stay at a kibbutz. This is a cooperative farm run by volunteers. It is often situated in difficult countryside, rough, barren and uncultivated, where Jews are attempting to make the wilderness blossom like a rose, as the prophet Isaiah said. For these people the pilgrimage is one of work, attempting to establish a nation.

Yad Vashem. Other pilgrims may go to Yad Vashem, a place in Jerusalem which is a memorial to those who died in the holocaust and to the 'righteous Gentiles' who courageously helped some Jews to survive. Yad Vashem means 'eternal memorial', and the name was inspired by other words found in the Isaiah scroll:

217

'Instead of the thorn shall come up the fir tree, and instead of the brier shall come up the myrtle tree: and it shall be to the Lord for a name, for an everlasting sign that shall not be cut off.'

(Isaiah 55:13)

Perhaps the most moving experience for those who visit Yad Vashem is that of standing in the bare room, lit only by a single flickering candle, and looking down to read the names, embedded in the floor, of the concentration camps. There are hardly any British Jews who have not lost a relative or friend in the holocaust, and therefore a pilgrimage to Yad Vashem is a particularly poignant experience, whether or not they can bear to visit the Holocaust Museum which is part of it.

Masada. In the year 73 CE, the strong fortress of Masada finally fell to the Tenth Legion of the Roman army. A small band of desperate defenders, with their families, had held out there for three years and were only beaten when the Romans built a massive artificial mound against the cliffside in order to overwhelm the defences. Many people visit Masada as tourists, but those who go as pilgrims remember the dedication of the Jews who sought refuge there and commit themselves to maintaining their faith and their heritage. Often this takes the form of support for the cause of Zionism, the protection of the Jewish homeland, now the state of Israel. Their feelings may be summed up in the slogan 'Masada shall not fall again', carried on stamps and medals struck in 1973 to mark the two-thousandth anniversary of the heroic defence of the fortress.

The Western Wall. The feeling of the pilgrim when he comes to the most significant site in Israel is very different. That place is the Western Wall of the Temple in Jerusalem, and the mood is probably one of lamentation and piety. This is all that remains of the Temple, rebuilt by Herod the Great and his successors on the site of the temple of Solomon, which had been destroyed when the Jews were taken captive to Babylon in the sixth century BCE. Sometimes it has been nicknamed 'the wailing wall', because it is possible to find pilgrims overcome by grief as they stand before this last relic of the building that features so prominently in the Bible. Some will press their lips to the stones as they offer prayers.

In the book of Daniel is the story of how that great Jew was commanded to cease praying to the God he believed in. When Daniel knew of the royal edict we read that, 'He went to his house where he had windows in his upper room open towards Jerusalem,

218

and he got down on his knees three times a day and gave thanks before his God as he had done previously.' (Daniel 6:10). The Temple was in his mind as he prayed. The Ark, the cupboard in which the scrolls are kept in the synagogue, is set in the wall nearest the Temple. Not surprisingly, then, it is the desire of many Jews to offer their prayers at the one remaining wall of the Temple. Although pilgrimages to Israel have become very popular since 1947, there are many records of Jews throughout the centuries making their way on foot to Palestine, even from places as far away as Spain or Baghdad. Praying at the Western Wall was the high point of their pilgrimage.

Pilgrims at the Western Wall, Jerusalem. It is the only surviving reminder of the massive building work undertaken by Herod the Great.

Pilgrimage in Buddhism

Buddhists are not obliged to go on physical pilgrimages to sacred places, but they should follow the Eightfold Path, a basic piece of Buddhist teaching which uses the image of a journey and is set out in Chapter One. Making the effort to visit a teacher is more important than going to a specific place, but pilgrimages to holy places are not discouraged if they help people to understand or practise their religion better. There are many famous pilgrimage centres. Some of them are described below.

Four important places in Gautama Buddha's life

Before he died, Gautama Buddha said that four places which had been important in his life could be visited with feelings of reverence. These sites flourished until Buddhism faded out of India between the seventh and twelfth centuries CE. They then became derelict. In the late nineteenth century CE, with the help of a new society—named after the great temple at Bodh Gaya, and called the Mahabodhi Society—a Buddhist called Anagarika Dharmapala went from Sri Lanka to India to restore these notable centres.

1. The Lumbini Grove. This is near Kapilavatthu, in present-day Nepal, and is the birthplace of the Buddha. The event is marked by an inscription on a pillar translated 'here the Buddha was born'. The pillar was put there by the Emperor Ashoka in the third century BCE. There are a few monks, two temples, and a pool at this remote site. The journey from the nearest railway station is half-an-hour by local bus, and then hour after hour on a cycle rickshaw, or on foot. For a Buddhist, the more effort a pilgrimage involves the greater the blessing brought by the journey. There is a very real sense of walking 'in the footsteps of the Buddha', even though the rural landscape is more arid than in his time. A woman described what she did while she was there:

> 'I sat for half an hour by the pool and meditated, thinking of the Buddha's birth and also the death of his mother soon after. Eventually, after he became Buddha, he was able to find her in the heaven she had gone to, and could teach her Dharma so that she could gain liberation. I thought to myself, "What greater thing can one do for one's mother than this?"'

The great Bodhi Tree at Bodh Gaya which is honoured by the meditation of pilgrims. In the foreground the Buddha's presence is symbolised by footprints in large circles of stone.

2. Bodh Gaya.   Near Gaya in Bihar, this is the site of the Buddha's enlightenment. It is the most sacred place of pilgrimage in the Buddhist world. There is a descendant of the very tree—called the Bodhi Tree or Bo Tree for short—under which the Buddha sat at the time of his great experience. Buddhists feel that the place 'where it actually happened' must be full of spiritual power, which is intensified by the constant flow of pilgrims. Visiting Bodh Gaya earns merit for a better rebirth, bestows blessings on the pilgrim and makes a karmic connection with the place where, some Buddhists believe, all buddhas are enlightened. The pilgrims walk round the tree in a clockwise direction. This practice is called circumambulation (from 'circum'—'around', and 'ambulation'—'walking'). The tree is made the focus of their respect and attention. They also make flower offerings, decorate the tree with prayer flags printed with sacred texts and meditate underneath it.

Next to the Bodhi Tree is the Mahabodhi, or Great Enlightenment Temple. Its foundations date from the second or third century CE, but there were earlier buildings, and this one has been constantly reconstructed. It has a fifty-nine-metre tower, and houses an image of the Buddha at the moment of enlightenment. Here pilgrims offer light, incense and flowers. They also make offerings to members of the Sangha, who are fellow pilgrims or who live there, and meditate on the meaning of enlightenment.

There are many rest-houses at Bodh Gaya. They are associated with the different Buddhist countries, and run by monks from the different traditions. This gives visiting Bodh Gaya a social dimension, and Buddhists feel part of a world-wide community in this microcosm of the Buddhist world.

3. The Deer Park at Sarnath.   Situated a few kilometres from Benares or Varanasi in Uttar Pradesh, this is where the Buddha preached his first sermon. The focus for the pilgrim is a statue of the Buddha preaching, which is in the Mulaganghakati vihara there.

4. Kushinara. Here, near modern Kasia in Uttar Pradesh, is the site of the Buddha's death. A temple commemorates the Buddha's final Nirvana. There are also modern Tibetan, Burmese and Chinese monasteries and the ruins of many ancient stupas, dominated by one huge mound fifteen to eighteen metres across. When the Buddha died he was cremated, and his ashes divided into eight parts. These were taken to various sites and burial mounds or stupas, built over them. The stupa has become a distinctive architectural feature of the Buddhist world. (Chapter Three describes them in detail, and a diagram appears on page 147). The text which gives an account of the Buddha's death says about the stupas:

> 'Whoever shall place there garlands or perfumes or paint or make salutation there, or become in its presence calm in heart—that shall long be to them for profit and joy.'

Buddhists circumambulate stupas three times in honour of the Buddha Dharma and Sangha, and also use them as a focus for meditation. To see a stupa in ruins may even add to its meaning. One Buddhist said that the stupa by which she chose to meditate was reduced to ground level—almost nothing there at all—but the blessing was the same. Seeing it made her think of impermanence, and of how lucky she was to follow Dharma when old age made her life difficult, and concentrate on the things that are undying.

Further sites which are important to Buddhists. Buddhists who are unable to visit the sacred sites in India have always had more local alternatives. Cuttings from the Bodhi Tree, for example, have been taken all over the Buddhist world. One of the most famous is at Anuradhapura in Sri Lanka. It is hung with offerings of pieces of cloth and approached with bare feet and head, in the same way as the one at Bodh Gaya.

The original relics of the Buddha in eight stupas were further divided by Ashoka into many parts, and relics have travelled to all parts of the Buddhist world, including England. Burma has a hair relic which is in the great stupa in Rangoon called the Shwe Dagon Pagoda. Lay Buddhists who visit the pagoda buy a little gold leaf to be placed on its beautiful roof to honour the memory of the Buddha. Another famous relic is in a miniature stupa in the Tooth Relic Temple in Kandy, Sri Lanka. This is honoured at an annual festival with a parade of ceremonial elephants (see Chapter Five). The relics, which are placed in portable reliquaries as well as in the centre of stupas, may be of a great Buddhist teacher, or a fragment from an old scripture, as well as of the Buddha. What matters is that these are a reminder of the Dharma, and that these reminders help the pilgrim to grow closer to the Buddhist goal of Nirvana. The motive of the pilgrim is very important. Buddhists stress that there are different levels of intentions and goals. The first is the search for practical help with sickness or personal problems. The second is the desire to gain merit for a better rebirth. These are lower goals than the third, which is the search for that wisdom, loving-kindness and compassion which will lead to Nirvana. The reminders of the Buddha, Dharma and Sangha which the pilgrims see help them along their path.

Other famous places of pilgrimage

Adam's Peak or Sri Pada in Sri Lanka. Some spots have been considered 'holy places' for so long in a country's history that it is not possible to say when, or even quite why, worship or pilgrimage began there. Often when the religion of the country changes the place is just taken over by a new group who 'recycle' it for their own purposes. Such places are often of outstanding natural beauty, or in a commanding natural position. Adam's Peak is a mountain over 2243 metres high. At the top of the mountain is a mark in the rock which looks like a giant footprint. For Buddhists this represents, or is a symbol of, Gautama Buddha who, they believe, visited the island three times during his lifetime. On the last occasion the tradition says he landed on this mountain and the footprint records this. Strictly speaking, the Buddhist name for the mountain is Sri Pada. 'Sri' is a title which can be translated 'honourable' or even 'holy'. 'Pada' means 'a footprint' and right from earliest times a footprint has represented the Buddha and his teaching. There is a famous one near the Bodhi Tree at Bodh Gaya which is strewn with flowers by devotees.

The fact that the commonest name for the mountain is Adam's Peak, despite the fact that Sri Lanka is predominantly Buddhist, shows how a pilgrimage site can be shared. Muslims say that the mark was made by Adam, who landed on this mountain when he was hurled out of paradise. This acknowledges the age of the site as a sacred place. Hindus associate the footprint with the god Siva or Saman, and the Portugese Christians linked it with Thomas the Apostle.

A mountain pilgrimage site is difficult both to reach and to climb, but for the Buddhist the more difficulties there are, the greater spiritual benefit the pilgrimage will bring. Every pilgrimage should involve effort. The 'classical' route from Ratnapura is not possible in the wet season. Most people go in March. From Ratnapura it is twenty-five kilometres to the top of the peak. The first fourteen kilometres can be covered by vehicle, but the last eleven have to be on foot. This last part is usually climbed during the night, and the steps are nowadays illuminated with electric light bulbs. There are frequent places where pilgrims can rest and have refreshments, but many prefer not to. The ideal is to set all worldly comforts on one side.

At the top, the pilgrims ring a bell to mark their arrival. The climax of the night ascent is to see dawn break from the top of the mountain. Often the triangular shadow of the peak is superimposed on the surrounding countryside in the dawn light. The struggle and tiredness of the night gives way to a joy in a completed task and the beauty of sunrise. This dramatic coming of light is symbolic of enlightenment itself, towards which the pilgrim is moving.

Borobudur.   This is a place in Java. Buddhism arrived here in the fifth century CE. In the eighth and ninth centuries an elaborate and highly symbolic stupa was built. Buddhism has declined in Java since the fifteenth century CE and the stupa has been restored in the last twenty years to save it from decay. It is still visited by many Buddhists, and has been called the greatest Buddhist monument outside India.

The general shape of a stupa can be seen from the illustration on page 147. At Borobudur the shape is set in circular and square terraces, so that the pilgrims can walk round and up from the bottom to the top. This means they circumambulate it and climb it at the same time. The four lower terraces, square in shape, are carved with vivid scenes from the Buddha's lives in animal and human forms, when he was working towards enlightenment. His is the example that the pilgrims hope to follow, and there are occasional Buddha images to remind them of the goal. Above the square earthly terraces are three round 'heavenly circles'. On these

A view of the pilgrim terraces around the great stupa at Borobodur in Java.

round terraces pilgrims will see a decreasing number of small stupas in stone latticework—thirty-two, then twenty-four, then sixteen. Inside each is a stone Buddha. At the very top is one, imageless stupa. The pilgrim has passed from the hectic, intricate scenes of the world, to the simpler calm of the Buddha images and on to the perfect, formless circle of Nirvana. Each pilgrim gains something different from the climb. Some spend most of their time on the lower carvings and take away a vivid moral inspiration. A monk might climb straight to the top and sit in meditation. There is something for everyone.

✝ Pilgrimage in Christianity

In Christianity, as in Judaism, pilgrimages are not regarded as essential. Indeed many Christians, mostly Protestant, see no worth in such expressions of piety. Before the sixteenth-century Reformation, when the Western Church became divided, pilgrimages formed an important aspect of the spiritual, social and economic life of the Church. Those who undertook long journeys believing that prayers offered at the English shrines of Thomas Becket, or St. Alban or that of St. Peter at Rome were particularly meritorious and helpful for themselves and their loved ones, also expressed their devotion by making gifts to enrich the churches. The money they paid for board and lodging on the way often made inns situated on the pilgrimage routes extremely wealthy. Clearly, advantage could be taken of the piety of the pilgrims, and sometimes even the travellers had mixed motives, as anyone who reads Chaucer's *Canterbury Tales* will know. The author pokes fun at some of the pilgrims and is justly critical of them, but he respects the sincerity of others.

The Reformers in their zeal saw only the worst side of such practices as pilgrimage — the superstition of the faithful, but not their piety, and the get-rich-by-any-means tactics of those who had custody of the holy places. Nowadays, though the shopkeepers of Rome or Canterbury may treat pilgrims like all other tourists, the churches are careful to avoid the charge of commercialism. They provide special facilities for pilgrims, opportunities for quiet meditation, spiritual guidance and a variety of acts of worship.

Holy sites, past and present. Christian places of pilgrimage vary as much as those of other faiths. Some of the holy wells of Ireland and other parts of Europe are sites which were regarded as holy long before the appearance of Christianity. What has happened is that these places have been 'Christianised'. Instead of being dedicated to a local deity or the spirit of the place, they are now called St Mary's, St Cuthbert's, or St Bridget's Well. Many sites commemorate important episodes in Christian history. For example, it is highly likely that St Peter's Basilica in Rome is built over the grave of Simon Peter, the apostle. In England Alban, a Roman citizen,

This illustration of the martyrdom of Thomas Becket was probably produced within forty years of his murder. (*By courtesy of the Trustees of the British Museum*)

was beheaded on a hilltop north of the city then called Verulamium. There can be little doubt that St Alban's cathedral now stands where he suffered a martyr's death and the city is now named after the saint. On the other hand, Canterbury cathedral already existed before it became a famous centre of pilgrimage. In 1170 its archbishop, Thomas Becket, was killed inside the abbey. Within three years he was proclaimed a saint and soon pilgrims were flocking to his tomb, and churches were dedicated to him throughout England.

During the nineteenth and twentieth centuries many new pilgrimages have become customary to places where people have seen visions of the Virgin Mary, the mother of Jesus. Knock in Ireland, Fatima in Portugal and Lourdes in France, are examples.

Knock. Pilgrimages to most Christian shrines may be made at any time of the year, but anniversaries are regarded as particularly important. For instance, Pope John Paul II visited Knock in 1979, exactly a century after some of the local people were granted a vision of Mary.

Knock is a small village in County Mayo in the Irish Republic. It would have remained unknown had it not been for the events of 21st August 1879. Shortly after seven o'clock on that Sunday evening Margaret Beirne locked up the church and began to make her way home. She became aware of a bright light, but ignored it in her eagerness to get home to welcome her mother who was expected back from a holiday. Half an hour later the priest's housekeeper passed the church and noticed on the gable:

> 'a wonderful number of strange figures or appearances at the gable; one like the blessed virgin, another like Saint Joseph, another a bishop. I saw an altar. I was wondering to see such an extraordinary group, yet I passed on and said nothing, thinking that the archdeacon had been supplied with these wonderful figures from Dublin and had said nothing about them, but had left them outside in the open air. I saw a bright light about them . . . I thought the whole thing strange.'

The housekeeper, Mary McLoughlin, was on her way to see Margaret Beirne and stayed with her for about half an hour. When she left Margaret walked with her some way along the road, a natural Irish gesture of politeness. She, too, saw the figures on the church and asked who had placed them there. It was only then that the housekeeper realised that the archdeacon could not have installed them. He had been away in another parish all day. Looking at them carefully, they noticed that they were moving. The women now realised that this was a vision and fetched others, who shared their experience. Not long afterwards a Commission of Investigation was set up by the Roman Catholic church, and efforts were made to ensure that the visions were neither hoax nor hallucination. Meanwhile pilgrims began to converge on Knock and to remove stones and even pieces of mortar from the church walls. A little later, a man whose deafness had not responded to the treatment even of a leading specialist, went to Knock and returned cured. The specialist was the father of the famous Irish dramatist Oscar Wilde. Though church officials were reluctant to support the claims of Knock to have been the site of a holy vision, the curious, the pious and the hopeful sick continued to come and many went away with their health restored. Since the Pope's visit to Knock in 1979 it has become the most famous modern place of Roman Catholic pilgrimage in the British Isles.

Lourdes. This French town at the foot of the Pyrenees is the most important international centre of modern Christian pilgrimage. It was here that a girl called Bernadette, born in 1844, had a series of visions of Mary the mother of Jesus between February 11th and July 16th 1858. There were eighteen appearances in all. Each took place at the Grotto of Massabiele. The first occurred when Bernadette was playing with two friends. They had gone ahead of her along the river bank and she was about to follow when she became aware of a movement in the grotto, then of a golden cloud of light, and finally, to quote Bernadette, of 'a lady, young and beautiful, exceedingly beautiful, the like of whom I had not seen before.'

Bernadette later described what happened next, in giving her account of her first vision:

> 'She looked at me immediately, smiled at me and signed to me to advance, as if she had been my mother. All fear had left me, but I seemed to know no longer where I was. I rubbed my eyes, I shut them; but the lady was still there continuing to smile at me making me understand that I was not mistaken. Without thinking of what I was doing I took my rosary in my hands and went on my knees. The lady made with her head a sign of approval and herself took into her hands a rosary which hung on her right arm. When I attempted to begin the rosary and tried to lift up my hand to my forehead my arm remained paralysed, and it was only after the lady had signed herself (with the sign of the cross) that I could do the same. The lady left me to pray all alone; she passed the beads of her rosary through her fingers, but she said nothing; only at the end of each decade did she say the Gloria with me. When the recitation of the rosary was finished, the lady returned to the interior of the rock and the golden cloud disappeared with her.'

When Bernadette's friends returned to find her praying they teased her. When her mother learned the story from Bernadette's

Pilgrims bearing candles sometimes bigger than themselves stand at the Grotto of the Holy Virgin at Lourdes. A group of gypsies is represented by a caravan on a pole.

sister she scolded her and told her never to go near the grotto again. The young girl felt called by an inner voice to return to the grotto and at last her mother gave her permission. Her sister, her mother, and aunt and various other people accompanied her on her visits, and as the rumour spread crowds waited at the cave for her arrival. No one shared her experiences, and on 16th July they came to an end. Only two pieces of 'evidence' survived – a spring of water which had begun to flow at a place indicated by Mary during the ninth apparition, and Bernadette's conviction that she had really met the Virgin. Those who questioned her on behalf of the church authorities eventually accepted her account of the events she described.

Bernadette Soubirous became a nun, a member of the Sisters of Charity at Nevers, and died there in April 1879. She was canonised in 1933. However, long before her death the little village of Lourdes had attracted the notice of the outside world. As early as 1864 the first organised pilgrimage took place and its popularity has increased spectacularly ever since. By 1908, fifty years after the appearances to Bernadette, it is estimated that five million pilgrims had been to the grotto. In 1958 the railway company serving the area said that a million travellers were then using it to reach Lourdes every year. The hotels of Lourdes provide accommodation for 30 000 people, about six times the village's own population. The centenary celebrations in 1958 and 1979 brought an especially large influx of pilgrims.

Many of the pilgrims who go to Lourdes are seriously ill or severely handicapped, for Lourdes, like Knock, has become a place where in numerous cases the sick have been restored to health. Between Easter and December each year two 'jumbulances' travel from Britain to Lourdes weekly. These are large ambulances, capable of carrying twenty-four passengers, including a doctor, three or four nurses, a chaplain, other helpers and about a dozen sick pilgrims. The ambulances pick up their sick passengers at motorway service stations and then take them to Lourdes, a journey of about twenty-one hours from London. The help given by the jumbulance team is voluntary, and a trust also pays for the accommodation of the pilgrims at a chalet called 'Across' in Lourdes. Pilgrims come in an almost endless flow, interrupted only by the harsh winter weather between Christmas and Easter.

Other shrines, Holy Island and Iona. Seasonal considerations also influence visits to other Christian shrines, such as Holy Island in Northumbria and Iona in Scotland. These are sites associated with the so-called re-conversion of Britain. Christianity had probably remained in Wales and Cornwall, and probably in the Galloway region of Scotland. However, when the Roman government of Britain came to an end in 410 the non-Christian invaders of the rest of the island had extinguished it elsewhere. St. Patrick, a Briton, evangelised Ireland, and his successors assumed the task of reviving the faith in his homeland.

St Columba came from Ireland, landing in Iona about 563, and, as a result of his work, a monk named Aidan began preaching to the people of Northumbria in 635 from his base on the island of Lindisfarne, known to many as Holy Island. Both places became the centre of monastic life until the sixteenth-century Reformation. Recently Iona has become the focal point of a group known as the Iona Community, and Christians of many denominations go to the island during the summer to spend a day, or a number of weeks, seeking spiritual renewal. Holy Island is more of a tourist centre. The monastery is in ruins and no community has reconstructed it or its life. However, occasionally, in summer, the Anglican diocese of Newcastle may organise a pilgrimage on foot, at low tide when the island can be reached by means of a causeway linking the island with the mainland. A service is then held in the grounds of the abbey.

231

The Archbishop of Canterbury preaches to pilgrims in the grounds of Walsingham Abbey, a famous medieval place of pilgrimage.

Jerusalem and Rome. Iona, Lindisfarne, Canterbury and Walsingham are reminders of past periods in British Christianity. Two other places of this kind, both in Europe, still attract pilgrims from all over the world. One is Jerusalem, where Jesus ended his earthly ministry, and the other is Rome, where Peter and Paul were martyred and which became the medieval centre of the Christian world. Both cities draw pilgrims to them throughout the year, but, for each, Easter is particularly important. At this time Christians in Jerusalem walk in procession along the Via Dolorosa, the route taken by Jesus to his execution at Calvary, and on Easter Day they visit the empty tomb from which he rose again to life. In Rome they gather in St. Peter's Square to receive the Pope's Easter blessing, 'urbi et orbi'—to the city (of Rome) and to the world.

Though these pilgrimages still have considerable significance for the Christians who make them, one feels that at Rome it is a sight of the Pope that gives the faithful most pleasure and satisfaction, and that those Christians who continue to find spiritual strength and comfort in pilgrimages probably do so much more at places hallowed by recent visions than at historic shrines, either local or international.

Pilgrimage in Islam

The Hajj. Probably the most famous pilgrimage in the world is that which a Muslim should make once in a lifetime to Mecca and certain places nearby 'if wealth and health permit'. The Hajj, as it is called, is an obligation. It is one of the five Pillars of Islam upon which the faith is built. A Muslim who has completed this journey of a lifetime may prefix the word Hajji to his name, so Cassim Muhammad will become Hajji Cassim Muhammad. However, though the Hajj is important and every man and woman in the community of Islam one day hopes to make it, nevertheless, there is the reservation 'if wealth and health permit'. In other words, a poor man cannot be expected to go, neither can a sick man, nor one who has family responsibilities. Nowadays the pilgrimage is comparatively safe and comfortable. One can fly to Jeddah, not far from Mecca, and then travel by bus or car. The dangers of shipwreck or highway robbery which were all very great in the Middle Ages have gone. Though the government of Saudi Arabia makes provision for food and sanitation for the two million or so pilgrims who descend on Mecca during a single week in the twelfth month of the Muslim year, there is still the danger of heat stroke and exhaustion.

There was a Ka'ba at Mecca before Islam. Different traditions are associated with the prophets Adam and Abraham. Muhammad, who taught that his was the religion revealed to Adam, but later perverted, regarded the pilgrimage which Arabs made to the Ka'ba during a month of truce as a relic of the old original religion, though its meaning had by then been lost. Under Islam the Hajj was reformed by being given a new significance.

The meaning of the Hajj. The word Hajj means 'to set out with a definite purpose'. The first people who did this were Abraham and his son Ishmael. Abraham had a vision that he should take his son to a certain place and there sacrifice him. When Ishmael was told of the vision he said that his father should do what God had

233

commanded. Abraham therefore took him to a place now called Mina and prepared to kill him. The Qur'an gives this description of the incident:

> 'Oh my Lord, grant me a righteous son (prayed Abraham). So we gave him good news of a boy ready to suffer patiently. Then when the son reached the age of serious work he said, 'My son, I see in a vision that I offer you in sacrifice: what is your view of this?' The son said, 'Father, do as you are commanded, you will find in me one who practises patience and constancy, if God wills'. So when both had submitted their wills to God and Abraham had laid him with his forehead on the ground, we (God) called out to him, 'Abraham, you have already fulfilled the vision. Thus do we reward those who do right. This was a test, and we ransomed him with a momentous sacrifice: and we left this blessing for him among generations to come, 'Peace and salutations to Abraham'.'

(Sura 37:100–109)

The Muslim who embarks upon the Hajj has this willingness to sacrifice and be sacrificed very much in mind. The pilgrimage is his act of sacrifice. Therefore, as Mecca is approached, the pilgrim stops, puts on the garments of Ihram, and expresses his intention:

> 'O God, I intend to make Hajj, and I am taking Ihram for it. Make it easy for me and accept it from me.'

Ihram is the pilgrim's dress. For a man it is two pieces of white unsewn cloth. One part is worn to cover the lower body to the ankles, the other is thrown over the shoulder and covers the upper part of the body. The head must be left bare and the only footwear permitted is a pair of backless sandals. Women dress in a single piece of white cloth which covers the head and reaches to the ankles, with long sleeves to cover the arms. The purpose of this simple clothing is to stress equality, single-mindedness and self-sacrifice. The attitude which should accompany it is one of peace and brotherhood.

The stages of the pilgrimage: The Ka'ba   The pilgrimage begins with a circling of the Ka'ba seven times. As the pilgrims enter the great courtyard in which it stands they say:

> 'O God, you are peace and the giver of peace; so our sustainer, give us peace and admit us to the Garden, Paradise, the abode of peace.'

They walk round the Ka'ba seven times in an anti-clockwise direction. As they pass the Black Stone set in one of the walls those who are near enough kiss it, or at least touch it: the rest raise their hand

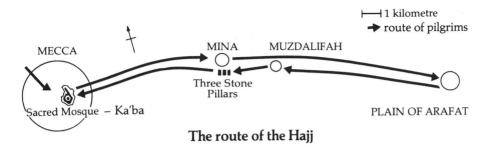

The route of the Hajj

towards it. It is said that the Black Stone was originally white in colour when it was given to Abraham, the builder of the Ka'ba, but it turned black during the period between Abraham and Muhammad when the Arabs forgot God and began to worship idols.

as-Safa and al-Marwa. From the Ka'ba the pilgrims proceed towards as-Safa and al-Marwa. These are two small hills in the centre of Mecca. They, too, are associated with the prophet Abraham and his son Ishmael; Abraham, at God's command left Ishmael and his mother Hagar there. She ran between the two hills searching for water and the pilgrims imitate her by going along the same path seven times. Now the ground is paved and a roofed corridor links the two hills.

While Hagar was looking for water her son found it. As the baby Ishmael scuffed his feet in the sand he unsealed a hidden spring. Its discovery made Mecca an oasis and soon local tribesmen came and joined the mother and her child. The spring is now a well called the Zam Zam, and from it pilgrims drink during the Hajj. At the end of the pilgrimage they wash the clothes they have been wearing in the well. These will be worn again as their shroud when they die. Bottles of Zam Zam water are often taken home for relatives and friends who have been unable to make the Hajj.

Mount Arafat. After sunrise on the ninth day of the month the pilgrims set out for Mount Arafat, some thirteen miles (20 km) away. Some will walk, others will ride. The Hill of Mercy which rises up from the plain is said to be the place where Adam and Eve met and were reconciled after the separation which resulted from their expulsion from Paradise. Here the pilgrims offer the noon and mid-afternoon prayers, remembering the Prophet Muhammad's comment that 'The best of prayers is that of the day of Arafat'. They now turn back towards Mecca and assemble at Muzdalifah, about eight miles (12 km) from the city, to say their evening prayers and camp for the night.

Mina. Next morning they journey on till they reach the small village of Mina in which there are three stone pillars. These mark the spots where the devil tried to persuade the prophet Ishmael to rebel against his father and refuse to be offered as a sacrifice. It is said that the boy drove off the devil with stones; in imitation the pilgrims stone the three pillars. Stoning of the first pillar is followed by the killing of a sheep, goat or camel by individuals or groups of Muslims. This is done in remembrance of Abraham's sacrifice of a ram instead of his son. It is regarded as an act of sacrifice, but it must be remembered that any slaughter of an animal is an act of sacrifice in Muslim eyes, for all life belongs to God. Whenever an animal is killed prayers should be offered over it. The meat of the animals slaughtered at Mina is shared among the poor as well as the pilgrims and the day of this celebration is one of the feast days of the Muslim year, Eid-ul-Adha, the Feast of Sacrifice. All Muslims, whether they are performing the pilgrimage or not, share in this festival in all parts of the world.

During the Hajj as many as three million Muslims may gather to say their noonday prayers at the Ka'ba.

For the pilgrims the Hajj is at its climax and almost at an end. The other pillars are stoned, and a second circling of the Ka'ba takes place, either on the day of the sacrifice or the following morning. Once that has been done the restrictions of the Hajj are over, the pilgrims may dress in normal clothes and make the journey home, though most visit Muhammad's tomb, the magnificent mosque at Medina and other historic sites of Islam before returning to their own countries.

In March 632 CE Muhammad himself led the pilgrimage, and on Monday, June 8th of that year he died. The route of the Hajj is said to follow that taken by the Prophet, so the Hajji returns, conscious that not only the most difficult Pillar of Islam and command of God has been obeyed but that he or she has followed in the footsteps of the Prophet Muhammad.

Pilgrimage in Sikhism

The Sikh Gurus saw so much of what they regarded as superstition at Indian places of pilgrimage that they condemned the practice, with such comments as:

'If a man goes to bathe at a place of pilgrimage with the mind of a crook and the body of a thief, his exterior will be washed by bathing, of course, but his inside will be twice as unclean. He will

The most famous Sikh shrine, the Golden Temple at Amritsar.

237

be like the gourd, clean on the outside but full of poison within. The saints are pure without such washing. The thief remains a thief even if he bathes at pilgrimage places.'

(AG 789)

What they felt was needed was a change of heart, a renewed outlook and attitude to life; therefore they encouraged meditation on the inner presence of God. Guru Nanak was asked, 'Should I go and bathe at pilgrimage places?' and replied:

'God's name is the real pilgrimage place which consists of contemplation of the word of God, and the cultivation of inner knowledge.'

(AG 687)

However, pilgrimage of a sort has grown up in the Sikh tradition, though not all Sikhs would accept this statement and certainly would not go on pilgrimages themselves.

The third Guru, Amar Das, established his headquarters at a village called Goindwal and commanded his followers to meet him there at three great festival times in the Hindu calendar, Magha associated with Shiva, Diwali, the festival of the Vaishnavites, and Baisakhi, the spring festival in April. He had an artificial pool constructed at Goindwal with sixty-four steps leading down to the water, rather like the ghats on the bank of the Ganges at Benares. Those who came to visit would also bathe in the pool. Sikhs, like Hindus, take a bath every morning, but they insist that the reason is only hygienic, and has nothing to do with ideas of purification. They would say that this was the only purpose of bathing in the Goindwal pool. However, it must have gone some way to reassuring any half-hearted Sikhs who had a lingering belief in the value of bathing at holy places.

Amritsar. Eventually Amritsar became the centre of the Sikh faith, and it is to the Golden Temple there that Sikhs now travel. For some the journey is a pilgrimage. They will bathe in the pool, or tank, as they usually call it, and they will cross the causeway to the building. There they will file past the Guru Granth Sahib, and listen to the continuous readings which begin before dawn and end late at night. Early visitors will see the procession carrying the Guru Granth Sahib from the building where it has been kept for the night to the Golden Temple where it is read.

Whether or not the visit that a Sikh would like to make to Amritsar some time in his or her lifetime is a pilgrimage must depend on the participant's attitude of mind. Some go in such a spirit of devotion that it is truly a pilgrimage. For others, it is more than part of a sight-seeing tour of the Punjab—for this is the Sikh homeland where their Gurus were born, lived and preached. These travellers, however, may not necessarily seek or derive any spiritual satisfaction or reward from their journey.

Attitudes to pilgrimage

The Sikh attitude to pilgrimage is perhaps the appropriate one with which to conclude this section. There is a scepticism directed at all suggestions that something is gained from visiting a holy place, no matter whether the pilgrim is sincere or not, yet there is a recognition that any journey undertaken with devotion can become a pilgrimage. Probably Guru Amar Das was astute enough to believe that the idea of pilgrimage was so deep in the Indian subconscious that it had to be directed rather than suppressed.

Pilgrimage remains a strange phenomenon. One man's journey is the deeply-felt devotional act of a lifetime. Yet to a casual observer it could seem nothing more than superstition. Another type of pilgrim will undertake the journey in a mundane spirit, purely for the interest of seeing new places. The experience of pilgrimage and the rewards it may bring vary enormously with each individual.

Questions

1. Why do people make pilgrimages? Describe **one** pilgrimage and explain its importance.

2. Describe **two** places of pilgrimage of two different faiths. Explain why members of those faiths might journey to them.

3. What makes a place a centre of pilgrimage? Illustrate your answer with reference to more than one.

4. Explain why some religious people consider pilgrimage important while others do not.

5. What makes a journey a pilgrimage? What kinds of places do pilgrims visit? Illustrate your answer with reference to at least **two** religions.

6. Describe the historical growth of pilgrimages and discuss their role in the world today.

CHAPTER FIVE
FESTIVALS

The character and purpose of festivals

A festival is an occasion when a community celebrates something which is important and meaningful to it. The occasion may be secular, like American Independence Day, which has purely patriotic significance, or it may be a religious festival, such as the Jewish Passover. A festival may occur annually, and frequently it is a time for rejoicing and happiness. Celebrations of the same event can vary considerably from one country to another. The reasons are many, and they include climatic differences. For example, Australians celebrating Christmas in a hot southern hemisphere summer could not possibly place the same emphasis on snow scenes and hot foods to keep out the cold as do people in the northern hemisphere.

This chapter will mention the main components of religious festivals wherever they are observed and will consider their origins and meaning. Often the significance of the occasion can be summed up in a word, like 'birthday', or a phrase, 'the victory of good over evil'. For the believer, the story told at the time of the festival, and the various observances are ways of conveying that simple meaning. The celebration becomes a deep and moving experience, affecting the heart and body as well as the mind and soul. Many festivals are local or regional, but we shall concentrate on those which are celebrated throughout the world by members of the five faiths.

Most religions have their own calendars. Often these are based on the moon and begin in spring or autumn. They are totally unrelated to the solar Gregorian calendar which begins on 1st January and is now used in many countries of the world to date everyday events. Also, of course, the year 2000, which some people consider a landmark in history, will have no significance for much of the world's population. For Jews it will be 5760, for Muslims 1421, and for some Hindus 2057, while for others it will be 1921, or 1401.

ॐ Hindu festivals

Hindus may use any of at least three religious calendars, depending on the part of India in which they live or originally came from. All these calendars are lunar, so although the number of the year may differ and there may be disagreements about the date of New Year's Day, nevertheless each month begins with one new moon and ends just before the next. The names of the months have also become standardised, as has the practice of inserting an extra month in every third year to keep the calendar in phase with the seasons of spring, summer, autumn, and winter which are determined by the sun.

Lunar months subdivide into the light part, when the moon is waxing, called shuklapaksha, and the dark half, when it is waning, called krishnapaksha. As the following list shows, Hindu festivals tend to occur at new moon, when the moon is full, or at the darkest period of the month just before it reappears.

Table of Hindu Festivals

HINDU MONTH	GREGORIAN EQUIVALENT	FESTIVAL
Chaitra	March/April	Ugadi (first day)
		Ram Navami (ninth day)
Vaisakha	April/May	
Jyestha	May/June	
Ashadha	June/July	
Sravana	July/August	Raksha Bandan (full moon)
		Krishna Janamashtami (eighth dark day)
Bhadrapada	August/September	
Asvina	September/October	Navaratri (first nine days)
		Dussehra (tenth day)
		Diwali (last three of dark part and first two of light in next month)
Karttika	October/November	Diwali ends
Margasirsha	November/December	
Pausa	December/January	
Magha	January/February	Mahashivaratri (day before new moon)
Phalguna	February/March	Holi (full moon)

241

Ugadi.   People often talk of beginning life afresh, making a new start, or turning over a new leaf. The new year—Ugadi—provides an opportunity for making changes. Most of the activities associated with the Hindu new year festival are inspired by the idea of renewal. Families rise even earlier than usual, often well before dawn, to clean the house and sweep the courtyard before decorating it with patterns made of flour, designed to bring happiness and good fortune. The morning bath provides an opportunity to rub the body with sweet-scented oils to welcome the new year. For the same reason new clothes are worn. The poor, who may not be able to afford them, are often given clothes as presents by the rich, for this is a time when everyone should be able to look to the future with hope. Some Hindus eagerly consult astrologers to discover what lies before them in the next twelve months. Members of the twice-born higher castes, Kshatriyas, Vaishyas, and especially Brahmins —who were admitted to their caste by a special ceremony in which the priest put a thin thread over their left shoulder, reaching to the waist on the right hand side—renew their sacred thread at this time of year.

Ram Navami.   The birthday of Rama, one of the gods of the Hindu tradition, falls on the ninth day of the year. It is likely to be observed by readings of the Ramayana and worship offered in front of pictures or sculptures of this god, who was one of the many forms taken by Vishnu in helping mankind in its continual struggle against evil. It is a fast day, which means that certain foods — for example, everyday vegetables, cereals, and salt — are not eaten. Other things, however, are permitted, so the day is one on which more unusual delicacies are enjoyed which families cannot normally afford.

Raksha Bandan.   This festival on the full moon of Sravana is associated with threads in two ways. This, as we have seen, is when the twice-born castes should replace their sacred thread with a new one. They, and other male Hindus may also be given a string or tinsel bracelet to wear on their right wrist. This is a reminder an ancient story describing the way in which the god Indra's wife saved him from the attack of the demon Bali. His efforts to defeat Indra were thwarted by the magic string which his wife had fastened round his wrist. Nowadays sisters tie rakhis on their brothers' wrists, and a Hindu girl may put one on any man's hand to claim him as her protector. The lucky man or brother is expected to pay for the privilege of being her protector by giving her a present. Needless to say, this custom is still popular among Hindus and

242

Sikhs wherever they are living. Sometimes rakhis are sent by relatives living in India as a token of affection to brothers, cousins, or nephews in England.

Krishna Janamashtami or Krishna Jayanti (sometimes called Janamashtami). The birthday of Krishna In Sravana is celebrated much like that of Ram but over a longer period and perhaps with even greater enthusiasm. Krishna was born at midnight, so most Hindus stay up keeping a vigil, waiting for that hour to come. When it does they greet the baby Krishna with singing and dancing. No one seems to go to bed that night. Sometimes cinemas which show Indian films put on special all-night programmes which are attended by those who do not care to spend the night in the temple. After midnight everyone in the temple shares sweet foods, the kind of things given to an Indian mother just after childbirth. The following day is a fast, followed in the evening by a feast. During the festivities the many stories of Krishna are told and songs and dances describe his exploits.

The three major festivals of the month of Asvina Navaratri, Dussehra, and Diwali, are also the most celebrated of all those in the Hindu calendar. There is a considerable overlap in the stories which are used to explain the significance of the festivals. It is likely that ancient new year and coronation festivals have been combined to produce a long and glittering period of celebrations.

Navaratri. The puja holiday, as this period is sometimes called, begins with a nine-day festival devoted to Durga, the divine symbol of motherhood. Navaratri means nine nights, and it is in the evenings that most of the celebrations take place. An important element of these is dancing around a shrine of Durga which may have been specially erected for the occasion. Outside India Hindu communities often hire school halls for their festival or hold them out of doors if the climate is warm and dry. If possible, newly married daughters return to the home of their parents at this time. Those Hindus who hold Durga in special veneration fast, taking only a single daily meal of fruit and sweet foods made with milk.

The story underlying the whole of this time of puja is that of Rama and Sita as told in the famous epic of Valmiki, the Ramayana, Rama not only lost his kingdom, but by a trick his wife Sita was also stolen from him. In order to obtain the necessary strength to overthrow the demon Ravana, he turned to Durga for help. It is his period of worship that is remembered at Navaratri. Perhaps another explanation for the festival may be guessed from the stick-dances which are a feature of it. The sticks probably represent sickles, and indicate that this was once a harvest celebration. The swaying of the rows of dancers is reminiscent of the corn and the movements of those who cut it by hand.

Dussehra or Vijaya Dashami. 'Das' means ten in various of Indian languages. It forms part of both names given to this 'tenth-day' festival. On this day the Spirit of God departs from the statue of Durga which has been made by the villagers. The statue is taken to the river in a joyful procession and put into the water. As it sinks beneath the water the people rejoice, believing that it has carried away with it all unhappiness and ill-fortune.

The festival also has another meaning. On this day Rama, attended by his brother Lakshman and Hanuman, the king of the monkeys, rescued his wife Sita from the clutches of the evil demon Ravana. In Delhi the great Ram Lilla celebrations are held at which an effigy of Ravana is burned as the central feature of a gigantic firework display. The statue, which stands over thirty metres high, is traditionally built by a group of Muslim workmen, and the entertainment is enjoyed by people of all faiths. Some years ago in Leeds when the festival coincided with the English bonfire night celebrations Ravana and Guy Fawkes perished together on the same pyre. In India presents are often given, especially to children.

On the 'glorious tenth' (Vijaya Dashami), the ten-headed Ravana was defeated by Rama, strengthened by Durga. Good triumphed over evil, the loyalty of Lakshman, and the fidelity of Sita were seen to be virtues that Ravana could not destroy. Underlying the story is a strong emphasis on friendship. Now is the time when Hindus forget their differences and try to make up any quarrels that have divided families or villages during the year. This period is the climax of the Hindu religious year. The festival is a reminder of God's love and protection, of the belief that good is more powerful than evil, and that people should be loyal and friendly to one another.

Diwali, or Deepavali. The climax of the Asvina celebrations spreads over into the next month, Karttika. That is simply another way of saying that Diwali is a five-day festival, beginning in the last three days of the dark period of the month and welcoming the new moon for two further days. Diwali means 'cluster of lights' and takes its name from the most characteristic aspect of the festival, the decoration of homes, cowsheds, temples, and many other buildings with coloured electric light bulbs or clay lamps containing a wick floating in oil.

A thirty-metre high statue of Ravana being prepared for burning at Ram Lilla celebrations in New Delhi.

There are several stories associated with the festival. One is that the goddess Kali (Durga in another form) was born at this time. Another is that the goddess Lakshmi, the consort of Vishnu, visits homes bringing gifts and prosperity for the coming year to those who welcome her with their houses cleaned and brightly lit. Sometimes the period is called Naraka Chaturdasi, in memory of Krishna's defeat of a demon called Naraka who lived in Assam. Krishna went all the way from his palace at Dwarka in the west of India to subdue the spirit which was causing trouble on the other side of the country. Such is the love of God. When Naraka was beaten and dying he asked a boon of Krishna, who quite properly promised to grant it. 'I was a wicked person all my life,' said the demon, 'so no-one should mourn me. On the anniversary of my death everyone should be happy, wear new clothes, let off fireworks, take oil-baths, burn lights to brighten the night, and send one another greetings. May it be so?' Krishna granted the request, and those rituals, which would never normally take place when someone dies, have been performed ever since, for Naraka's sake.

Vishnu's defeat of the demon Bali, the one from whom Indra's wife protected him by putting the rakhi round his wrist, is another reason given for celebrating Diwali. Bali, sometimes called King Bali in this story, had gained control of the world. He decided to perform a great sacrifice to enable him to become master of the heavens and the gods as well as the earth. Indra and the other deities were at their wits' end until Vishnu then came forward with a cunning idea. He caused himself to be born as a deformed dwarf, and when he had grown into a boy went to Bali who was famous for his generosity and begged alms from him.

Bali said he would give the dwarf anything he wished. The disguised Vishnu asked for as much land as he could cover in three strides. Bali laughed, agreed and waited for the dwarf to leap a few centimetres. Instead the dwarf grew so large that he was able to cover the whole earth in two strides. King Bali had promised him as much land as he could pass across in three strides — therefore, Vishnu said, the king had failed to keep his promise! Bali was banished as a punishment, but allowed to return for one day each year — the first day of the Karttika New Moon. This festival, coinciding with Diwali, is therefore sometimes called Bali Pritipada. The story of Vishnu's trickery of King Bali may not seem a very moral tale, but its moral really is that everyone should know his place: mortals should not try to play God.

Perhaps the best-known reason for celebrating Diwali is the triumphant return of Rama to Ayodhya to claim the throne which had remained vacant for fourteen years. In Benares, where the story of the Ramayana is serialised over a period of thirty days throughout Asvina, the climax is reached with the short pageant of the heroes' victory procession. The local raja, believed to be an incarnation of Shiva, watches this last scene of the Ramayana from his state elephant.

Some of the events which take place at Diwali have already been mentioned in the brief description of Lakshmi's visit to Indian homes or the words which Naraka addressed to Krishna. Others are continuations of entertainments which began during Navaratri or earlier still. Families which have not yet succeeded in coming together will try to do so now, and it will be the turn of the son-in-law who has brought his wife home to see her parents to be given presents. On the last day of Diwali fortunate boys will be given a feast or party by their sisters and cousins, especially if they were generous at Raksha Bandan.

That this was a new year festival in north India may be seen from the emphasis upon renewal. New clothes are given. Homes are cleaned and decorated. Paint and whitewash is as much in evidence as the clay lamps outside the house. Even the animals are washed, groomed and decorated; and they have bells put around their necks and a special mash to eat. Businessmen try to settle their accounts so that no one goes into the new year in debt. Children may be lectured on imitating their elders in trying to turn over a new leaf. However, the spiritual meaning of this festive time of year is probably summed up in the words of the Upanishad:

From the unreal lead me to the real,
From darkness lead me to light,
From death lead me to immortality.
May God protect us both at the same time,
At the same time support us both,
May both of us at the same time apply our strength,
May our learning be illustrious,
May there be no hatred between us,
May all here be happy.

(Brihadaranyaka Upanishad 1.3.28)

Though unrelated to this time of puja, these words probably express the hopes of all Hindus in the autumn days before the coming of the cold winter nights.

In some other parts of the world Diwali celebrations may be less public than in India, but there will be no less enthusiasm. Sometimes the outdoor fireworks are absent because Hindu communities do not like to offend people who live near the temples and who may have experienced sufficient noise for one year on bonfire night and may not be too tolerant of the ways of strangers. Instead there will be dances, speeches and parties, with temples and homes lit as brightly as Christian houses at Christmas time. Indeed it is not unusual to hear Hindus describe Diwali as 'our Christmas'. Presents are exchanged and Diwali cards are sold in the shops and sent to relatives in India or East Africa. Some are received from these parts of the world and may be seen on the mantelpiece of Hindu homes, though the sending of cards has not yet become as popular among Asians in Britain as it is among the Christian and Jewish communities.

Mahashivatri. The thirteenth day of the dark part of every month is sacred to Shiva, the manifestation of God which reminds Hindus that, as well as being the creator, he is also destroyer and recreator of life. In the month of Magha the occasion is regarded as specially important. Some say Shiva married his wife Parvati on this day; others remember that he drank the poison which a demon had prepared in order to kill mankind. The origins of the festival are lost in pre-history, and it is not possible to guess at its ancient meaning. It is celebrated by a fast until about 4.00 p.m., when puja is offered to Shiva, and even afterwards no cereals or curries are eaten. Popular constituents of the fast-breaking meal are sweet potatoes and cucumbers. It is believed that unmarried girls should keep vigil throughout the night of festival so that Shiva will enable them to find a suitable husband. 'The great night of Shiva' is followed by a day of feasting. Because the night includes part of two consecutive days some books say that the festival actually occurs on the fourteenth of the month; another name for it is, in fact, Chaturdashi, 'the fourteenth'.

Holi. This is one of the most riotous and notorious festivals celebrated anywhere. It is essentially an outdoor occasion to welcome the coming of spring, but its popularity has led to its being observed in Britain in the middle or end of a cold February. In India village bonfires are lit, around which babies are sometimes carried in a clockwise direction by their mothers who are eager that Agni, the god of fire, will bless them with a successful life. Children fill buckets with coloured water and use bicycle pumps to squirt anyone who comes in sight. It is not a time for those who dislike practical jokes to be out of doors, or for wearing one's best clothes.

The end of winter is a sufficient reason in itself for merrymaking, for although India is free of frost, fog and snow, nevertheless nights are very cold and everyone looks forward to the appearance of the spring harvests. There is, however, a story from Hindu mythology which explains the festival of Holi. It is about another dream, this time their king, Hiranyakapishu by name. He issued a command that no one should worship anyone else but him. His son Prahlada, though very small, refused to obey him. So religious was the boy that he even memorised his alphabet with the aid of the names of the gods—V for Vishnu, K for Krishna, S for Shiva, A for Ambaji . . . This was too much for his father, who asked his daughter Holika to get rid of the boy. She possessed magic powers which enabled her to walk through fire without being burned so she picked up Prahlad and carried him into the fire. Holika was destroyed in the fire because she did not know that her power was only effective when she entered the fire alone. Prahlad emerged unharmed, because all the time he had been in the fire he had chanted Hari Krishna, the names of God, and these had saved him. Ignorance is the greatest fault that anyone can possess, except perhaps for pride. These faults prevent a person from recognising the truth. Consequently, Holika died, while her brother who trusted himself to God lived. This is the moral that Hindus would draw from Holi, as they change into some dry clothes.

There is almost no end to the festivals of Hinduism. These are only some of them. The myths associated with them, too, are apparently endless and Hindus accept and retell the one which they prefer. This does not mean that they deny the truth of the other story to the one they treasure: Hinduism is not at all exclusive. All are acceptable and can contain the truth, just as all rivers are ways of reaching the sea.

✡ Jewish festivals

The Jewish religious calendar has points of resemblance with that of the Hindus, being based on the moon, and uses a system of leap years to maintain agreement with the solar calendar and the seasons. However, the beginning of the year does not coincide with spring, but with autumn. It falls in the months of September or October according to the Gregorian calendar used throughout the world. Judaism dates its years from the supposed beginning of creation. The year 2000 C E will be 5760 by Jewish reckoning, and 5761 will be celebrated in the autumn of that year.

Table of Jewish Festivals

JEWISH MONTH	GREGORIAN EQUIVALENT	FESTIVAL
Tishri	September/October	Rosh Hashanah (day 1)
		Yom Kippur (day 10)
		Succoth (days 15–21)
Marchevan	October/November	
Kislev	November/December	Chanucah (day 25, for eight days)
Tebet	December/January	
Shebat	January/February	
Adar	February/March	Purim (days 13 and 14)
Nisan	March/April	Pesach (days 14 to 21)
Iyyar	April/May	
Sivan	May/June	Shavuot (day 6)
Tammuz	June/July	
Ab	July/August	
Elul	August/September	

Rosh Hashanah.   The Torah refers to the month Nisan as the first month of the year, but an ancient tradition says that God began his work of creation in Tishri, the seventh month. Rosh Hashanah, Jewish New Year's Day, therefore remembers this occasion. When the world actually began no one knows, and such dates as 5740 or 5760 are not to be taken seriously, but the belief that this is God's world is. The principal theme of the prayers offered on this day is the sovereignty of God.

The commandment contained in the Torah is:

> In the seventh month, on the first day of the month, you shall observe a day of rest, a memorial proclaimed with a blast of the horn, a holy convocation. You shall not do any servile work.

> (Leviticus 23:24-25)

In response to this, everyone who can gathers in the synagogue where the shofar, an instrument made of ram's horn, is blown (unless the day is a sabbath when the blowing of the horn is omitted). The man who sounds the shofar recites a special blessing;

> Blessed art thou, Lord our God, king of the universe, who has sanctified us with your commandments and commanded us to hear the sound of the shofar;

to which the congregation replies, 'Amen'.

A hundred notes of the horn are blown during the services. Each is regarded as a call to penitence. Indeed, though Rosh Hashanah is an occasion for well-wishing and saying to one's friends and relatives, 'May you be inscribed and sealed for a good year,' and one may eat a slice of apple dipped in honey with the wish, 'May it be the Lord's will to renew us for a year which will be good and sweet,' the day is one when everyone looks forward to a period of soul-searching. From now until Yom Kippur is a time known as the Ten Days of Repentance, when Jews should be reconciled with anyone they have wronged or quarrelled with, and should try to put their affairs in order so that on the Day of Atonement, being at peace with the world, they can make their peace with God.

Yom Kippur. God forgives all sins committed against him, provided that the sinner repents sincerely. This is a fundamental teaching of Judaism. Therefore a special day is set aside for this act of penitence. This does not mean that a Jew cannot make his peace with God at any time, but only that he is more likely to do so if provision is made for it. Just as he has sought forgiveness from his neighbour, for only he can forgive offences committed against him,

Blowing the shofar on Rosh Hashanah. The rabbi or minister dresses in white on high holy days.

so he now approaches God for pardon. The Torah is again the instructor, saying when the day shall be observed and how:

> The Lord spoke to Moses saying, 'On the tenth day of this month, (Tishri) is the Day of Atonement (Yom Kippur in Hebrew). It shall be for you a time of holy convocation, and you shall afflict your souls. . . . And you shall do no work on this same day; for it is a day of atonement, to make atonement for yourselves, before the Lord. . . . .It shall be a sabbath of solemn rest, and you shall afflict yourselves; on the ninth day of the month, beginning at evening, from evening to evening shall you keep your sabbath.

(Leviticus 23:26-32)

The word 'affliction' is the one which probably remains most firmly in the reader's mind. The form taken by this affliction is a total abstinence from eating and drinking for about twenty-five hours, for the period begins on the ninth day, about an hour before sunset, and continues till the end of the tenth. In all respects but perhaps two, Yom Kippur is like a Sabbath, so much so that it is called the Sabbath of Sabbaths. However, on the Sabbath fasting is forbidden, for it should be a day of rest and joy; and much of Yom Kippur is spent in the synagogue, much more than is customary on the Sabbath.

In ancient times the High Priest symbolically placed his hands on the head of a goat, the idea being that it could be clearly seen through a ritual act that his and the nation's sins had been removed. The goat was then led away and killed. Later it was fairly common for a chicken to be treated in the same way and then given to a poor family, but gradually the practice has lapsed. It is still remembered, however, in the use of the word 'scapegoat' for one who innocently carries the blame for something. Judaism does not see the need for guilt to be taken away in this kind of way, nor, now that there is no longer a Temple, the need for a High Priest to perform this symbolic ritual. On Yom Kippur each person must offer his or her own contrite act of repentance.

Succoth. Immediately after Yom Kippur preparations begin for celebrating Succoth. This was an ancient grape and fruit harvest festival but, as with Pesach and Shavuot, it is linked in Jewish teaching with the Exodus from Egypt. At this time many Jews forsake their houses for simple huts or shacks made of tree boughs and leaves which they have erected in the garden or on the flat roof of a house. Branches of palm, myrtle, or willow leaves are woven together for the roof, to represent the bunch of branches, called a lulav, which is waved at the synagogue service on Succoth. Citrus fruits are hung from the roof, and these are known as the Etrog.

In the service the waving branch symbolises God's care for the whole world as it waves in every direction. The Etrog shows God's care in providing food for mankind. Jewish tradition teaches that during the journey from Egypt to Canaan the Hebrews built themselves rough shelters and the purpose of the festival is to remember with gratitude God's deliverance. In English Succoth is called either Tabernacles or Booths. The commandments relating to the keeping of Succoth are to be found in the Book of Leviticus (23:39-43).

Chanucah.   This eight-day festival falling in the month of Kislev is regarded as being of minor importance. It is not mentioned in the Torah and was not one of the three occasions when Jews should go up to the Temple. Chanucah means dedication and on 25 Kislev a special act of this kind is remembered. In 168 BCE the Greek ruler of Syria and overlord of Palestine embarked on a policy of Hellenisation. He was a Greek in language and culture and, like Alexander the Great over a century earlier, he had the dream of making Greek as much of the world as he could conquer. He also believed himself to be the embodiment of God. His name was Antiochus IV, but on his coins he added 'theou Epiphanou' which means 'God Manifest'. This alone was enough to prevent devout Jews using them, especially as Temple offerings, for they were tokens of blasphemy. However, Antiochus also decided to suppress Judaism for the sake of Greek culture. For the Jews his dream became a nightmare when his army invaded Jerusalem in 168 and he sacrificed a pig on the high altar of the Temple. His soldiers went through Palestine compelling Jews to eat swine's flesh and sacrifice to the God-King. Many Jews died rather than submit to the madman. Instead of Epiphanes they called him Epimanes, 'madness manifest'. At last a revolt broke out. To everyone's surprise the Greeks were defeated, Jerusalem was liberated and the Temple restored and rededicated on 25 Kislev 165.

There is a further story associated with the festival. The Talmud says:

> 'What is Chanucah? The rabbis teach: On the twenty-fifth day of Kislev the days of the Feast of Chanucah begin. There are eight of them, days on which there may be no public mourning or fasting. When the Greeks entered the Temple they desecrated all the oil in the Temple. After the leaders of the House of the Hasmoneans (the family leading the Jews) had overcome and defeated them, they searched all over and found just one little cruse of oil still bearing the seal of the High Priest: just enough oil to last for one day. But a miracle happened, it burnt in the candelabrum for eight days, (until fresh oil could be prepared). The following year it was

ordained that these days be observed with songs of praise and thanksgiving.'

(Shabbat 21b)

For this reason nine-branched candleholders, called menorahs, are lit in Jewish homes during the Chanucah festival. First, the servant candle, the shamach, is lit, and then one other is lit from it on the first night, two on the second, and so on through the festival. Special dishes are prepared, parties are given, Chanucah songs are sung, and the gloom of winter relieved by a period of enjoyment. Though the festival may not be mentioned in the Tenakh, it is nonetheless popular, and since the holocaust, the wholesale extermination of Jews in the Second World War, which was the most recent attempt to destroy Judaism, it has acquired a greater significance.

The symbolism of the feast is the victory of good over evil, of light over darkness; it may be that even before Chanucah was celebrated there was a winter solstice festival to which the events of 165 BCE gave new meaning.

Purim. Like Chanucah, this is not one of the main festivals commanded by the Torah. Also, like Chanucah, it commemorates an act of deliverance. The heroine is Esther, the Jewish queen of Xerxes, king of Persia, also known as Ahasuerus. The story is told in the Biblical book which bears the heroine's name. One of the king's advisers plotted to kill the Jews, but his plan was brought to the notice of Esther who turned the tables on him so that he died on his own gallows. When the tale is read—from a handwritten scroll of Esther at the evening service on Purim, and the following morning—children are encouraged to wave rattles similar to those used at football matches (Haman gregers), to drown the sound of the villain's name. It is customary at this time to celebrate with feasting but also to send presents to the poorer members of the Jewish community. The name Purim means 'lots' and is given to the festival because lots were cast to determine the day when the Jews should be put to death.

Pesach. According to the Torah this is the first festival of the Jewish year beginning in the month Nisan. It has certainly become the most important of the three major feasts. Originally there may have been pastoral and grain harvest rites which were distinct but now there is one celebration which commemorates the occasion when God 'with a mighty hand and outstretched arm' delivered the Hebrew people from Egypt. Pesach is the independence day of the Jewish faith and nation.

The word Pesach means Passover. The name is linked with the command of Moses that each Hebrew family in Egypt should smear the doorpost of its house with the blood of a lamb and so avert the plague which was to befall the Egyptians, the death of their first-born children. This account, found in the book of Exodus Chapter 12, is probably an historical reinterpretation of a ritual already practised by sheep farmers to protect their spring lambs. Now the meal associated with it was given a new meaning. It was the last meal of slaves about to be given their liberty.

Another name for the festival is the Feast of Unleavened Bread. To prevent flour from the newly-harvested corn being contaminated by that from the previous harvest, the two were kept separate. The old bins were completely cleared out. To provide a clean break between new and old no yeast was added to the new dough for a period of seven days. A safety precaution of this kind may well lie behind the Feast of Unleavened Bread. However, in Exodus, Chapter 12;14-20 the custom is again linked with the deliverance from Egypt.

The high point of Pesach is a meal which is accompanied by a service. Before this can take place, however, the home—for Passover is essentially a festival of the home—must be prepared. It must be spring cleaned. Everything containing grain must be thrown away, for the old leaven, called hametz, must be removed. This should even include whisky and perhaps starch. To ensure complete cleanliness many Jews will put their normal cooking utensils and dishes on one side and use special ones brought out only once a year at Passover time. Before the meal takes place the children of a family will make a final search for any remaining unleavened bread, and a prize will be given to the one who finds the piece which has been hidden.

The Passover celebration is called a Seder. The word means 'order' and indicates that a particular pattern is to be followed. All over the world Jews will eat the same foods, and say the same things, at this meal. The table is laid in a special way. A fine cloth will cover the table and the best dishes will be placed on it. There will be silver candlesticks, if the family can afford them, and a wine glass for everyone, including the children. In addition to these, each person will probably have a copy of the Haggadah, a small book containing the story of the Passover. In the centre of the table there will be the Seder Plate, near the head of the household. The plate has three matzos on it (thin wafers of unleavened bread), and an arrangement of foods; a roasted shank bone, an egg, sprigs of parsley, bitter herbs (usually horseradish), and haroset, a mixture of apples, nuts, cinnamon, and wine. There will also be a dish of salt water or vinegar, and an extra glass which is not used at all during the meal.

Each of these items has a symbolic meaning:

The roasted shank bone represents the Passover lamb. It is not eaten.

The egg is a reminder of spring and the hope of new life and resurrection; though outwardly it appears dead, within there is life. It too remains uneaten.

The parsley is an appetiser; dipped in the salt water or vinegar it is a reminder of the tears of the Hebrew slaves and of the salt sea.

The bitter herbs are also a reminder of the bitterness of slavery.

The haroset, tasty though it might be by itself, is eaten with the herbs and symbolises the mortar used by the Hebrew slaves, and the idea of bondage.

The Seder, or ritual Passover meal, in which children play a full part, especially by asking what its significance is. What items are placed on the Seder dish? What do they represent?

The cup from which no one drinks awaits the coming of Elijah the prophet, who, according to the Book of Malachi, will come before the great day of redemption and will be its herald (Malachi 4:5). The presence of the cup shows that redemption, expressed in the promise, 'I will bring you into a land' (Exodus 6:8), is no idle dream, nor does it simply refer to the settlement of the Jews in Israel. Though they are now established there the cup is still placed on the table to signify the eventual redemption of all mankind and the establishment of God's kingdom of justice and peace.

The service begins with the mother of the family lighting the candles and making the blessing. Then everyone drinks a cup of wine, after which father washes his hands ceremonially and distributes the parsley. After a blessing the parsley is eaten, and then the father takes and breaks the middle of the three matzos in two. He puts the larger part away, and holding the other piece he says, 'It is like the bread which our forefathers ate in the land of Egypt. All who are hungry, let them come and eat. All who are needy, let them come and celebrate the Passover. Now we are here, next year may we be in the land of Israel. Now we are slaves, next year may we be free men.' The future has a prominent place in the Seder. Not only is it thought of in the words just mentioned, but also at one point in the service a child opens the door so that Elijah may enter.

At the end of the meal, after the grace, these words are said:

Ended is the Passover Seder according to statute, law and order.
Just as we were worthy to celebrate it here so may it be in the future year.
O pure one, in heaven your dwelling place, give to the people of Israel grace. Soon, as the planting of your choice be Zion redeemed and in song rejoice.

Then everyone says, 'Next year in Jerusalem,' even those who are fortunate enough to be living there—which is another indication that the real hope is for the kingdom of God, not merely settlement in Israel, important though that may be.

Past and future come together in the present in the Passover meal. Interestingly, it is the youngest boy, the one who belongs more than anyone else to the future, who is responsible for bringing the past to mind; for he has the task of asking four questions. These are written down in the Haggadah:

Why is this night different from all other nights?
Tonight we eat no bread, only matzah.
On other nights we eat herbs of many kinds; tonight we

257

eat only bitter herbs,
On other nights we do not dip our herbs even once; on this night why do we dip them twice?
On other nights we sit upright or lean to eat, why do we eat in a leaning position only tonight?

The father answers the questions by telling the story of the first Passover, the escape from Egypt, the meal eaten in a hurry so that they had not time to sit properly at table. (Now this is simply part of the story and everyone sits normally, as at any other meal.)

Passover keeps alive memories and hopes, but perhaps most of all it is a witness to the continuing journey of the Jewish people to the Promised Land.

Shavuot. Fifty days after the cutting of the first sheaf of corn at Passover came the last of the year's festivals, and the third of those mentioned in the Torah. Its name means 'weeks' because it takes place seven full weeks after Passover, but it is also known as Pentecost, the 'fiftieth-day' festival. The original significance of the occasion is remembered by the reading of the beautiful Book of Ruth in the synagogue service, but the real celebration is that of the giving of the Torah to Moses at Sinai. This is regarded as the anniversary of that event. Therefore, the chief lesson drawn from the Book of Ruth is that of the heroine's dedication to Judaism and her faith in God. Though her husband had died and she would have had every justification for returning to her own people, she said to Naomi, 'Where you go I will go, and where you lodge I will lodge; your people shall be my people and your God my God.' (Ruth 1:16). She later remarried and her son was the grandfather of the great king David.

Buddhist festivals

Buddhism began in India, and the stages of the moon are important in the Buddhist calendar, as in the Hindu calendar. Months are lunar. The first and fifteenth days, when the moon is new and full, are called uposatha days. The word means 'entering to stay', and refers to the fact that on these days lay Buddhists should join the monks in a day of fasting, devotion and meditation in the vihara. The eight days following each new and full moon are slightly less important uposatha days. At these times, as well as at major festivals, lay Buddhists take Eight Precepts, or even all Ten.

Buddhist festivals, too, are associated with the stages of the moon and occur around a full-moon day. Even if Buddhists cannot go to a vihara for all or some of the four monthly uposatha days, they will try to go at festival times. Ways of celebrating these in Buddhist countries are as different as the languages of those countries. In fact cultural activities are a sort of 'language' in their own right. The Buddha told his followers to teach in the language of the people, and so the sheer variety of Buddhist festivals and practices at those festivals is in keeping with the way Buddhism adapts itself. In the west Buddhists often celebrate festivals or observe uposatha days on the Saturday or Sunday nearest to the full moon, so that as many people as possible are free from work and can come together at a Buddhist centre.

The Buddhist Calendar—Two Examples

Note: The names of the months are different in each Buddhist country and not used universally, so the English month which approximates to the time of the year is given instead.

	BURMA	JAPAN
April	New Year three days with water festival on first two. Washing away sins. Making merit	Hana Matsuri Flower Festival marking Birth of Buddha Sakyamuni
May	Buddha day, usually called Wesak: birth/enlightenment/death of Gautama Buddha	
July	Rainy Season Retreat begins, usually called Vassa	Obon Helping Remembering the souls of the dead Way lit with lanterns
September		Autumn Higan 'Other-Shore' Ceremony
October	Rainy Season Retreat ends Gifts to Sangha Festival of Lights	
December		Jodo-e Enlightenment of Buddha
January		Joyo no Kane New Year
February		Nehan-e Nirvana of Sakyamuni Buddha
March		Spring Higan 'Other-Shore' Ceremony

All the Buddhist countries have a slightly different calendar, and have developed a distinctive set of festivals which they have brought to the west. As a result there is a Thai, Sri Lankan and Burmese (all Theravadin), as well as a Japanese (Mahayana) and Tibetan (Vajrayana) way of doing things. The Buddhist new year falls at different times in different countries. Mahayana Buddhists focus on bodhisattvas and cosmic buddhas, as well as on Gautama Buddha, or on a national saint like the twelfth-century Japanese Shinran Shonin, whose festival is in May. For Sri Lankans, Poson—the full moon in June—marks the coming of Buddhism to their island in the third century BCE, and an annual perahera (procession) in June/July is held from the Rock temple at Aluvihare, which is the traditional site of the Council which committed the Pali scriptures to writing. There is some overlap with pre-Buddhist fertility rites in the Burmese Water Festival, which is part of their new year in April. Pre-Buddhist mythologies emerge in the Tibetan dance-dramas.

All festivals involve monks and lay Buddhists. The monks are expert in the sutras appropriate to the festival theme, and chant them during the devotions. They also lead the meditation, and give a Dharma talk. Lay Buddhists bring gifts of food for the monks at the beginning of their visit to the vihara, and also flowers, light and incense for the shrine. At the end of the Rainy Season Retreat, outlined later in this chapter, they bring more substantial gifts. Among them are cooking utensils; cloth for robes and parasols or umbrellas, which monks use to shade them from the sun. Other offerings will supply any particular needs of the monastery in the coming year.

Festivals relating to the life of Gautama Buddha

Buddhists honour Gautama Buddha for what he discovered about the meaning of life and the way to true happiness. They try to remember what he taught and follow his example along the path to enlightenment all the time. All daily meditation and worship, and especially the practice of mindfulness, helps with this. Buddhists are very much aware that most monks spend more time thinking about and disciplining themselves to follow in the footsteps of the Buddha than do lay Buddhists, who have jobs and families to worry about. So festivals act as a reminder for busy people of the importance of the life of the Buddha and its relevance for Buddhists today. The activities of a festival can be a lively and enjoyable way of teaching children, and reminding adults, of the events of the Buddha's life and the Dharma (teaching) which it illustrates. Festivals also bring a holiday, a sense of joy and a release from normal routine which anticipates the spiritual joy that a religion has to offer its followers.

Wesak. This is the Theravada festival, a threefold celebration of the birth, enlightenment and death of Gautama Buddha. Its name comes from the Sri Lankan month in which it takes place, corresponding to the English months of April or May. Other forms of the word are Vesak, which is closer to the way it is pronounced, and Vesaka-puja. The Burmese also call it Buddha Day, and it takes place at the full moon, which is said to have marked the three events and the enlightenment of all buddhas. Even Buddhists who do not visit the temple at other times will go for Wesak. First thing in the morning they will take gifts of food for the monks and make their own offerings in the shrine room with words like these:

> 'With this lamp which blazes with firm strength, destroying darkness, I make offering to the truly enlightened lamp of the world, the dispeller of darkness.' (*light*)

> 'With this fragrant smoke full of perfume I make offering to the one worthy to receive them.' (*incense*)

> 'I make offering to the Buddha with these flowers, and through this merit may there be release. Even as these flowers must fade so my body goes towards destruction.' (*flowers*)

At Wesak Buddhists honour the memory of the Buddha wherever there are shrines, bodily relics in stupas, Bodhi trees or Buddha statues out-of-doors. When they remember him they remember the truths which he taught. With their offerings they hope to gain merit for a better rebirth. The fragile beauty of the flowers reminds them how short life is. The symbol of light in the candles and lamps reminds them of the hope in the Buddha's message and encourages them to follow the Dharma. On the day of the festival lay Buddhists renew their vows by taking the Three Refuges and Eight or Ten Precepts.

The rest of the day will be spent in the kind of programme outlined in the section on worship. The laity will join the monks in their meditation and teaching will be given various forms. There is usually sutra chanting and preaching, and in the east perhaps a dramatic performance. In the west some films may be shown about life in Buddist countries. The themes of all of these are related to the

A greeting card sent by
Buddhists at Wesak.

theme of the festival. Sutras will be about the birth, death and
enlightenment of the Buddha. The Jataka stories are also retold or
enacted. They are stories of his previous births which illustrate the
long moral and spiritual climb through many births which is
necessary before a person is worthy of enlightenment. These stories
are enjoyed especially by the children since they contain many
animal characters.

Many Buddhists send each other Wesak cards which are
decorated with a lotus, symbol of purity; or a picture of the
Buddha's birth, enlightenment or death or perhaps a Bodhi tree.

The Three Japanese Festivals for the Buddha's Life. In Japan the
birth, enlightenment and death of Sakyamuni Buddha, which is the
name they use for Gautama Buddha, are celebrated on three
different days. Hana Matsuri is in April. This is one of the many
Japanese flower festivals and that is the literal meaning of the
name—and it marks the birth of the Buddha. Models of the
Lumbini Gardens, where The Buddha was born, are set up in the
courtyards of the temples. In the middle is a statue of the Buddha as
a child. He is standing up, because the stories of his birth are full of
unusual events, including the fact that he was able to stand and take
some steps straightaway. Another story says that the gods provided
perfumed water from heaven for his first bath. In the temple models
there are bowls of delicately perfumed tea and a ladle. The children
remember the story, and honour the image by ladling some of the
sweet-smelling tea over it. Sometimes there is a large papier-mâché

262

A model in a Japanese temple courtyard at Hana Matsuri. This shows the garden where the Buddha was born. A child ladles perfumed water over an image of the baby Buddha.

white elephant standing near the model garden. White elephants are rare and became a symbol of royalty, and, moreover, the Buddha's mother dreamed of a white elephant at the time of his conception. So the model elephant is a reminder of that incident.

At this and other festivals the temples are full of crowds in festive mood. As well as the more obviously religious activities there is a great sense of a holiday, and people enjoy folk-dancing, watching acrobats, listening to story-tellers and buying articles from stalls.

The two other Japanese festivals which mark events in the Buddha's life are Jodo-e in December, which commemorates his enlightenment, and Nehan-e in February which signifies his entrance into final Nirvana at his death.

The Rainy Season Retreat

The technical term for this is Vassa, which is a Pali word. The Vassa began in the time of the Buddha. The rainy season, which occurs between July and October in the east, makes travelling difficult. There were complaints from the farmers that the Buddhist monks, who were travelling around to teach people, were treading

263

on the young rice shoots growing in the flooded fields and accidentally damaging them. So it became the custom for monks not to travel to teach at this time, but to stay together in a monastery and concentrate on study and meditation. This is what is called a 'retreat' in English. The custom has continued, even where there is no rainy season. This in itself is not a festival, but the beginning and end of the period is marked by Buddhists with special celebrations. Laymen often join the monks for some or all of the retreat, and although ordination (the ceremony for joining the Sangha) can take place at any time, it is often at the beginning of this period.

Three kinds of activity can mark the beginning of the Rainy Season Retreat:

1. Initiation. Boys, and sometimes girls, between the ages of eight and twenty go through a special 'coming of age' ceremony. They are dressed as princes and princesses, and parade through the village, riding on an animal or being carried. The procession includes village musicians and the family is joined by as many relatives and friends as possible. It is often an expensive occasion for the parents, who have to feed all these people as well as the monks involved in the ceremony. At the monastery the boys ask for admission. All their finery is abandoned, their heads are shaved and they stay with the monks for a night or longer. The ceremony is an enactment of Gautama Buddha's birth as a prince and his renunciation of this life to take up a spiritual quest. Boys can make this ceremony the beginning of a period of education in the monastery as a novice monk. This is the first step to full ordination and it was important for general educational reasons when the monasteries were the main centres of learning.

2. Ordination. Boys are not allowed to be fully ordained as monks until they are twenty, but they may become novices. They stay in the monastery for a matter of months or years, and some take full ordination and remain for life. This ceremony may be part of an initiation or may be taken years afterwards.

3. Renewal of vows. Lay Buddhists often try to be more observant in their religion during the rainy season. They renew the five precepts, and often take eight or even all ten. Many of them actually stay in the monasteries for a few weeks. This is the easiest time of the year for farmers in countries like Burma, and people are freer to think of religious things.

The end of the retreat. This is the part of the Vassa which is most like a festival and involves the whole village. The monks are given a special feast, which is more than the daily offering of food. As we have seen, they also receive presents of necessary items for their religious observances and for the upkeep of the monastery. In addition to those mentioned at the beginning of this section, gifts of razors, blankets and begging bowls may be made. The laity who come for the 'giving' ceremony take the precepts at this time, and those who have been with the monks for the Rainy Season return home.

New Year festivals

Theravada. The new year falls at different times in different Buddhist countries, although Buddhists in the west are happy to adapt to a western calendar. In Burma and Thailand it is in April, and is especially associated with water and activities which may pre-date Buddhism. Bowls of cool water are offered to revered people in the community, and there is bathing of Buddha images and monks. Water is also thrown over people in the streets. This goes on for two days. The water symbolises purification and the readiness for a new start. On the third day, which is the beginning of the new year, Buddhists go to the temples to renew their religious commitment by giving to the monks, making offerings in the shrine room and taking the Three Refuges and Five Precepts. Extra merit is gained by freeing animals and fish from capitivity. This demonstrates typical Buddhist respect for all living things.

Mahayana—the example of Japan. Japan observes the same calendar as the west, so New Year's Day is on 1st January. It is 31st December, however, that is more important to Buddhists than the first day of the new year. The celebration on this day is called Joya no Kane, or The Evening Bells Ceremony. Bells are a distinctive feature of Buddhist temples all over the world. Japanese bells are struck on the side with a large stick, and at Joya no Kane the old year departs when temple bells are struck 108 times. Buddhists also have 108 beads for prayer and meditation. The number is $2^2 \times 3^3$, or 9×12, and has astrological associations going back into Indian culture, which do not always concern Buddhists any more. The number, however, remains. On this occasion, Buddhists hear the bells, visit the temples and think of the many evils of the year that is passing and the blessings that could be part of the new year. Evils are such things as greed, hate and ignorance, and actions like lying, stealing and killing which flow from them. Blessings are friendliness, helpfulness, kind words, generosity, love, compassion, sympathetic joy and stability.

Japanese festivals

Higan. This means 'other shore', and is an image for Nirvana or enlightenment. On 21st March and 23rd September, when the seasons change, Japanese Buddhists think about harmony. Harmony and naturalness are important ideas in Japanese culture. They are expressed in the way the Japanese use wood in their buildings, arrange flowers, paint pictures and even take tea. This harmony, tranquillity and peace can be realised both in nature and in ourselves and is another way of talking about Nirvana. At Higan, Japanese Buddhists visit the temples and also the graves of ancestors. They pour water from wooden ladles over the tombstones. This is an act of love and compassion towards the dead, as the pouring of water in this case is to transfer merit to them and help them to the further shore. At the temples there is the feeling of going on an enjoyable outing, as Buddhists make the usual offerings of flowers and incense, and enjoy walking round the beautiful temple grounds. There is a special emphasis on the six virtues which are especially important for anyone on his way to the 'other shore'. These are generosity, non-harming, patience, effort, meditation and wisdom.

Obon. If you were in Japan just before 15th July you would notice that many people were planning to return to their native village or town or to see their parents. This is 'going home for Obon', which is a joyful ceremony and is also called Ura-Bon-e. The theme of joy comes from the story of the Buddha's compassionate release of the mother of Moggollana, one of his followers. Her son had the power to visit other worlds, and when he saw her suffering in one of the many Buddhist hells he asked the Buddha to help her, which he did. One tradition says he used a rope to haul her out, so many villages remember this with a tug-of-war. At this festival Buddhists offer fruit and flowers to the Buddha and ask for his compassion on themselves and their ancestors in future lives. This very serious theme is surrounded by the happiness of family reunions. Villages hold fêtes with side-shows, toffee apples, lucky dips and folk-dancing. One distinctive dance is performed by a large group of people in a circle. This gentle dance has given its name to the festival. Celebrations go on into the night, and lanterns become another characteristic part of the scene and make it another one of the many religious 'festivals of light'.

The Tooth-Relic festival

Kandy, Sri Lanka. Most festivals mark a particular time of the year, or an event. This festival is in honour of a tooth relic of Gautama Buddha, kept in a special temple in Kandy. It is a great tourist attraction every year, because there are fifteen days of colourful processions in the streets. Dancers, musicians and decorated elephants take part and the festivities lead up to the last night, when the relic is honoured. The streets are crowded, and there is a great sense of national pride and joy at this reminder of the island's religious heritage.

The relic is kept in a special temple in a miniature stupa. The temple itself is not in the form of a stupa. At the temple there are daily acts of devotion to this reminder of the Buddha, but nothing that rivals the annual festival. The tooth relic is said to have been brought to the island from India in the fourth century CE. It was taken to the great ancient capital Anuradhupura, which is now in ruins. Even then, an annual procession and festival were held in its honour. It moved when the capitals were changed and is now in Kandy. The present festival of fifteen nights in July/August—called Esala in Sri Lanka, and Esala Perahera is another name for the festival—is an eighteenth-century mixture of Hindu elements and ancient court ritual. The Hindu gods are incorporated as guardians of the four quarters of the world, and the relic is treated as if it were a king, riding on an elephant with a court of attendants to escort it. The actual tooth relic is too precious to leave the temple, and a lesser relic is used in an exact copy of the stupa reliquary. On the fifteenth day, at the climax of the festival, the tusked elephant, which is dressed to carry the stupa, is accompanied by whip-crackers, flag-bearers, lines of musicians, dancers, drummers, temple attendants and also many other elephants.

✠ Christian festivals

The Christian calendar evolved over a period of about six centuries. In New Testament times Sunday, known as the Lord's Day was observed but it was not until the reign of the Emperor Constantine that it was declared a day of rest. The anniversaries of

Jesus' crucifixion and resurrection at Passovertide and Pentecost were probably also observed by the early church. Not until the sixth century did the church observe Advent, which is now regarded as the beginning of the Christian year. Even now, the Orthodox Christians of Eastern Europe, and the Western churches have different calendars. They celebrate Christmas and Easter on different dates and the Advent season is longer in the east than in the west. However, in this section it is the significance of the festivals, not their dating, that will concern us most.

The year begins in November with Advent, which means 'coming'. Four Sundays before Christmas Christians begin to prepare for the coming of Jesus. Sometimes Advent candles are lit or homes use special Advent calendars to mark the approach of the festival of Jesus' birth. In the Eastern church it is a forty-day long period of penitence. The West tends to emphasise this aspect rather less, though services have preparation as their theme.

The outline below indicates that the Christian year has two dates which determine all its festivals and special occasions. One is the fixed date of Christmas, always 25th December in Britain; the other is Easter, a variable feast whose date is related to the full moon after the spring equinox and can be as early as 21st March or as late as 25th April.

The main red-letter days—and in old calendars they were actually printed in red ink—of Christians in Britain, celebrated by all churches are the following:

The Christian Year

MONTH	FESTIVAL OR SEASON
November/December	Advent
December	Christmas (25th)
February/March	Lent
March/April	Easter (21st March–25th April)
May/June	Ascension Day (Thursday after fourth Sunday after Easter)
	Pentecost or Whitsuntide (seven Sundays after Easter)
June	Trinity Sunday (Sunday after Whitsunday)

Of these festivals, Christmas, Easter and Whitsuntide are of outstanding importance and they will be considered in turn.

Christmas.　No one knows when Jesus was born, either the year or even the time of year, and for about three hundred years the church did not seem to care. A calendar dated to 336 shows that it was the custom of Christians in Rome to celebrate the festival on 25th December by then. That date was regarded as the Natalis Solis Invicti, (Birthday of the Unconquered Sun), by the worshippers of Mithras, one of Christianity's greatest rivals. It seems probable that the church took over that date. Also in the Roman world, on 17th December a festival of Saturn was held when presents were given and slaves were freed for a short time to share in the merrymaking. Elements of this festival may have crept into the Christian observance. Underlying all these may be celebrations throughout the northern hemisphere to ensure at the darkest time of the year, the winter solstice, the victory of light over darkness and the eventual return of spring after the bleakness of winter. Christmas is probably a 'Christianising' of all these things.

The message.　The belief which prompts Christians to celebrate Christmas is that God sent his only son into the world to bring his message of light and love. They sing special hymns which contain such words as:

> Love came down at Christmas,
> Love all lovely, love divine;
> Love was born at Christmas,
> Star and angels gave the sign.
>
> Worship we the Godhead,
> Love incarnate, love divine;
> Worship we our Jesus:
> But wherewith for sacred sign?
>
> Love shall be our token,
> Love be yours and love be mine,
> Love to God and all men,
> Love for plea and gift for sign.　　　　(Christina Rossetti)

There can be no disputing that love is the key word of this poem, God's love for man, man's love for God and for one another. This the poet sees as the message of Christmas. Jesus, born in a stable in Bethlehem, heralded by the angels who spoke to shepherds, and by a star which guided Gentile wise men from the east, is God's token of love. Perhaps the author had these New Testament words in mind when composing her poem:

> Beloved let us love one another; for love is of God, and he who loves is born of God and knows God. He who does not love does

269

not know God; for God is love. In this the love of God was made manifest among us, that God sent his only son into the world, so that we might live through him.

(I John 4:7–9)

The idea of light overcoming darkness is also present in the Christian explanation of the meaning of the life of Jesus. His life was the light of men, (John 1:4); Jesus is called the light of the world, (John 8:12) and in King Herod's attempt to kill the infant Jesus (Matthew Chapter 2), we read the first of many incidents describing the struggle of darkness and evil to extinguish love, light, and goodness.

The customs. These three ideals are shown at Christmas in the giving of presents, in family gatherings, and the serious attempt to keep the Christian spirit — that is, to be kind and considerate. Quarrelling is forgotten and collections are made for poor people and those in institutions and hospitals. A real attempt is made to ensure that everyone can enjoy Christmas. However, of the things seen at this time of year perhaps only one is really Christian, the crib. In many churches, homes, town hall squares, city centres, and outside large department stores, a representation of the crib may be seen — the child Jesus lying in a bed of straw, the crib, which was actually a manger, and around him Mary, Joseph, perhaps the wise men and shepherds, and some animals. The tableau represents the scene in Bethlehem at Jesus' birth, the stable—or probably cave —where he was born 'because there was no room in the inn' (Luke 2:7).

The Christmas tree is pre-Christian. Being evergreen, it may have been used to symbolise the belief that life would survive the darkness and cold of winter when most of nature seemed to be dying. Other evergreens, like holly and ivy, may have had similar significance. The lights on Christmas trees are reminders of ancient festivals of light, also. The large meals and the presents, too, are more to do with the Saturnalia than with Jesus. However the church has Christianised them all, with one exception. Mistletoe is not supposed to be used in the decoration of churches. It was associated with the Druids, whose practice of sacrificing human beings made them intolerable, even to the Romans. Christianity shared this disgust, and had no wish to encourage the survival of anything to do with the cult. The fact that we still find mistletoe decorating homes at Christmas shows the power of ancient traditions to survive.

Christmas is a good example of a religion's ability to give new meaning to old customs, while permitting the practices to live on.

Easter. The most important festival for Christians is Easter. It commemorates the death and resurrection of Jesus. Christians believe that the crucifixion of Jesus was not the tragic end of the ministry of a good man, or one of many examples of political executions. It was more than either of these things. They believe that Jesus acted in obedience to the will of God. On the night of his arrest, only a few minutes before his enemies — led by one of his own disciples, Judas — came for him, Jesus prayed in the Garden of Gethsemane, 'Father, if you are willing, remove this cup from me; nevertheless, not my will but yours be done.' (Luke 22:42).

Why was the death of this innocent and good man God's will?

Christmas, a joyful Christian festival celebrated by parties as well as special services.

271

That is a question that has been examined by Christians ever since it happened, but it would only have been asked as a matter of idle curiosity had Jesus' death been the end of the story. However, Christians believe that on the following Sunday the man who had died on the Friday appeared to some of his disciples, and to others during the next few weeks. The resurrection convinced them that the crucifixion had some special purpose. What might it be?

The meaning of the crucifixion.   One theory is that it was to show the greatness of God's love. To the Christian, Jesus is God. By dying he showed that there is no possibility of man's hatred making God lose his patience and destroy him. By overcoming death he showed that love is all-conquering. Connected with this view is the belief that Christians should live like Jesus, loving their enemies, refusing to resist evil by evil means. As Jesus suffered, so his followers should be prepared to suffer in the service of God and mankind. Jesus is a moral example.

Another theory is that Jesus died to pay the price of man's sin. In the Garden of Eden story at the beginning of the Bible, Adam and Eve are seen to be living a life of perfect bliss. However, when they disobey God, life changes. It becomes hard and wearisome, ending in death. Even if we do not take the Genesis story absolutely literally, we can still accept the principle that death is some kind of punishment. Many societies still execute criminals, suggesting that to deprive someone of life is the severest retribution that can be exacted. According to this theory, God's justice demanded the death penalty. The innocent Jesus by dying paid the price for everyone who believes in him. For Jesus' sake God forgives mankind. This view of Jesus' death is, of course, very different from the first one.

Perhaps most Christians believe something between the two. They want to see both the love of God and the sin of man as being responsible in some way for the death of Jesus. Many of the New Testament writers make use of the symbol of the Day of Atonement scapegoat upon which the High Priest placed his hands as a token that Israel's sins were forgiven, before it was killed. In John's gospel the death of Jesus takes place when the Passover lambs are being killed (John 19:14), and Jesus is described as 'the lamb of God who takes away the sin of the world' (John 1:29).

Lenten observance.   Whatever Christians believe about the death of Jesus, they all agree in calling the day that he died Good Friday (or Holy Friday), because it proves the victory of good over evil; otherwise there would have been no resurrection. Good Friday also reminds us of man's disobedience and therefore it is preceded by a period of just over forty days which is called Lent, a length of time given to penance. This begins on Ash Wednesday, so called because traditionally the palm crosses from the previous year's Palm Sunday were burned then, and when Christians went to church on Ash Wednesday to begin Lent the ash from the crosses was used to mark a cross on their foreheads. The custom is less observed now than in past times. During Lent people fasted, eating no meat and sweet foods; on the Monday before Lent, they used up their meat, so it was called 'collop Monday', a collop being a piece of meat. On the Tuesday people feasted to eat up all the good things that they might have in the larder — hence Pancake Day. It is also known as Shrove Tuesday because people confessed their sins to the priest and were shriven, or absolved from sin, before attending church on Ash Wednesday. Lent is also associated with Jesus' period of forty days in the wilderness before he began his ministry, but Lent lasts a little longer than forty days because it includes days like Mothering Sunday which are not fast days. Lent as a strict fast is now observed more by Roman Catholics than by other Christians.

Although most people enjoy hot cross buns on Good Friday, and chocolate eggs on Easter Sunday, the festival is kept more by Christians than by the general population. In this respect it differs from Christmas—a time when everyone celebrates something. The hot cross buns were intended to break the fast, for they are sweet and contain spices and currants; they are not merely a kind of bread. The cross is, of course, a reminder of the crucifixion. The egg represents new life; Christians are reminded of Jesus rising from the tomb in which he had been placed after his death. They may have got the idea from the Jewish Passover meal, or both may owe it to some ancient spring custom belonging to a tradition and religion long since forgotten. However, Easter is another example of how Christianity 'Christianised' a festival, this time the Jewish Passover, though, of course, Jesus actually did die at this time.

In the years shortly after his ministry the new sect of Christians, all of whom were still Jews, would celebrate the Passover but give it a new meaning. It is probable that the Last Supper, described in the gospels as the final meal which Jesus ate with his disciples, was the Passover Seder. Instead of remaining an annual festival it became a daily celebration, remembering his self-sacrifice and looking forward to Jesus' coming in power (Acts 2:46, I Cor 11).

Whitsuntide. According to the Acts of the Apostle, seven weeks after Jesus' resurrection during the festival of Passover, another

273

important event took place, on the day of the Pentecost festival. This was the giving of the power of the Holy Spirit to the disciples. In the Hebrew Bible there are many references to the spirit of God inspiring the prophets to speak the words God gave them and to perform acts which demonstrated the power of God. There was also the promise that this inspiration, given to only a few men and women, would be 'poured out on all flesh' one day (Joel 2:28–29). This is what Peter and the other Christians experienced at Pentecost, so in future years, while their Jewish friends and relatives continued to celebrate the giving of the Torah at Sinai, they would thank God not only for the Torah but for the Holy Spirit which inspired it and Moses.

This festival might be called the birthday of the Christian community or church. Therefore it was once a popular time for admitting new members into it through the rite of baptism. These men and women would dress in white, a colour symbolising newness. Consequently the day came to be called White Sunday, then Whit Sunday. In Britain this third important Christian festival is now much less regarded than the other two and has ceased to be a public holiday. Instead, in the hope of good weather, the spring bank holiday has been fixed as the last weekend of May. Perhaps the church will move its celebration of Pentecost to that date eventually. Already it seldom coincides with its Jewish parent or with Eastern Orthodox Pentecost. Therefore little might be lost and much gained by bringing the festival back to a time when everyone has a weekend holiday. Meanwhile there have been discussions for some time over the issue of fixing the date of Easter, perhaps observing it on the first or second Sunday in April.

Trinity Sunday. This day is mentioned for only three reasons. First, it is an occasion when some denominations ordain men who have completed their training to the ministry. Secondly, the church year from that Sunday until Advent is counted in terms of Sundays 'after Trinity'. Thirdly, and most important, it is a reminder that Christians do not believe in three Gods but only in one. The festivals of Christianity all make this claim and it is appropriate that the last one of the church calendar should be devoted to remembering it particularly.

Muslim festivals

The Muslim year is based on a system of lunar months, like other religious calendars, but does not make use of leap years to bring it in line with the Gregorian solar calendar. Consequently, the Muslim year in effect moves backwards through the secular year. For example, in 1970 the Muslim new year fell on 8th March, and in 1980 it was celebrated on 9th November. In 1979 Muslims greeted the year 1400, the beginning of a new century. They date their era from 622 of the Common Era, the date when the Prophet Muhammad left Mecca to become leader of the people of Medina. Clearly 1400 plus 622 does not add up to 1979, but 2022. Therefore a mathematical formula is required for calculating the corresponding common or Christian or Muslim years. It is:

$$AH = \frac{33}{32} (CE - 622) \text{ or conversely, } CE = \frac{32}{33} (AH + 622).$$

AH stands for 'Anno Hijra' or 'After the Hijra', just as AD represents 'Anno Domini'. 'In the year of our Lord', for a Christian.

It is obviously impossible to put the months of the Muslim year against their January to December counterparts. Together with the festivals they are as follows:

Muslim Festivals

MUSLIM MONTH	FESTIVAL
Muharram	Hijra to Medina
Safar	
Rabi' al-Awwal	Muhammad's birthday (12th)
Rabi'ath-Thani	
Jamadi al-Awwal	
Jamadi al-Akhir	
Rajab	
Sha'ban	
Ramadan	complete month of fasting Night of Power
Shawwal	Eid-ul-Fitr
Dhul-Qa'da	
Dhul-Hijja	Eid-ul-Adha

Muharram. Muharram was declared to be the first month of the Muslim year by Umar, the second Caliph, after discussions with other companions of the Prophet. It commemorates the Hijra to Medina and therefore Muslims rejoice over the foundation of their community and a new year at the same time. It is a time for exchanging greetings and telling stories about the Prophet and his companions.

The Prophet's Birthday.   This day, the twelfth of the third month, is another occasion for thanksgiving. In many ways it is regarded as the most important day in man's history since creation, for it was through Muhammad that God gave mankind his final revelation, the message of the Qur'an. The whole month is a time for remembering his ministry.

Ramadan.   All other events in the calendar are overshadowed by this and the two feasts which will be described after it. Ramadan is a whole lunar month of fasting. From dawn until dusk—or, more precisely, from the moment it is possible to distinguish a white thread from a black thread laid alongside it until the moment this is no longer possible—the Muslim must fast. This means obtaining not only from food, but even from water, from smoking, and from indulging in unkind remarks and quarrels.

The origin of the fast is not known. Muslims observe it as one of the five Pillars of their faith explicitly mentioned in the Qur'an:

> You who believe, fasting has been prescribed for you, just as it was prescribed for those before you, so that you may do your duty on days that have been fixed. Any of you who is ill or on a journey should choose a number of other days. For those who can afford it, making up for it means feeding a poor man; if someone offers even more, it is even better for him; although it is better for you to fast.

(Sura 2:183–184)

The reference to those before you is probably to the Jews fasting on the Day of Atonement, or to Christians keeping Lent. An important feature of the Muslim fast is the concession to those who might find it hard to observe — travellers and the sick. Though going without food and water for a whole day, either in an Arabian summer or perhaps a British winter is an ordeal, the intention is to impose discipline, not cruelty. The compassionate element of God's nature is seen in these relaxations of the regulations. It can be found even more in the practices of Muslims. Some years ago a Muslim friend invited the author to his home for a meal after the Friday noon prayers at the mosque. The imam came but did not eat anything. When asked why, he said that his wife had not been well during part of Ramadan, which had just ended, and she was now completing the fast. Because it would be a strain on her to cook him food while she was fasting, and to show his love for her, he, too, was keeping extra days of fast.

During Ramadan, especially in Muslim countries, even the more lax Muslims are more regular in their religious observances. In the

276

evenings the men will gather in the mosque to say their prayers, and most will keep the fast. The pace of work will slow down and during the day many people will find an opportunity to sleep. However, this is not a practice confined to Ramadan. In lands with hot climates, like India or Pakistan it is customary and necessary to rest in the middle of the day. In some other parts of the world, however, most of the population is unaware that its Muslim members are keeping Ramadan and they are expected to work as hard as anyone else. Even children in school try to observe the fast, to be, like their parents, good Muslims, even though they should not begin to fast until they are in their teens.

Ramadan is not only a month of fasting and seriousness. It is also a time for rejoicing. Ramadan is the only month referred to in the Qur'an and it is mentioned for two reasons — the fast and the giving of the Qur'an:

> The month of Ramadan is when the Qur'an was sent down as guidance for mankind, and with explanations for guidance, and as a standard (for judging between right and wrong).
>
> (Sura 2:185)

One night in the month, which has come to be known as The Night of Power, Lailat al-Qadr, Muhammad received the first revelation from the angel Gabriel. Probably it took place on the night before the 27th of the month, but the precise date is not known. Therefore, many Muslims devote the last ten days of the month to reading the Qur'an and offering extra prayers besides the obligatory five each day. The Qur'an says:

> The Night of Power is better than a thousand months. Thereon descend the angels and the spirit (Gabriel) by God's permission on every errand. There is peace until daybreak.
>
> (Sura 97:1–5)

The fast ends with a festival, Eid-ul-Fitr, but before Ramadan ends a final obligation must be observed, that of making a special contribution for the care of the poor, Zakat-ul-Fitr, 'the charity of Fast-breaking'. Generosity, caring for the poor, is one of the great virtues encouraged by Islam. The purpose of this requirement is to ensure that no Muslim is unable to break his fast. Ramadan has as one of its aims the reminding of the rich of what it means to go hungry. The thirty-day experience ought to make them thankful for their wealth, and more prepared to share it with those in need. The fast also stresses the equality of everyone, for when all go without food there are no rich and no beggars, and all share the same duty to obey God by keeping this Pillar of the faith. These are the other

277

meanings of the fast in addition to its being a healthy discipline, teaching self-control.

Eid-ul-Fitr (Id-ul-Fitr). The sighting of the new moon signifies the beginning of the month of Shawwal and the end of Ramadan. The feast which follows is made even more enjoyable when the Muslim has faithfully observed the fast. As the Prophet Muhammad said:

> 'A fasting person will have joy and happiness twice; when he breaks the fast he will be full of joy because it is at an end, and when he meets his Lord on the Day of Judgement, because he has kept his obligation.'

The feast begins with special congregational prayers in the morning between dawn and noon. These are held in as few mosques as possible, to encourage Muslims to gather in large groups. Sometimes a village may have two or even three mosques; it is likely that on this day only one would be used. After the prayers families and

Cards such as these are sent at the festival of Eid-ul-Fitr which follows the end of Ramadan, the month of fasting.

friends come together in their homes. Everyone wears new clothes, there is a party, and presents are given. In Pakistan swings are often tied to trees for the children to enjoy themselves, while adults who have not met for a long time exchange news. A mother may send a tray of food to her daughter who has married and is living in a nearby village. The poor are not forgotten either. They will be sent gifts of food or grain. At the end of the day the hosts give their guests sweets as they depart for home.

Eid-ul-Adha (Id-ul-Adha). This is the high point of the Hajj for those who have been able to make it. It takes place at Mina, where Abraham showed his readiness to sacrifice Ishmael, but where a ram was offered instead. The name of the festival means 'feast of sacrifice' and it is celebrated throughout the Muslim world, not only by those who are at Mina in Arabia. On the tenth morning of the month of pilgrimage, which is what Dhul-Hijja means, each family sacrifices a sheep or other animal, or perhaps a group of families will offer a cow. Sacrifice signifies the giving of oneself to God; the animal is not a substitute, but only a symbol. There is no idea of appeasing an angry God through this act. Indeed the Qur'an clearly states:

> 'It is neither their meat nor their blood that reaches God. It is your piety that reaches him. He has made them (animals) subject to you so that you might glorify God for his guidance to you. Proclaim the good news to all who do right.

> (Sura 22:37)

Congregational prayers follow the killing of the animals. Sometimes in Britain it is necessary to hire a school hall or some other large building to accommodate the crowd of people who attend. After the prayers friends and relatives wish one another 'Eid Mubarak', a happy festival and celebrate with their families. Though the meat of the slain animal is eaten by the family, at least one third of it should be given to the poor. Sometimes British Muslims kill only a token number of animals and instead send money home to their relatives to pay for their goat or sheep. In past years, though rarely now, some Muslims have been brought to court for killing a sheep or cow in their own backyard. In many countries this is perfectly permissible, but in Britain slaughter must be carried out in an abbatoir in accordance with strict rules. Now that Muslim communities are well-established in Britain, arrangements are usually made for the slaughter to be carried out at the abbatoir by a Muslim in the presence of an inspector, though a few years ago when Eid fell on a Sunday communities found it difficult to persuade authorities to open the abbatoirs. Unaware that the animals must be killed on the tenth of Dhul-Hijja, they thought that the meat could be put into the refrigerator after being killed on Friday.

This is the most important festival of the year, but perhaps because of its solemnity it is not celebrated quite as joyously as Eid-ul-Fitr, when cards may be sent and parties are held. However, both Eids are occasions when children should not go to school and adults should not go to work so that all may worship God.

Sikh festivals

About ten million of the world's Sikh population live in the Punjab region of India. Therefore they use the Hindu calendar which runs from Chaitra to Phalguna though their religious new year begins on the first day of Baisakhi, in April. This has become a fixed festival, the only one in the Sikh calendar, falling on 13th April. (In 1975, however, it was observed on the 14th. This occurs once in every thirty-six years.) The rest, being based on Hindu lunar months, are variable. Sikh festivals are of two kinds, melas, which are meetings or fairs, and gurpurbs. The latter are the anniversaries of the birth or death of one of the ten Gurus; the melas correspond to Hindu festivals and are reinterpretations of them. Only four gurpurbs are regularly observed in Britain—the birthdays of Guru Nanak and Guru Gobind Singh, and the martyrdom days of Guru Arjan and Guru Tegh Bahadur, though such events as the five hundredth anniversary of Guru Amar Das's birth are specially commemorated. The Sikh festivals occur in the Hindu and common calendars in the following order.

Sikh Festivals

HINDU MONTH	GREGORIAN CALENDAR	FESTIVAL
Vaisakha	April	Baisakhi mela
Jyestha	May/June	martyrdom of Guru Arjan
Asvina/Karttika	October/November	Diwali mela
		birth of Guru Nanak
Pausa	December	martyrdom of Guru Tegh Bahadur
Magha	December/January	birth of Guru Gobind Singh
Phalguna	February/March	Hola Mohalla mela

At least two of the melas were probably observed by the Sikhs before any of the gurpurbs, so it is with the former that we shall begin. A characteristic of all three Sikh melas included in our list is a joyful spirit and considerable hustle and bustle. Crowds come from afar on foot, on carts pulled by tractor or by horse, or on public transport. They play games, organise races, buy and sell animals, listen to speeches about the Gurus, and visit local places of interest and religious significance. Each mela has a slightly different emphasis.

Baisakhi at Amritsar is very much a fair, at which farmers sell all kinds of domestic animals from camels to pigs, though horses seem to predominate. Hola Mohalla at Anandpur, where the festival has taken deepest root, stresses competition of many kinds, wrestling, archery, but also music and poetry. Diwali at Amritsar sees the Golden Temple illuminated by hundreds of coloured lights, firework displays and a general atmosphere of carnival. Though the melas were devices for weaning Sikhs away from Hindu practices, Diwali still owes much to its Hindu counterpart, though there are no effigies of Ravana burned and no stories of Lakshmi or Rama told. Instead each mela has its own significance for Sikhs.

Watched by her mother and some friends, a Sikh ties a rakhi on her young brother's wrist. Though the custom is Hindu in origin it is observed by Indians generally regardless of belief.

Baisakhi. This is the beginning of the Sikh religious year. Gurdwara committees are elected at this time, but the date has a greater significance than that in the story of Sikhism. Guru Amar Das was the first leader to command his followers to assemble before him on that occasion and his successors maintained the tradition. He also summoned them at Mahashivatatri and Diwali, so it was clearly his intention to ask them to decide whether they were Sikhs or Hindus. They could not be both.

On Baisakhi day 1699 the tenth Guru, Gobind Singh, summoned the Sikhs to him at Anandpur where he happened to be. Standing in front of his tent with a drawn sword, he asked which of them was willing to lay down his life for his Guru. At last one man came forward. He was taken inside the tent, from which the Guru emerged alone, his sword dripping blood, a few moments later. Again he made his request, with the same result. Each time there was more hesitation before a volunteer came forward, and the crowd grew steadily more restive. When the fifth man had been taken into the tent Guru Gobind Singh reappeared with them all, alive and unharmed. The blood had been that of a goat. The drama which his followers had witnessed was a way of telling them that the hard times they were living in demanded self-sacrifice, that the Sikhs must be resolute and loyal to their faith.

The Guru now made a nectar of sugar crystals dissolved in water, sprinkled it on the five men, gave them some of it to drink, and then asked them to perform the same ceremony for him. His wife submitted to it also, and by the end of the day most of the Sikhs present had been initiated in the same way. Those who refused did so either because they saw no need to undergo this rite with men and women of inferior castes, as they regarded them, or because they disapproved of the use of force which the Guru was sanctioning.

For almost a hundred years some Sikhs had taken arms in an independence struggle against the Mughal rulers of India. Now the Guru was bringing the war bands under his control. To those men who were initiated into the organisation, which came to be called the Khalsa (the pure, or dedicated ones), he gave the common name Singh, lion, and the women came to be called Kaur, princess. The men adopted a common uniform, based on five elements known as the five 'Ks', for the Punjabi words for them each begin with that letter; they are uncut hair, a comb to keep it tidy, a wrist band on the right arm, (probably to protect it in battle), a sword, and trousers (instead of the loose skirt or dhoti often worn in North India). To these they also added the turban, which has become the most important distinguishing mark of the Sikh. Women, too, have adopted the five 'Ks' and some, especially American converts, are beginning to wear the turban.

Baisakhi might be regarded as the birthday of Sikhism as we now know it. Initiation ceremonies, when new members join the Khalsa, are often held at this time of year. After celebrating the festival, farmers in the Punjab turn to the work of harvesting their first corn crop, for there is a tradition that this should not begin until Baisakhi has ended.

Diwali. The sixth Guru, Hargobind, enjoyed mixed relationships with the Mughal authorities. This is not surprising when it is remembered that his father, Guru Arjan, had died while in their custody. Though sometimes Guru Hargobind was the Emperor's guest at court and went hunting with him, on other occasions he was suspected of treachery. It was at such a time when the Guru found himself a prisoner in a fortress at Gwalior. With him were no fewer than fifty-two Hindu princes. The Emperor Jehangir personally investigated the charges which his officials brought against the Guru, rejected them, and ordered him to be released. Guru Hargobind, however, refused to leave prison unless he could take the other princes with him. Jehangir replied that as many rajas could go free as could hold on to the Guru's clothes as he walked along the narrow passage leading out of the prison. The Guru asked for a cloak to be brought which had long tassel like ends. These the princes held and so gained their freedom. This happened at Diwali time, which for the Sikhs commemorates the safe and triumphant return of their Guru. With bonfires and fireworks they salute a festival of freedom.

Hola Mohalla. In 1680 Guru Gobind Singh introduced this assembly to divert Sikhs from the Hindu Holi festival, usually dedicated to Krishna in their part of the Indian subcontinent. It is only seriously observed in Anandpur, but must be mentioned here as another example of the Sikh practice of reinterpreting Hindu festivals, and to draw attention to the fact that Sikhs in Britain and other parts of the world tend not to join in the Holi festivities of their Hindu neighbours.

Gurpurbs. 'Pur' is a syllable signifying 'holiday', therefore a gurpurb is a holiday associated with a Guru. In India there are many such holidays, but they are usually observed only in the places where a Guru was born or died, with the exception of the four included in the list at the beginning of this section. Open air processions, carrying the Guru Granth Sahib round the village or city, lectures, and langar characterise the celebrations in India. In Britain, partly for climatic reasons, the occasion is more subdued. However, on the anniversary of Guru Arjan's death which falls in summer, Sikhs have been known to present oranges or apples to people who visit or remain for langar, the meal served in the dining hall of the gurdwara.

There are three features common to all the gurpurbs and only one difference. The difference is simply that the speeches or lectures at a gurpurb take as their theme the particular Guru who is being commemorated in the day's celebrations.

The first common element is that the gurpurb will be celebrated on the weekend after the anniversary, unless the day falls on a Sunday. This allows as many people as possible to attend. As we have seen, it is customary among Sikhs to adopt the weekly holiday of the country in which they are living and use it as their day for worship, though many go to the gurdwara every evening. Secondly, after diwan (the service), everyone will be invited to remain for langar, the meal served afterwards. Some may have langar every Sunday and all gurdwaras will make it part of their gurpurb celebrations. Thirdly, and most important, at each gurpurb a continuous reading of the Guru Granth Sahib is held. This begins about forty-eight hours before the Sunday diwan and is undertaken by a relay of readers. Such a ceremonial reading of the scriptures is called an Akhand Path. During the two days Sikhs will attempt to attend it for some time each day, but will make a special effort to be present when the final pages are read on the Sunday morning. Diwan, which follows, will concentrate on the Guru whose gurpurb is being remembered.

Questions

1. *What is a festival? Describe* **two** *festivals from different faiths saying when, how, and why they are celebrated.*

2. *Describe* **two** *festivals which have light as a theme. How do the stories (myths) and practices of these festivals bring out this theme?*

3. *Sometimes festivals change their meaning. From different religions name and describe* **two** *festivals which were once based on nature but now have a different significance.*

4. *Describe* **two** *of the following festivals saying when, how, and why they are celebrated: Holi, Baisakhi, Eid-ul-Fitr, Wesak, Whitsuntide, and Passover.*

5. Discuss the purpose and importance of fasting in the Jewish and Muslim faiths.

6. Festivals are described as a time of celebration. Show how the elements of rejoicing and love of one's neighbour appear in the festivals of two of the faiths you have studied.

7. How do festival celebrations differ from normal worship in **two** of the religions you have studied?

EPILOGUE
e Coming Together
of Religions

One of the features of the world of the late twentieth century is that each day it is in effect growing smaller. The distance between London and Brazil or Arabia may not have changed for a million years but they can now be reached from London in a few hours. News pictures of these distant countries can appear on our television screens almost as soon as the events happen, and if their prices for coffee or oil go up, prices in our shops increase overnight as a result. The world has become a global 'village'. Britain is part of that village in two respects; first, her economy is influenced by what takes place elsewhere in the world, just as life in Africa or India used to be affected by wars taking place in Europe. Secondly, her former subjects have settled in Britain as citizens. This book has described faiths and cultures of great antiquity and worth, all of which have played their part in the development of human society and experience. Even the youngest of them is over five hundred years old, but it, and the others, tended to be ignored because they were far away. Now all the world's religions are close at hand.

Things common to the six religions

In its approach, considering messengers, worship, scriptures, festivals and pilgrimages, this book has highlighted the similarities between the six faiths. However it has not exhausted the areas of agreement. Here are some other things that they have in common.

All the religions believe that there is one transcendent, ultimate reality, which five of them call God. The Hindu may be prepared to describe it in non-personal form, or as a personal God in many forms, female as well as male, but the ultimate belief, like that of the Trinitarian Christian, is that reality is one.

It is a very important belief of the faiths that this reality makes itself known to mankind, and that the various scriptures contain its message to humanity. Through this message, whether it be the

Qur'an or Jesus, the believer is sure that peace with God can be obtained in this life and in the world to come. In other words, the six religions all believe in a quality of life based on faith which transcends death.

Many Buddhists and some Hindus would be unhappy to speak of God, but they would certainly subscribe to belief in an eternal, unchanging reality. They call it the state of Nirvana or Nibbana. That faith results in obligation is another fundamental belief of these religions. The obligations include a command to worship or meditation, and also a requirement to care for one's fellow human beings. A belief that we are responsible for our neighbours is a strong teaching of all the world's great religions.

Something else that they share is the difficulty of persuading people of the truth of eternal values, like love and truth, in a secular, materialistic society which is not inclined to take religion very seriously. The problem may seem greater in America or Britain, but it is just as real in Egypt, Pakistan or Israel.

The differences between the religions

The areas of agreement between the world's faiths must not be underestimated; they may well have more in common than they have differences. However, dissimilarities cannot and must not be ignored, and perhaps they should not always be regarded as tragic and deplorable. Some differences may appear unimportant to out-siders. Does it really matter, for example, if some people sing hymns during worship and other remain silent, speaking only if they feel the spirit of God moving them? Does the worth of one's prayers depend on facing Mecca or Jerusalem, or only on turning one's heart towards God and Nirvana? These issues must not be dismissed as insignificant. The Jew and the Muslim are calling to mind ancient and treasured traditions, as well as the teachings of their men of God. They may well say that once one ceases to be concerned about the direction in which one should face the time will soon become unimportant, and before long the practice of prayer itself will be forgotten in the busy rush of modern life. It is the individual Jew, Muslim, Buddhist, Christian, Hindu, or Sikh, who must decide what matters, following the guidance of the community to which he belongs, and not uninvolved observers. Nevertheless, each faith is being challenged by the modern world to say what its priorities are.

As members of the religions meet to share experiences and

287

problems, to discuss their similarities and differences, in Birmingham, London, or Leeds, mutual respect is growing between them. The Muslim learns that the Christian does not believe in three gods. The Christian discovers the richness of Jewish ritual and the deep faith of his Jewish friends. The Sikh explains why the turban is important to his sense of identity, and the Hindu teaches them all that their ideas about him as an idol-worshipper are wrong. The Buddhist asks each of them to think carefully what they mean by the word 'God', and to be concerned for all living creatures, not just the human species. The goals of his religion are not selfish. The differences are put into perspective. The history of persecution and bitterness—for often religions have met only to fight—is put aside.

This does not mean that questions of religious truth have been forgotten. Hindus, Jews, and Sikhs, are not missionaries. They share the belief that God has created them as they are. He has given the Jew the covenant to obey and the Torah to live by. Similarly the Hindu and the Sikh have their codes and insights to witness to, but they do not believe that the faiths of other men are in any way false or inadequate. Buddhists believe truth to be more important than a system labelled Buddhism. Traditionally, Christianity and Islam stand together against the rest. Jesus is the Light of the World; Muhammad is the last Prophet and the Qur'an God's first and last word. Even these standpoints are being modified by many Muslims and Christians as they learn to respect one another and members of other faiths. It must be remembered that only a few years ago Baptist, Roman Catholic, or Anglican Christians each believed that only they were right, and all the other denominations were not true Christians. Attitudes can change as people talk to one another.

Towards a new understanding

Some Christians and Muslims are still missionaries, seeking to convert one another and also Jews, Buddhists, and everyone else to their beliefs. Others keep themselves to themselves, adopting a 'live and let live' approach to the other religions that are being practised alongside them. A third group spends much of its time in dialogue. This means more than talking to Hindus or Muslims. There are various kinds of dialogue, all of which are important in promoting understanding between people of different faiths. There is the 'dialogue' of a Hindu and Christian young woman who worked in the same office, were about the same build and exchanged clothes. The English girl learned how to wear a sari and how to prepare curries, the Hindu was a vegetarian, but became very good at cheese dishes.

Sometimes groups combine to fight against racism or to seek the improvement of playing facilities in inner city areas. The International Red Cross has its Jewish and Muslim equivalents, flying the Star of David, and the Red Crescent, but being part of the one world-wide organisation. Interfaith groups also study together. Some of the subjects discussed are the meaning of prayer, the idea of forgiveness, the place of the family in twentieth-century society and the relevance of religion in our world. In Bradford, Birmingham, and elsewhere they have worked together to produce religious studies syllabuses for use in schools, and interfaith services are by no means uncommon. In some schools assembly has become very much a sharing of ideas and beliefs between the different faiths and ideologies represented in the school, instead of something acceptable only to Christians.

The question of truth

To the question of which religion is right or true there is no answer that will convince members of other faiths or those who have no religious stance. If someone says that he or she believes Islam to be the true religion, that would be because the speaker is a Muslim. Someone else says Christianity, because that person is a Christian. Perhaps in a hundred years' time one of these religions will be alive and the rest dead. That might be thought to show that it was true, for we usually say that truth will win in the end. Or a last judgement may come when God will give us the answer, though from the way that most religions have fallen below the standards of their messengers or their scriptures few members of any of the faiths can look forward to being congratulated. The author's view, for what it is worth, is that the truth lies within all these religions, and beyond them as well. It is possible to be a member of any of these faiths and others besides, and know God or fail to know him.

Hinduism teaches:

'The life, or self, of this whole universe, is the same as that tiny seed from which it came. You are that self.'

(Chandogya Upanishad 6:12:3)

Judaism teaches:

'The Lord is near to all who call upon him, to all who call upon him in truth.'
(Psalm 145:18)

Buddhism teaches:

'Not to do any evil, to cultivate good, to purify one's mind, this in the Teaching of the Buddhas.'

(Verse from the *Dharmapada*)

Christianity teaches:

'The kingdom of God is within you.'

(Luke 17:21)

Islam teaches:

'We (God) are nearer to him (man) than his jugular vein.'

(Sura 50:15)

Sikhism teaches:

'Wherever I look I find no one but you and if I were to leave you I would perish.'

(AG 25)

It is the challenge of statements like these that the faithful of the religions have to consider, for while they argue among themselves about questions of truth the voice of those who say that they are all victims of an illusion grows stronger.

Here we have simply tried to understand some of the elements which are to be found in some of the major religions at the present day, so that we may begin to appreciate the place which religious belief has for those who consider it important. The debate about whether a reality to whom men give the name God exists or not lies beyond the scope of this book. It is the most important question of all.

Questions

1. *List and explain four similarities and four areas of difference which exist between the religions you have studied.*

2. *Is it correct to say that the religions you have studied believe that they are all paths leading to one destination?*

3. *Why are some religions called missionary religions but others are not?*

4. *Discuss in broad terms how people who practise and believe in any of the faiths you have studied in this book may differ in their lives, attitudes and behaviour from those who have no religious beliefs.*

Reading List for Teachers

This bibliography has been compiled with two needs in mind. First, many teachers will have been trained traditionally, in Biblical Studies, as the authors were. The books marked with an asterisk should help teachers to extend their own education confidently. Secondly, they will wish to supplement the material in this book, for a textbook can never replace an informed and enthusiastic teacher.

Attention must also be drawn to the Open University Course AD 208, Man's Religious Quest, which covers the six religions and many others. It is now open to qualified teachers who may become associate students.

Finally, the Shap Working Party on World Religions in Education organises courses and provides an information and advisory service for teachers. Letters (with SAE, of course) should be sent to the Secretary, West Sussex Institute of Higher Education, Bishop Otter College, Chichester, or the Information Officer, City of Liverpool College of Higher Education, Liverpool Road, Prescot, Merseyside.

General Books

Dictionary of Non-Christian Religions by Geoffrey Parrinder (Hulton Educational). Comprehensive illustrated reference book on religions, deities, philosophies, etc.

Man and His Gods, edited by E. G. Parrinder (Hamlyn). A well-illustrated encyclopaedia for teachers; also for the library.

The Concise Encyclopedia of Living Faiths, edited by R C Zaehner (Hutchinson). Excellent sections by specialists in each tradition (no Sikhism).

Penguin Handbook of Living Religions, edited by J. R. Hinnells (Penguin).

The Religious Experience of Mankind by Ninian Smart (Fontana). A useful and sound introduction, though its interpretation of Sikhism must be treated with caution.

World Religions: A Handbook for Teachers, edited by W. O. Cole (Commission for Racial Equality). Provides a comprehensive list of audio-visual aids for use in the classroom, and also addresses of Jewish, Muslim and other sources. This guide is frequently revised and updated and is most easily available directly from the Commission for Racial Equality, Elliot House, 10/12 Allington Street, London SW1 5EH.

ॐ Hinduism

There is a dearth of books describing festivals, pilgrimage and worship. Hindus do not need to write them and Westerners concentrate on theology and philosophy.

Hinduism, edited by J. Hinnells and E. J. Sharpe (Routledge & Kegan Paul).

The Hindu Religious Tradition, by T. J. Hopkins (Dickenson). Useful on the classical period.

The Hindu Tradition (Argus Publications). Has sections on aspects of the living faith.

My Village, My Life, by P. Mohanti (Davis-Poynter).

Hindu Myths, by W. D. O'Flaherty (Penguin).

Gods, Demons and Others, by R. K. Narayan (Heinemann). An anthology of myths which pupils might enjoy reading.

Krishna, Myths, Rites and Attitudes, by M. Singer (Chicago). Has an excellent and amusing chapter on the Holi festival in an Indian village.

Hindu and Christian in Vrindaban by K. Klostermaier (SCM). A very sensitive introduction to Indian religious life.

✡ Judaism

A History of the Jewish Experience, by Leo Trepp (Behrman).

The Jewish Tradition (Argus Publications).

Guide to Jewish Festivals (Jewish Chronicle Publications).

Introduction to Judaism, by I. Fishman (Valentine-Mitchell).

Everyman's Talmud, by A. Cohen (Dent).

The Jewish World by Elie Kedourie (Thames and Hudson)

Buddhism

The Buddhist Religion (Third Edition), by R. H. Robinson and W. L. Johnson (Wadsworth). Excellent survey with diagrams, maps, charts, lists of scriptures and further bibliographies.

Buddhism, its Origin and Spread in Words, Maps and Pictures, by E. Zurcher (Routledge & Kegan Paul). Useful overviews.

What The Buddha Taught, by W. Rahula (Gordon Fraser: paperback). A thorough survey of the material in the Pali Canon by a Sri Lankan scholar working in England.

Buddhist Ethics, by H. Saddhatissa (George Allen & Unwin). A basic Theravada account of the meaning of taking refuge and observing the precepts, the relationships of the laity to the Sangha, and the ultimate goals of Buddhism.

The Way of Zen, by A. Watts (Penguin Books Ltd). This shows Buddhism's capacity for cultural adaptation.

Cutting Through Spiritual Materialism (Second Edition), by C. Trompa (Shambala Publications, Boulder, Colorado). A modern Tibetan working in the west presents the Dharma.

Buddhism and Society, by M. Spiro (Campus [University of California Press]). A fascinating account of Buddhism in Burma by a social anthropologist. Includes festivals and rites of passage.

The Buddhist Directory and information on Buddhist groups in Britain. Apply to The Buddhist Society, 58 Eccleston Square, London SW1.

✝ Christianity

The Phenomenon of Christianity by Ninian Smart (Collins). Almost the only book to examine Christianity in the way that religions are approached. Most writers assume they are writing to the informed faithful, while the rest produce historical surveys. This book still presupposes considerable 'inside' knowledge of Christianity.

Festivals – an Anthology by Ruth Manning-Sanders (Heinemann).

Christmas Book, by James Reeves (Heinemann).

Islam

Islam, by H. A. R. Gibb (Oxford University Press). A good and sound introduction.

293

Muhammad, Prophet and Statesman, by W. M. Watt (Oxford University Press). An excellent and readable biography and introduction to Islam.

Sikhism

The Sikhs, Their Beliefs and Practices, by W. O. Cole and P. S. Sambhi (Routledge & Kegan Paul). Covers in great detail all aspects discussed in the present volume.

The Guru in Sikhism, by W. O. Cole (Darton, Longman and Todd). A study of the central and distinctive concept of Sikhism.

The Scriptures

The Hindu scriptures, like so much else to do with the religion, are not very well represented in English.

The Hindu Scriptures, by R. C. Zaehner (Dent/Everyman). Covers the Upanishads and the Bhagavad Gita well but not interestingly. The Vedas are scarcely represented.

The Upanishads and the Bhagavad Gita, translated by Juan Mascaro (Penguin). More readable.

The Hindu Tradition (Argus Publications). Contains articles which frequently quote from the Hindu scriptures.

The Wisdom of the Forest, by E. G. Parrinder (Sheldon). A readable introduction to the Upanishads.

The Ramayana, by R. K. Narayan (Viking Press). An attractive version of that epic; there is nothing similar on the Mahabharata.

Buddhist scriptures. These are very large, and so anthologies give the best overall spread. *The Buddha's Philosophy of Man*, by T. Ling (Dent). Theravada only. *World of the Buddha*, edited by L. Stryk (Doubleday Anchor). A very full range over all the schools. *Buddhist Scriptures*, by E. Conze (Penguin Books Ltd). *The Teachings of the Compassionate Buddha* by E. A. Burtt (Mentor).

The Bible. When deciding which translation of the Bible to use, it is most satisfactory to choose one which best answers your purpose. For academic studies the Revised Standard Version and New English Bible are recommended. Jews find most translations acceptable, apart from the Jerusalem Bible, because of the use it makes of the Divine Name.

The Qur'an. The same applies to the Qur'an. Muslims naturally prefer translations made by Muslims. Of these the best currently available is an anthology. *The Qur'an, Basic Teachings,* published by the Islamic Foundation, Leicester. Its sectional divisions should be a great help to teachers. Meanwhile a full translation is being prepared by the same team of scholars.

Sikh scriptures. Similar anthologies of the Sikh scriptures exist and these are better than the expensive complete translations in awkward English. *Selections from the Holy Granth,* by G. S. Talib (Vikas, India) and selections from The Sacred Writings of the Sikhs (Allen & Unwin) should provide ample material for the teacher to use.

Lectionaries. *The Daily Book of Prayer for Judaism, The Book of Common Prayer* (Anglican) and similar lectionaries will also be helpful. *Many Lights,* edited by Donald Butler (Chapman), includes many readings from important non-scriptural sources.

Lectionaries. The Daily Book of Prayer for Judaism, The Book of Common Prayer, Alternative Service Book (Anglican) and similar lectionaries will also be helpful. *Many Lights,* edited by Donald Butler (Chapman), includes many readings from important non-scriptural sources.

NOTE: Teachers might also find the following books helpful:
World Faiths in Education, by W. Owen Cole (Allen & Unwin)

Further titles by Geoffrey Parrinder—
A Book of World Religions (Hulton Educational)
Themes for Living (Hulton Educational)
The World's Living Religions (Pan)
What World Religions Teach (Harrap)
Comparative Religion (Sheldon)
Jesus in the Qur'ān (Sheldon)
Upanishads, Gītā and Bible (Sheldon)

Books for Pupils

Supplementary information about the topics covered in this book and other aspects, such as family life, or weddings can be found in the following series:

The Way of the Hindu, by Swami Yogeshananda
The Way of the Sikh, by W. H. McLeod
The Way of the Muslim, by Muhammad Iqbal
The Way of the Buddha, by C. A. Burland
The Way of the Christian, by J. C. Allen
The Way of the Jews, by Rabbi Dr. Louis Jacobs
(all Hulton Educational Publications Ltd.)

Understanding Your Sikh Neighbour, by P. S. Sambhi
Understanding Your Hindu Neighbour, by John Ewan
Understanding Your Muslim Neighbour, by M. and M. Iqbal
Understanding Your Jewish Neighbour, by Myer Domnitz

Thinking about Sikhism, by W. Owen Cole
Thinking about Christianity, by Richard St. L. Broadberry
Thinking about Islam, by John B. Taylor
Thinking about Judaism, by Myer Domnitz
Thinking about Hinduism, by Eric J. Sharpe
Thinking about Buddhism, by D. Naylor

Looking at Myth, by John Rankin
Looking at Symbols, by John Rankin
Looking at Worship, by John Rankin
Looking at Festivals, by John Rankin
(all Lutterworth publications)

The Many Faces of Religion, by F. Dicks (Ginn & Co. Ltd)

Glossary

The purpose of this glossary is to enable the reader quickly to understand the passage which is being read. The subject index on page 313 will often indicate the place in the book where fuller explanations can be found. Festivals are listed in that index, not in the glossary. The abbreviation (q.v.) indicates that the word against which it appears is also in the glossary and should be consulted.

Abhidharma
(Pali Abhidhamma)

Further or higher teaching. One of the three baskets (pitakas) of the Pali Canon. Also the name given to the continuation of this style of organisation and explanation of Buddhist ideas.

Abraham

the first well known historical figure of Judaism. Respected by Muslims as a prophet and hanif, that is, worshipper of the one God.

ascetic

a person or way of life. This involves discipline in eating, drinking, clothing, accommodation and sexual activity. See also fasting.

Adi Granth

literally 'first book'. The scripture of the Sikh religion.

Advent

literally 'coming'. Preparation for the coming of Jesus. Beginning of the Christian year in November, or early December (the Sunday nearest November 30th).

Akhand path

a continuous, literally 'unbroken', reading of the *Guru Granth Sahib* on an important domestic occasion or gurpurb (q.v.). It lasts about forty-eight hours.

Aleynu

literally 'adoration'. A prayer at the end of synagogue worship reflecting the task, dedication and hope of every Jew.

Amidah

literally 'standing'; the name given to a prayer silently offered by members of a synagogue congregation as they stand facing Jerusalem.

Anglican

the name given to a member of the Church of England or to the Church of England itself.

Apocrypha

books included in the Greek version of the Jewish Bible but excluded from the Hebrew Bible.

apostle	literally 'one who is sent'. The name given to the eleven disciples of Jesus, and St. Paul, who were sent out to preach the message of Christianity.
apse	a semicircular recess in a church or temple.
Arabic	the language of the Arabs in which the sacred book of Islam is written and Muslim prayers are said.
Ardas	the formal prayer offered before a Sikh wedding or at the conclusion of a Sikh service.
Ark	(1) the boat in which the family of Noah was saved from the Flood. (2) the chest which held the Hebrew tablets of the Law. (3) a cabinet in the synagogue where the sacred scrolls are kept.
arti	a form of Hindu worship in which lamps are waved in front of statues of the gods.
Aryans	invaders of northern India about 4000 years ago. Other Aryan tribes settled in Iran and even penetrated as far as Ireland (Eire).
Ash Wednesday	the first day of the Christian penitential season called Lent which leads up to Easter.
atman	other self, or individual soul, in Hindu thought. Buddhists teach that the eternal and ultimate reality is not to be identified with the atman.
avatar	literally a 'descent'; incarnation of a deity, sometimes in human form; most commonly used of Vishnu.
ayat	literally 'a sign'. The smallest division of the sacred book of Islam, a verse.
azan	the name for the Muslim call to prayer.
baptism	Christian rite of initiation.
Baptist	member of a Christian denomination which practises adult baptism by total immersion.
baptistry	an artificial pool in a church where people are baptised.
beth din	literally a 'house of law': one of the functions of a synagogue (q.v.).
Bhagavad Gita	'The Song of the Lord'. The most famous and popular Hindu scripture in which the god Krishna reveals himself to the warrior Arjuna. Composed about three centuries before the Common Era.
bhajans	devotional hymns forming a major part of bhakti worship (q.v.).
bhakti	devotion to a personal God; an attitude of loving devotion which develops into ardent worship, usually in the form of hymn singing and sometimes dancing.

298

bhikkhu (Pali bhikshu) literally almsman, someone who is supported by the voluntary sharing or almsgiving of others. In Buddhism it is usually translated as monk. The word nun translates bhikkhuni (Pali bhikshuni).

Bible literally 'book'. For the most part used of the sacred writings of Christianity. Sometimes also used of the Jewish scriptures.

bimah a platform in the centre of a synagogue from which the Jewish sacred scrolls are read.

bodhisattva a being who is on the way to enlightenment, e.g. Gautama in previous lives and before his experience under the Bodhi Tree. In Mahayana the title is used for those who deliberately postpone their own entry into Nirvana in order to help others to that goal.

Book of Common Prayer collection of services, orders and other materials approved for use by the Church of England, authorised in 1662.

brahma charya a celibate student of Vedic knowledge.

Brahma the Hindu creator god and communicator of divine knowledge.

Brahman the holy power, implicit in the Universe, the indescribable ultimate reality, God. The term is neuter.

Brahmin the priestly class of Hindu society. Not all Brahmins perform as priests, but they possess the right to exercise priestly functions.

Buddha a title meaning awakened. It refers to the state of enlightenment and insight which was reached by Gautama under the Bodhi tree, a state which is possible for everyone.

Buddhist one who follows the teachings of Gautama, the Buddha (literally enlightened one) who lived 2500 years ago. See above.

Caliph a word meaning 'successor', applied to the men who succeeded Muhammad as leaders of the Muslim community.

calligraphy literally 'beautiful writing': the use of writing as an art form, especially in the decoration of Muslim places of worship. It was also developed in Chinese and Japanese Buddhism.

canon literally a norm or measuring rod. The term is used for the written works in the different religions which are accepted as sacred scriptures.

cantor a trained singer who leads worship in Jewish places of worship.

catacomb	subterranean cemetery where Christians often met to worship.
catechumen	a Christian convert who is being trained in preparation for baptism.
catechism	instruction by question and answer given to a person being prepared for Christian baptism.
circumambulation	walking round a person or sacred place to show respect and to concentrate one's attention on it. Muslims go in an anticlockwise direction round the Ka'ba at Mecca. Buddhists go round stupas clockwise, usually three times, remembering the Buddha, Dharma and Sangha.
chandala	the lowest of untouchable Hindu groups.
chapel	place of Christian worship.
charn-pahul	(literally foot-washing initiation). Water is poured over the Guru's foot and then given to the disciple to drink.
chauri	a sign of royalty or authority, made of peacock feathers tied together or of nylon or yak hairs embedded in wood or metal. Nowadays nylon fibres are sometimes used.
chela	disciple of an Indian spiritual teacher.
Chi-Rho	✶ the first two letters of the Greek word Christ; a Christian symbol.
Christ	the Greek word for Messiah (q.v.) applied to Jesus whom Christians believe to be the Messiah.
church	(1) the Christian community; hence – (2) a place where they meet for worship.
Church of England	the name given to the Christian denomination which is legally established in England.
Church of Scotland	the national Protestant denomination of Scotland.
clergy	people specially ordained to conduct religious services.
communion service (Eucharist or Lord's supper)	a Christian service originating from the Last Supper, the meal Jesus ate with his followers on the evening of his arrest.
confirmation	rite of admission into full membership of the Christian community.
consecration	an act whereby a building or person is set apart for sacred uses and responsibilities.
convert	one who changes from one religious faith to another.
covenant	an agreement, especially used of that established between God and the Jewish people.
Creed	a statement of belief.
crematorium	a place where the bodies of dead people are burned.

Darbar Sahib	the building constructed at Amritsar in which Guru Arjan installed the Adi Granth (q.v.). Now the name frequently applied by Sikhs to the Golden Temple.
Dasam Granth	a book containing the collected writings of the tenth Sikh Guru.
Day of Atonement	the most solemn day in the Jewish year when Jews fast and assemble in the synagogue to ask for God's forgiveness.
denomination	name given to the groups or churches into which Christianity is divided (e.g. Roman Catholic, Lutheran, Baptist).
Deuteronomy	the last of the five books of the Torah.
devil	the name given to the personification of evil by Jews, Christians and Muslims; also called Satan or Shaitan.
dharamsala	commonly a hostel or inn. In the early Sikh period used of Sikh places of worship. Later replaced by the word 'gurdwara'. Also a charitable religious hospice.
Dharma	conduct religious and moral appropriate to one's status in Hindu society. Most commonly used of the rules of caste behaviour; (Pali dhamma) in Buddhism can be translated as truth, law or teaching. This dharma is Buddhism, the vehicle or raft for taking beings to Nirvana.
Dharma-kaya	the truth-body of the Buddhas and bodhisattvas. It is a term for the one, ultimate Buddha-Nature which they all share.
dhoti	a garment made of one piece of cloth worn by some Indian men. The cloth is wound round the body and then drawn up between the legs.
dialogue	discussion or interaction between two individuals or religious groups.
disciple	literally, 'one who learns'. Used especially of twelve men specially chosen by Jesus to receive his teaching. (See also apostle.)
diwan	(literally a royal court). Name given by Sikhs to their act of congregational worship.
du'a	Muslim private prayer.
duhkha (Pali dukkha)	the 'dis-eased', suffering, unsatisfactory nature of life. The first of the Four Noble Truths in Buddhism.
Easter	Christian festival celebrating the rising of Jesus from death.
epic	a long poem with an historical and magnificent theme: used especially of the Hindu poems, the Mahabharata and Ramayana.

301

Exile	being forced to leave one's homeland. Used especially of the period spent by the Jews in Babylon (697–538 BCE).
Exodus	the name given to the journey made by the Hebrews (Israelites) led by Moses, from Egypt to Canaan. Also the name given to the second book of the Bible.
Eucharist	literally 'rejoicing'. A name given to the Christian service originating from Jesus' last meal with his disciples. (Also called Last Supper, or Holy Communion.)
evangelist	one who preaches in the hope of winning converts.
fast	going without food and/or drink or abstaining from certain foods, such as fish or meat, as a religious observance.
festival	an enjoyable, usually annual, celebration.
font	a bowl used to hold water used in the rite of baptism.
free church	a Christian community or denomination which is free from worshipping and organising itself according to the requirements of the Book of Common Prayer (q.v.) and its accompanying legislation.
Gabriel	an angel through whom the coming birth of Jesus was announced to Mary in the New Testament. The angel through whom God revealed the Qur'an to Muhammad.
Gandhi (Mohendas Karamchand)	a Hindu reformer (1869–1948).
Gayatri mantra	the key verse of the Hindu scriptures: sometimes called, 'the mother of the Vedas'. It is imparted to a member of the twice-born castes at initiation and should be recited daily.
Gentile	a name applied to people who are not Jews.
gompa	term used by Tibetan Buddhists, meaning 'a place apart' or 'monastery'; can also apply to a part of the vihara.
gospel	literally 'good news'. (1) the name given to the first four books of the Christian New Testament. (2) the good news, that is the Christian message of salvation.
Gregorian calendar	a solar calendar established by Pope Gregory XIII in 1582 and now widely used throughout the world.
grihastha	the second of the four stages of life of a Hindu of the twice-born castes. It entails being a householder and bringing up a family. For the Sikh it is the stage through which all material and spiritual goals are realised.
grotto	a small cave, often used for religious observances.

gurdwara	literally 'door, or house, of the Guru': a place of Sikh worship.
gurpurb	the anniversary of the birth or death of one of the ten Sikh Gurus, usually celebrated by an unbroken reading of the *Adi Granth*.
guru	Hindu religious preceptor who communicates knowledge and techniques enabling his chosen students to achieve spiritual liberation. In Sikhism of the ten historical leaders of the community, of God himself and of the Sikh scriptures.
Guru Granth Sahib	the sacred writings of the Sikhs.
gurmukhi	the script in which Punjabi is written: the original script used for the sacred writings of the Sikhs.
gyani	a trained religious teacher attached to a Sikh gurdwara.
hadith	tradition in Islam, often related to the example set by Muhammad and adapted by his companions and later Muslims.
hafiz	one who can recite the Qur'an from memory.
Harimandir	a building constructed at Amritsar in which Guru Arjan installed the Adi Granth (q.v.). Now the name sometimes given by Sikhs to the Golden Temple.
havan	modern Hindu act of worship focused on a sacred fire: based on ancient rituals.
Hajj	Muslim pilgrimage to the Ka'ba at Mecca and nearby places during the month of Dhul-Hijja.
Hijra	literally 'migration': used of Muhammad's migration from Mecca to Medina in 622 CE.
Hindu	name originally given by Muslims to non-Muslims living east of the river Indus in India. Now used of the dominant Indian religious tradition.
Holy Spirit	third person of the Christian Trinity.
Holocaust	suffering of the Jewish people between 1939 and 1945 during which six million were murdered.
hymn	a religious poem set to music and sung during worship.
Indus Valley	ancient and highly developed Indian culture which existed in the river Indus region of the Indo-Pakistan subcontinent 4000 years ago.
ihram	the simple clothing worn by Muslims while making their great pilgrimage.
imam	one who leads Muslims in prayer in the mosque.
Islam	literally 'peace' or 'submission'; the religion revealed to Muhammad: by obedience to its teachings believers attain peace.

303

Israel	(1) a name given to the Jews in Biblical times. (2) the ancient Hebrew kingdom. (3) the Jewish state established in 1948.
janam sakhi	literally 'birth evidences'. The name given to the hagiographic biographies which were written down by members of the Sikh community two or three generations after the death of Guru Nanak.
janeu	the sacred thread with which Hindu boys of the twice-born classes are invested on the day of their initiation. Sometimes the ceremony itself is called the janeu ceremony but the more appropriate term is upanayam.
Japji	one of the most important hymns of Guru Nanak. It should be said by Sikhs every morning. Guru Arjan made it the opening hymn of the Sikh sacred writings.
Jataka	birth story, usually of the previous lives of Gautama Buddha.
Ka'ba	cube-shaped building in Mecca: the focal point of Muslim prayer: according to Muslim tradition built by Abraham and Ishmael.
kaddish	Jewish prayer of sanctification which forms part of the synagogue service.
Kalimah	title given to the Muslim confession of faith, 'There is no god but God; Muhammad is the messenger of God.'
karah parshad	a food (karah, literally 'pudding') prepared from flour or semolina, butter, sugar and water, shared by Sikhs at the end of a service and after most other religious observances.
karma	(Pali kamma) literally 'actions'. Can be applied to ritual actions, e.g. sacrifices, or to moral. These deeds are believed by Hindus, Sikhs and Buddhists to be influential in determining the nature of their future rebirth—hence the Law of Karma: good actions procure a good rebirth, bad actions a bad rebirth.
Kaur	literally 'princess', the name given to all females initiated into the Sikh community.
Kaurava	one of the two rivals whose families featured in the Mahabharata (q.v.).
Ketubim	the writings, the third part of the Jewish Bible.
Khalsa	the Sikh order, brotherhood, instituted by Guru Gobind Singh in 1699. The word is said by Sikhs to mean either 'pure' or 'God's own', khalsa being a term used by Mughal Emperors to refer to land in their personal possession.
khanda	emblem of a double-edged sword, circle and two scimitars. Sometimes worn as a badge, seen on Sikh flag.

Kshatriya	protector or warrior class of ancient Indian society. Entitled to study but not teach the Hindu sacred writings.
khutba	sermon preached in a mosque on Fridays.
kirpan	knife worn by Sikhs.
Lailat al-Qadr	the Night of Power when Gabriel first revealed the Qur'an to Muhammad. Commemorated on the night before the 27th Ramadan.
laity	the collective name for lay members of a religion who are not ordained as priests, monks, nuns, etc. In Buddhism the ordinary householders are usually married with families.
langar	kitchen attached to a Sikh gurdwara where Sikhs eat together to express hospitality and the rejection of caste and class distinctions.
Latin	the language of the ancient Romans which became the language of the Western Christian church for many centuries.
Laws of Manu	Hindu code of conduct compiled about the third century BCE.
leap year	year with an extra day or days in it to keep it seasonally and astronomically correct. Especially necessary with many religious calendars which are moon based.
lectern	reading desk, used when reading the Bible in Christian churches.
Lent	period of fasting and penitence before the Christian festival of Easter.
liturgy	a form or order of public worship.
Lord's Prayer	prayer taught by Jesus and universally used by Christians in public worship and private devotion.
lunar	adjective meaning 'moon'. Used of months or calendars calculated by the movement of the moon round the earth.
Mahayana	the great or superior way. A name which includes various schools of Buddhism, such as the Pure Land and Zen. These claim to offer a wider variety of means to help beings to Nirvana, in contrast to the earlier schools, which they critically called Hinayana, small or inferior way.
mala	beads strung together to be used as an aid to concentration while meditating upon the name of God, or the Dharma for Buddhists. Sikh and Buddhist malas are made up of a hundred and eight units, either knots or beads. Christians call such an aid to meditation a rosary: Muslims use the name subha, tasbi or tasbir.

305

mandala
name given to the individual ten sections into which the Rig Veda (q.v.) is divided. It can also refer to a symbolic and sacred diagram used as an aid to meditation.

mandir
name given to a Hindu place of worship.

mantra
a sacred formula or chant believed by Hindus to possess mysterious qualities and powers. A hymn or verse which can aid meditation. Mantras are used in this way by Buddhists too. (The Sikh Mool Mantra is not a formula of this type but a statement of belief.)

martyr
someone who is put to death for remaining loyal to a belief.

Masoretes
a group of Jewish scholars who produced an accurate text of the Hebrew Bible in the eighth century CE.

menorah
a seven-branched candle-holder which stood in the Jewish Temple. Now found in synagogues.

meditation
a means of calming the mind and increasing one's perception of the true nature of things. People often begin by 'sitting quietly', but it is possible for the whole of life to be lived in a mindful and meditative way.

Messiah
literally 'the anointed one', the deliverer many Jews expect God to send.

mezuzah
literally 'doorpost'. A small container holding the Shema (q.v.) fastened to the doorpost of Jewish houses.

mihrab
the niche in a mosque which marks the direction of Ka'ba at Mecca.

mikvah
bath for ritual washing in a synagogue, important in days before it was normal to have a bath in one's own home.

minaret
the tower from which Muslims are called to prayer by the muezzin (q.v.).

minister
clergyman, usually nonconformist (q.v.).

Mishnah
collection of Jewish oral teaching compiled and written down in the second century CE.

Missal
book containing the order of service of the Roman Catholic Mass (q.v.).

Mithras
an important Iranian god widely worshipped by soldiers in the Roman army.

moksha
the Hindu term for liberation from the round of rebirths resulting in union with God. Sikhs more commonly use the word mukti.

monk	a man who has taken certain vows and become a member of a religious community.
monotheism	belief that only one God exists.
Mool Mantra	Sikh statement of belief.
mosque	Muslim building for public worship; derived from the Arabic masjid, a place of prostration.
muezzin	the person who summons the Muslim faithful to prayer.
Mughal	the Muslim rulers of India from the sixteenth to the nineteenth century.
mukti	Indian term for spiritual liberation – commonly used by Sikhs.
Muslim	one who submits himself to God by following the religion of Islam.
Nam simran	meditation upon the Name so that one attains God-realisation.
Nevi'im	second section of the Jewish Bible containing the prophetic writings.
nirmana-kaya	the manifestation body of a Buddha, that seen on the earth.
Nirvana	(Pali nibbana) the blowing out of the flames of greed, hate and delusion which keep human beings bound to the wheel of rebirth (samsara). This state of peace and joy is the ultimate reality for a Buddhist.
nishan sahib	Sikh flag flown over a gurdwara.
nonconformist	a Protestant Christian who does not conform to the form of worship, organisation and belief contained in the Book of Common Prayer (q.v.).
nun	woman who has taken certain vows and become a member of a religious community.
Om	a sound representing God in Hinduism. It is used in Buddhist mantras as a sound which draws together all meanings.
orthodox	(1) someone who accepts the established tradition: so –
	(2) a Jew who lives as fully as possible according to the teachings of the Torah (q.v.) and the traditions based on it.
	(3) Orthodox Church – a development from the predominantly Greek speaking branch of Christianity following the split between Eastern European (Orthodox) and Western European section of the Church (Roman Catholic) in 1054 CE.

Palm Sunday	the Sunday before Easter when Christians remember Jesus' entry into Jerusalem – the crowds welcomed him by waving palm branches.
Pandava	one of the two rival noble families featured in the Mahabharata (q.v.).
parable	story used to convey a spiritual or moral truth, or stimulate thought and reflection about it.
Pentateuch	the first five books of the Bible.
Pharaoh	the title used by Egyptian rulers, equivalent to king.
Pharisees	a group or party of devout, strictly observant and yet radical Jews active during the period from about 200 BCE to 200 CE.
polytheist	one who believes in the existence of many gods.
priest	(1) person authorised to officiate at religious ceremonies. (2) member of the family of Aaron responsible for officiating at worship in the Jerusalem Temple. (3) members of the Brahmin class in Hinduism who carry out religious ceremonies. (4) members of the Roman Catholic and Anglican churches ordained and authorised to administer the sacraments.
Psalter	a book containing the Psalms, poems found in the Hebrew Bible.
Protestant	Christians who do not acknowledge the authority of the Roman Catholic or Orthodox churches, so called after the 'protest' of the followers of Martin Luther against the withdrawal of a right to allow them to organise their own church (1529).
pulpit	name given to the place from which preaching is given in a Christian church.
purana	literally 'ancient'; collections of poems celebrating the power and works of the Hindu gods.
pyre	the fire upon which corpses are cremated.
qibla	the direction in which Muslims pray.
Quakers	see Society of Friends.
Qur'an	the sacred book of Islam.
rabbi	a title given to an authorised teacher of the Jewish Torah and traditions after intense training and examination.
Ramadan	ninth month of the Muslim calendar; a month of fasting.
Reformation	a movement to reform the western church (now called Roman Catholic), in the sixteenth century, associated with Martin Luther. It resulted in the split of Western Christianity.

Rig Veda	most important of the oldest Hindu scriptures, compiled in the second millenium BCE (literally 'Royal knowledge').
rishi	ancient Hindu seers who received the revelations contained in the Vedas.
romalla	a square of silk cloth used by Sikhs to cover the Guru Granth Sahib. Sometimes given by Sikhs as an expression of gratitude: sometimes given to them as a token of God's care after a bereavement or before going on a long journey.
Roman Catholic	community of Christians which acknowledges the Pope as successor of St. Peter and vice-regent of Christ.
rosary	beads used by Roman Catholics in their private devotions.
rupa	a form or body. Used for images of the Buddha.
sabbath	the name given by Jews to the seventh day of the week, their holy day. Now popularly used to refer to any weekly religious holy day or day of rest.
sacrament	an outward, visible sign of an inward, spiritual blessing obtained through the rites of the church.
Sadducees	Jewish priests who recognised only the written Torah (q.v.). They came to an end after the destruction of the Temple in 70 CE.
salat	ritual prayer in Islam.
Salvation Army	a Christian evangelical denomination founded by William Booth in the nineteenth century.
samsara	literally 'going through'; Hindu, Sikh and Buddhist term for the state of rebirth and going from one body to another.
sangat	the Sikh congregation assembled for worship.
Sangha	the Buddhist community. The term is used particularly of the monks and nuns.
Sanskrit	the sacred language in which the most ancient Indian scriptures are written.
scroll	a roll of parchment or paper used before the book form was invented. Still used by the Jews in public worship.
seder	the ritual followed at the Jewish Passover meal.
Sinai, mount	the place where, according to the Bible and Jewish tradition, Moses received the Torah.
Septuagint	the Greek version of the Hebrew Bible translated in the third century BCE.
sermon	a discourse delivered as part of a religious service.

Shema	the Jewish affirmation of belief.
shofar	the ram's horn trumpet blown in the synagogue at New Year and the Day of Atonement.
Shrove Tuesday	the last day before the beginning of the Christian season of Lent.
sin	disobedience or rebellion against the will of God. Often used of any moral failure.
Singh	literally 'lion'; the name given to all male members of the Sikh khalsa (q.v.).
smrti	literally 'that which is remembered'. Used of such Hindu writings as the Epics and Bhagavad Gita to distinguish them from the revealed scriptures.
Society of Friends	a Christian denomination which arose in England in the seventeenth century through the preaching of George Fox. It has no paid ministry, its members refuse to take oaths and reject warfare as a method of settling disputes. They worship in silence, broken only if someone feels moved by God to speak. Sometimes called Quakers.
solar	adjective meaning 'sun'. Used of months or calendars calculated by the movement of the earth round the sun.
stupa	mound or mound-shaped buildings, which contain relics and which are the distinctive monuments of the Buddhist world.
sruti	literally 'what is heard': the revealed Hindu scriptures, for example the Vedas.
subha	Arabic term for the string of a hundred beads used by Muslims in their private devotions. (Sometimes also called a tasbi or tasbir.)
sufi	a Muslim mystic.
sura	name given to the hundred and fourteen divisions of the Qur'an.
Sutra	(Pali sutta) literally a thread. The term used for the collection of the threads of teaching, sayings or discourses of Gautama Buddha. One of the three sections of the Pali Canon; also of Mahayana works, such as the Lotus Sutra.
swastika	an ancient Hindu symbol.
synagogue	Jewish meeting place for worship and instruction.
tallith	often called a prayer shawl: worn over the shoulders by Jewish men in private devotion and during synagogue worship.

310

Talmud	a major source of Jewish teachings consisting of the Mishnah (q.v.) and the commentaries upon it, compiled 200–500 CE.
Temple	(1) a place of worship. (2) the focus of Jewish worship in Jerusalem until its destruction in 70 CE.
Tenakh	the Jewish Bible.
tefillin (or tephillin)	small leather cube-shaped boxes containing the Shema (q.v.) which a male Jew wears on his forehead or left arm (or on the right if he is left-handed) when saying his prayers; in obedience to the words of Deuteronomy 6:4–9. They are not worn on the Sabbath. In the New Testament they are called phylacteries.
Theravada	the way of the elders. The term preferred by the remaining early Buddhist school which is found, for example, in Sri Lanka and Thailand. It is the school which the Mahayana call the Hinayana.
Three Jewels	these are the three 'precious things' of Buddhism; the Buddha, Dharma and Sangha. They are also called the three refuges.
Torah	literally 'teaching' or 'instruction': the first five books of the Bible: the authoritative scripture of Orthodox Judaism.
Trinity	the Christian doctrine that there is one God in three persons, Father, Son and Holy Spirit.
Tripitaka	(Pali Tipitaka) the threefold division of the Theravada Buddhist scriptures into Sutra, Vinaya and Abhidharma, which are called the three baskets.
United Reformed Church	Christian Protestant denomination.
Upanishad	ancient Hindu scriptures produced about 2500 years ago as a result of teachings given by Gurus (q.v.).
Vajrayana	literally 'thunderbolt' or 'diamond' vehicle. The vajra cuts through conventional ideas and the defilements that stop people attaining Nirvana. It is the title of the Tibetan Buddhist School, which can also be called tantric Buddhism.
Veda	literally 'knowledge'. The most ancient of Hindu scriptures, composed between 4000 and 3000 years ago.
Vinaya	the monastic rules which form one of the three sections or baskets of the Pali Canon in Buddhism.

Wesak the Sinhalese month in April/May during which Gautama Buddha's birth, death and enlightenment are celebrated by Theravada Buddhists. The month has given the festival its name.

yarmulka skull cap worn by Jewish males especially during synagogue worship, though many Orthodox Jews will always wear one.

Zam Zam spring near the Ka'ba at Mecca discovered by Ishmael, the baby son of Abraham, according to Muslim tradition.

Zionism nineteenth-century Jewish movement aimed at establishing a national homeland in Israel.

Zen this is the Japanese translation of the Chinese Ch'an and the Sanskrit dhyana, which all mean meditation. It is the name of a school of Mahayana Buddhism which began in China and now flourishes in Japan and various other parts of the world.

Index